# 1 MONTH OF FREE READING

## at
## www.ForgottenBooks.com

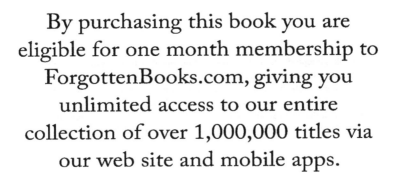

By purchasing this book you are eligible for one month membership to ForgottenBooks.com, giving you unlimited access to our entire collection of over 1,000,000 titles via our web site and mobile apps.

To claim your free month visit:
www.forgottenbooks.com/free894385

ISBN 978-0-266-82081-9
PIBN 10894385

*SPRING*

**1903**

## RELIABLE NORTHERN GROWN

# FARM & GARDEN SEEDS

**ORNAMENTAL SHRUBS**

**SMALL FRUIT PLANTS**

CLOVER GRASS MIXTURES
FOR PERMANENT PASTURES & MEADOWS
OUR SPECIALTY

# FARMER SEED CO.

## FARMERS & SEED GROWERS

### FARIBAULT.    MINN.

# A Few Words to our Friends and Customers.

In presenting our Annual Catalogue for the current year we wish to thank you all for your liberal patronage and ever-willingness to extend the fame of our Reliable Hardy Northern Grown Seeds. We gratefully acknowledge that to your kindness in this respect is due, in a great measure, the remarkable increase in our business, as this has more than doubled during the past three years. Our steady progress is also evidence that our seeds are of strictly first-class quality and that we fill all orders entrusted to us carefully and satisfactorily. Although we are located here in the Northwest, our old friends and patrons in the far Eastern States, who favored us with their orders when we were first located in Chicago (1890-1894) stay with us in spite of the higher freight rates. They acknowledge the superior quality of our Reliable Northern Grown Seeds.

To do justice to such a large trade naturally requires the best facilities and equipment, to which we have added again last year by putting in the most Perfect Cleaning Machinery available, which is one of the most important factors in a Seed Establishment. We have also added large Steam Drying Kilns for curing Seed Corn, and by making the main feature about Seed Corn we are better enabled to offer choice Seed Corn than ever before.

We are located in the best farming and seed producing section of the Northwest, and grow the most important part of the Seeds that we sell, ourselves. Improved Seed Grain, Seed Corn, Seed Potatoes and Vegetable Seeds are our specialty. No other section of this country produces Timothy and Clover of better and higher quality than Minnesota.

City seedsmen buy their Seeds in the open market like ordinary merchandise, the vitality and purity of which is always doubtful, and sell them under all sorts of big names at the highest price obtainable. This is what they call "SEED BUSINESS."

To entrust such Seed Dealers with your orders is very risky, for without good and reliable Seeds you cannot be successful, for "AS YE SOW SO SHALL YE ALSO REAP."

Everybody can easily see that we have the best facilities for supplying you with superior grades of the best varieties of Seed Grain and Vegetable Seeds. We do not claim, however, that we grow all the different varieties of seeds we sell. This would be impossible. Such seeds as cannot be successfully raised here we have grown from carefully selected Stock Seeds where they can be grown to the best advantage, and some we import. Everything is grown on good land, which is clean and free from all weeds, and from carefully selected Stock Seeds.

It is our aim to supply only the very best seeds to our brother farmers—Seeds true to name and of the best quality, such as will give the best satisfaction and that can be depended on for a crop.

We want all our brother farmers, who have not yet dealt with us and who receive this catalogue, to give our carefully selected Clover-Grass Mixtures, Seed Grain and Choice Vegetable Seeds at least a trial this spring and send us their orders, so we can demonstrate that nobody can supply better and more reliable Northern Grown Seeds than we can.

Yours to command,

**FARMER SEED CO., WM. KUEKER, Manager.**

# A Few Suggestions about Ordering—Please Read.

**CAUTION.**—Please be careful that you do not direct your correspondence to the Faribault Seed Co., but to the FARMER SEED CO., Faribault, Minn., otherwise we are not responsible for an answer nor for the amount sent.

The full address should be plainly written on every order sheet as well as on every letter sent to us, and no matter how often you have written to us, always give your full address.

**TERMS.**—With every order you send us please send the amount, as we do not fill orders unless the amount is sent with them. Money can safely be sent either by POSTOFFICE MONEY ORDER, BANK DRAFT ON CHICAGO OR NEW YORK, EXPRESS MONEY ORDER, or in a REGISTERED LETTER. We are responsible for all money sent us in this way. Do not send money loose in a letter without registering it, as it is not safe, and if lost we cannot be responsible for it. Silver coins should be sewed in cloth or pasted upon strong paper to prevent wearing through the letter. Do not send your check, as orders are held until the bank here reports it paid, besides it costs 15 to 25 cents to collect it. This all causes needless trouble, delay and expense in filling orders. Please do not send POSTAGE STAMPS, and if it is necessary, not in amounts over $1.00; we prefer the two-cent stamps. Be careful not to moisten them. Letters, also, will often get damp, causing the stamps to stick together, resulting in the destruction of the stamps and the order.

We notify our customers of the receipt of the order or of the shipment of the Seeds ordered. Orders sent by freight are notified by postal card of shipment, and if the amount of the order exceeds $5.00 we also send the shipping receipt, with a letter, advising that shipment has been made. As potatoes cannot be sent during the extreme cold weather, these orders are acknowledged and shipped as soon as the weather moderates, and customers are notified of shipment.

**QUICK SHIPMENT** is our motto. We have the facilities, and our experience and improved methods of packing and shipping give us the advantage of filling orders faster than any one else can. We have more than doubled our warehouse space and added other improvements during the past summer, which will enable us to fill all orders promptly.

**ABOUT SHIPPING.**—We send all heavy or bulky seeds, like Grass Seeds, Clover-Grass Mixtures, Seed Grain, Seed Potatoes and other heavy farm Seeds by freight, and the purchaser pays the transportation charges upon receipt of the goods. Large orders for Garden Seeds can also be sent by freight safely, and to good advantage, as we pack them securely. If customers will leave the way of HOW TO SHIP to us, we will use our best judgment in sending the order via the quickest and cheapest way, and think that, with our experience gained by shipping so many thousands of orders every year we can do well for you.

Our railroad connections are the very best, being located on such far-branching roads as the C., M. & St. P.; C. R. I. & P.; C. G. W., and securing through rates to nearly all points of the C. N. W.; C., B. & Q.; B. C. & N., and their branches. We also secure SPECIAL SEED RATES on the GREAT NORTHERN, NORTHERN PACIFIC, ST. PAUL & SAULT ST. MARIE RAILROADS, on GRASS and CLOVER SEED, MILLET and RAPE.

**PREPAID STATIONS.**—Frequently some of our customers live near railroad stations where there are no agents, and these are called Prepay Stations, and they should be kind enough to give the name of the nearest station, where there is an agent, on the order sheet. We do not pay the freight charges here on heavy seeds, but ship to the nearest station to this Prepay Station, which insures quick delivery and no danger of loss.

# INDEX.

# GRASS AND CLOVER SEEDS

Since the last three or four years, all the meat and dairy products have commanded a very high market price, so that most all intelligent farmers have given this more attention than ever before. The best breeds of cattle and swine obtainable are secured, almost regardless of cost, to bring the herds up to the highest point of perfection, which is business-like and surely a step towards success. As necessary as good breeding stock is, so essential are good Grasses and Clovers for your stock to feed and thrive on. Good Pastures and Meadows are the foundation for all successful Dairy and Stock farming. More and better grasses are required than Timothy, Blue Grass or Red Clover, which are in most sections the only grasses sown. The more grass we grow, the more cows and cattle we can feed, and the larger the income. Of all the crops produced, the grass crop of the world is by far the most important. No other crop is so necessary to the sustenance of the various forms of animal life, and in no other way can soil fertility and soil moisture be so easily maintained as by sowing the proper kinds of Grass and Clover Seed. No matter how large a variety of forage and fodder plants you may grow, you cannot replace a good Pasture or Meadow, for not any of these contain such nourishing and milk-producing elements than a good combination of Grasses and Clovers. We say combination, for one kind of Grass or Clover will not make a complete or balanced ration any more than single varieties of fodder plants, and as nearly all kinds of Grasses and Clovers supply different forms of nourishment, it is plain that the larger the varieties of Grasses and Clovers we sow for Pastures and Meadows, the better the feeding and milk-producing qualities will be.

Another important factor which should not be overlooked is that most all the different Grass and Clover plants subsist also on different soil elements, and it is therefore obvious that the larger the variety of Grass and Clover Seeds sown for Pasture or Meadow, the larger the yields of these will be.

We have for years already devoted a large part of our Catalogue to the description of the various kinds of Grasses and Clovers, and have carried on extensive experiments on our own farms to ascertain the varieties best adapted to the different kinds of soil and for the various purposes. These are not only garden plot tests, but are as extensive as conducted by anyone, devoting sometimes from five to fifteen acres to single varieties. Having studied Grasses and Grass Seeds from actual experience, we are in a position to know something about the habits of the different kinds and their nature. On this and the following pages we have given a full description of the most important Pasture and Meadow Grasses. Everybody can select therefrom, according to the requirements, such varieties as are best adapted for his soil and purpose. We have also put up Clover-Grass Mixtures for Permanent Pastures and Meadows, well considering the growth, maturity and adaptability to the different kinds of soil and for the various purposes, thus enabling our customer to make the right selection of the proper Grass Seed required for his particular soil and purpose. The utmost attention that we exercise in selecting and putting up these Clover-Grass Mixtures accounts for the great success our customers have with them, as the many letters received from them, of which we have a few printed on the enclosed circular, will prove.

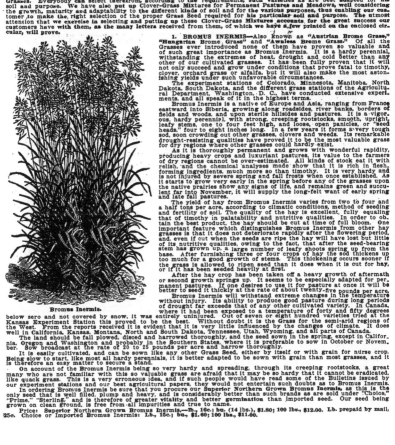

Bromus Inermis.

**1. BROMUS INERMIS**—Also known as "Austrian Brome Grass," "Hungarian Brome Grass" and "Awnless Brome Grass." Of all the Grasses ever introduced none of them have proven so valuable and of such great importance as Bromus Inermis. It is a hardy perennial, withstanding the extremes of heat, drought and cold better than any other of our cultivated grasses. It has been fully proven that it will not only succeed and grow under conditions that prove fatal to timothy, clover, orchard grass or alfalfa, but it will also make the most astonishing yields under such unfavorable circumstances.

The experiment stations of Colorado, Minnesota, Manitoba, North Dakota, South Dakota, and the different grass stations of the Agricultural Department, Washington, D. C., have conducted extensive experiments, and all speak of it in the highest terms.

Bromus Inermis is a native of Europe and Asia, ranging from France eastward into Siberia, growing along roadsides, river banks, borders of fields and woods, and upon sterile hillsides and pastures. It is a vigorous, hardy perennial, with strong, creeping rootstocks, smooth, upright, leafy stems, one to four feet high, and loose, open panicles, or "seed heads," four to eight inches long. In a few years it forms a very tough sod, soon crowding out other grasses, clovers and weeds. Its remarkable drought-resisting qualities have proved it to be the most valuable grass for dry regions where other grasses could hardly exist.

As it is thoroughly permanent and grows with wonderful rapidity, producing heavy crops and luxuriant pastures, its value to the farmers of dry regions cannot be over-estimated. All kinds of stock eat it with relish, and the chemical analyses made show that it is rich in flesh-forming ingredients, much more so than timothy. It is very hardy and is not injured by severe spring and fall frosts when once established. As it starts to grow very early in the spring before any of the grasses upon the native prairies show any signs of life, and remains green and succulent far into November, it will supply the long-felt want of early spring and late fall pastures.

The yield of hay from Bromus Inermis varies from two to four and a half tons per acre, according to climatic conditions, method of seeding and fertility of soil. The quality of the hay is excellent, fully equaling that of timothy in palatability and nutritive qualities. In order to obtain the best product, the hay should be cut at time of full bloom. One important feature which distinguishes Bromus Inermis from other hay grasses is that it does not deteriorate rapidly after the flowering period, and, even if cut when the seeds are ripe the hay will have lost but little of its nutritive qualities, owing to the fact, that after the seed-bearing stem has grown up, a large number of leafy shoots spring up from the base. After furnishing three or four crops of hay the sod thickens up too much for a good growth of stems. This thickening occurs sooner if the grass is allowed to ripen seed than it does when it is cut for hay, or if it has been seeded heavily at first.

After the hay crop has been taken off a heavy growth of aftermath or second growth springs up. It seems to be especially adapted for permanent pastures. If one desires to use it for pasture at once it will be better to seed it thickly at the rate of about twenty-five pounds per acre.

Bromus Inermis will withstand extreme changes in the temperature without injury. Its ability to produce good pasture during long periods of drought far exceeds that of any other cultivated variety. In Canada, where it had been exposed to a temperature of forty and fifty degrees below zero and not covered by snow, it was entirely uninjured. Out of seven or eight hundred varieties tried at the Kansas Experiment Station this proved to be the best. Without doubt it is the Grass for the semi-arid regions of the West. From the reports received it is evident that it is very little influenced by the changes of climate. It does well in California, Kansas, Montana, North and South Dakota, Tennessee, Utah, Wyoming, and all parts of Canada.

The land should be fall plowed, disced and harrowed thoroughly, and the seed sown in the spring, except in California, Oregon and Washington and probably in the Southern States, where it is preferable to sow in October or November. Sow broadcast at the rate of 20 to 25 pounds per acre and harrow thoroughly.

It is easily cultivated, and can be sown like any other Grass Seed, either by itself or with grain for nurse crop. Being slow to start, like most all hardy perennials, it is better adapted to be sown with grain than most grasses, and it is therefore an easy matter to secure a stand.

On account of the Bromus Inermis being so very hardy and spreading, through its creeping rootstocks, a great many who are not familiar with this so valuable grass are afraid that it may be so hardy that it cannot be eradicated, like quack grass. This is a very erroneous idea, and if such people would have read some of the Bulletins issued by our experiment stations and our best agricultural papers, they would not entertain such doubts as to Bromus Inermis.

In ordering Bromus Inermis be sure that you procure our Superior Northern Grown Bromus Inermis, as this is the only seed that is well filled, plump and heavy, and is considerably better than such brands as are sold under "Choice," "Prime," "Sterling," and is therefore of greater vitality and better germination than imported seed. Our seed being grown on clean ground, is free from all impurities and true to name.

Price: Superior Northern Grown Bromus Inermis.—lb., 10c.; bu. (14 lbs.), $1.80; 100 lbs., $12.00. Lb. prepaid by mail, 25c. Choice or Imported Bromus Inermis: Lb., 15c.; bu., $1.60; 100 lbs., $11.00.

# TIMOTHY—{*Phleum Pratense*

Minnesota Timothy.

**2. TIMOTHY—Phleum Pratense**—Timothy is so well known that it needs hardly any description, and there is scarcely a variety of our natural Grasses that is more generally cultivated than this. It is best suited for moist, rich, strong and loamy soils, where it grows to perfection and yields under favorable circumstances large crops of hay. If cut in due season, which is at flowering time, it makes a very good and nutritious hay, while for pasture it cannot be well recommended, as most every farmer well knows; its growth is not thrifty enough, and close pasturing is very injurious to it. Like all other grasses, it is hardier for either pasture or meadow if sown together with these, and only then one will get the best returns from it. For this reason we have added it to most all of our Clover-Grass Mixtures, where the circumstances allow it.

We would like to call the attention of our brother farmers here to the difference between Timothy Seed grown here in the most prosperous farming country in the United States, on good, rich bottom lands free from all kinds of obnoxious weeds, and Timothy handled by dealers in larger cities, sold through commission houses mostly, grown by everybody and anyone, on neglected farms, for the purpose, mainly, to subdue all kinds of foul weeds. Now, for a good and prosperous farmer it is too risky to buy such seeds, as there is more danger to get your farm infested with obnoxious weeds by sowing an inferior grade of Timothy Seed than with anything else, excepting Clover, with which the risk is just as great.

Besides we claim, and our customers have experienced this every year, that our Minnesota Grown Timothy is of a much thriftier growth, possesses more vigor and vitality and raises larger crops and better grass than Timothy Seed grown in a milder latitude. The large dairy and stock farmers in the Middle and Eastern States have recognized this long ago, and send us their orders as early as possible, very often in fall already, although they may not sow it until spring. On account of its high quality there is also always a large demand for our Minnesota Grown Timothy for export.

Price of our Superior Minnesota Grown Timothy: Lb., 10c.; lb. prepaid by mail, 18c.; peck., 65c.; bu., $2.30; 2½ bu., $5.50; 100 lbs., $5.00; grain sacks 16c. each extra.

**COMMON TIMOTHY**—Although this is free from foul seeds, we offer it at a lower price, as it has not the nice and bright appearance of our Minnesota Grown Timothy, but it is fully equal to such grades offered by other dealers as "Prime," "Strictly Prime," "Choice," etc.

Price of Common Timothy: Peck, 60c.; bu., $2.15; 100 lbs., $4.75; 2½ bu., $5.30; grain sacks 16c. each extra.

**3. TIMOTHY AND ALSYKE CLOVER MIXTURE**—This is a better combination for either pasture or meadow than Medium Red Clover and Timothy, as they will flower and ripen at the same time. Alsyke Clover can be sown to good advantage on moist soil where Med. Clover will soon perish, and will make a much finer hay than this, being free from fuzz and dust, and will not cause the horses to cough.

The Seed that we offer has been raised together, and being both of the same size, they cannot be separated, so that we have to sell it at a reduced price. The seed contains about a third to one-fourth of Alsyke Clover and the balance Timothy, or is as near in that proportion as we can tell, which is just the proper proportion for sowing. It should be sown at the rate of 8-10 lbs. per acre. Price: Lb., 10c.; prepaid by mail, 18c.; 10 lbs., 90c.; 25 lbs., $2.10; 50 lbs., $4.00; 100 lbs., $7.75; grain sacks 16c. each extra.

**Prices:** Owing to the prices of Timothy varying a great deal, and sometimes changing almost daily, we reserve the right to fill all orders quoted as above as long as the market permits us to do so; but should the market be lower or higher when your order is received, we will send seed to the full value of money sent. Buyers of large quantities should write for firm and lowest prices before buying, which we quote by return mail.

**4. MEADOW FESCUE—Festuca pratensis**—We regard this as one of the most valuable Grasses for several reasons. Chief among them is that it adapts itself to different conditions of soil and climate and does well all over the United States and Canada, and is also highly valued and largely cultivated throughout Europe. It gives a good amount of early and late feed of good quality, and yields heavily—from 2 to 4 tons of hay per acre, which is of fine quality and very nutritious, as a pasture grass it is particularly valuable, as it is a most persistent grower, and one of the earliest in spring and the latest in the fall. It never freezes out or winterkills, and is not affected by drought. It grows well on wet or dry bottoms, hillsides and tops, gravelly and loamy lands and clays, and having many fibrous roots running down 8 to 15 inches, resists the drought.

Meadow Fescue is also known as "Randall Grass," "Evergreen Grass" or "English Blue Grass." It grows about 3 feet high, stools out well, but never grows in tufts, and flowers in June. About 18 to 22 pounds of seed should be used per acre.

Owing to an unusually good season, the Seed crop turned out very good this year, and is therefore lower in price than it has been for years, of which our patrons should take advantage.

Price: Lb., 12c.; lb. postpaid, 20c.; bu. (14 lbs.), $1.40; 100 lbs., $9.25.

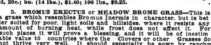

Meadow Fescue.

Crested Dogstail.

**5. BROMUS ERECTUS or MEADOW BROME GRASS**—This is a grass which resembles Bromus Inermis in character, but is better suited for poor, light soils and hillsides, where it resists any amount of burning heat, while frost does not affect it. For such places it will prove a blessing, and it will be of inestimable value to countries where the Clovers or other Grasses do not thrive very well. It should especially be sown by ranchmen and in range countries, as its introduction into those states means millions of money added to their wealth. Vilmorin, the noted agriculturist of France, says that 20 years ago he sowed this Grass on lands that have never been manured and the Grass still stands extremely well. Bromus Erectus grows well on land so poor where other Grasses cannot exist, is thoroughly permanent and remains for an indefinite period, affording large yields of hay, which on good land are as high as 4½ tons per acre, and furnishes excellent pasturage also. We can offer the seed at a reasonable price, and it would be well to send your orders as early as possible. The seed is sown the same way as Bromus Inermis, at a rate of 18 to 20 pounds per acre. Lb., 20c.; lb. postpaid, 28c.; bu. (14 lbs.), $2.25; 100 lbs., $15.00.

**6. CRESTED DOGSTAIL—Cynosorus cristatus**—For permanent pastures, especially on high land and hard, dry soils and hills, this Grass is invaluable. It produces an abundance of foliage, is very hardy, and but little affected by extreme drought or cold weather. It is tender and nutritious and relished by all kinds of stock. On account of its evergreen foliage and thick and close growing habit it is of particular value in a lawn mixture. It is a hardy perennial, 1 to 1½ feet high, flowering in June.

Lb., 30c.; lb. postpaid by mail, 38c.; bu. (14 lbs.), $3.50; 100 lbs., $24.00.

For prices on larger quantities of Seeds please write us.

Italian Rye Grass.

Hard Fescue.

**7. ENGLISH RYE GRASS—Perennial Rye. Lolium perenne—** It has become well known in this country, and is very largely sown, and has proven itself very valuable. It seems to be especially adapted for pastures, will endure close cropping, and is of strong and quick successive aftergrowth. It produces an abundance of foliage, which remains bright and green throughout the season, and for this reason is also much used for Lawn Grass mixtures. It is also well adapted f permanent meadows, and yields large quantities of very nutritious hay, which is well liked by all kinds of stock. It grows well on almost any soil, but prefers medium rich or moist land, such as will produce a good crop of corn, and gives the heaviest yields on such land. It grows 2 to 3½ feet high; when sown by itself about 20 to 22 pounds of seed per acre is sufficient. **Superior Grade: Lb., 10c.; bu. (14 lbs.), $1.00; 100 lbs., $6.75. Pound by mail, postpaid, 18c.**

**8. ITALIAN RYE GRASS—Lolium Italicum—** It is one of the Grasses not well known, but very valuable, and deserving more attention. It grows on almost any soil, but thrives best on rich, moist land. Where the ground is favorable, and especially if irrigated, immense crops can be produced, being cut 4 or 5 times, and yielding as high as 7 or 8 tons of dry hay per acre. It is well adapted for pastures, on account of its early growth in spring and its quick and successive aftergrowth when closely cropped. For this reason we found it very valuable to sow as a catch crop in clover fields where the clover had died or winter-killed. When mixed with Crimson Clover and sown on these bare spots in spring a full crop can be counted on from these fields. It grows 2 to

4 feet high, with an abundance of foliage, and is much liked by cattle and stock generally. When sown by itself or alone, about 20 pounds of seed per acre is sufficient. **Price, Superior Grade: Lb., 10c.; bu. (14 lbs.), $1.10; 100 lbs., $7.00. Pound by mail, postpaid, 18c.**

**9. SHEEP'S FESCUE—Festuca ovina—** This variety prefers to grow on light, sandy soil, and dry uplands or hillsides. It is deep rooted, and not affected by extreme drought. Sheep are especially fond of it, and in mixtures for permanent pastures on dry uplands, particularly if used for sheep grazing, it should be included, as it is highly relished by them, being one of the sweetest grasses and very nutritious. On account of its fine foliage and compact growth it is very desirable for lawn purposes. It is a hardy perennial, 1 to 2 feet high, flowering in June and July. **Lb., 15c.; bu. (14 lbs.), $1.50; 100 lbs., $10.75. Pound postpaid by mail, 25c.**

B.—Fremont Co., Ia.—You will probably remember that I bought 2 bushels of Minnesota Grown Alfalfa Clover of you last spring, which I sowed on six acres of ground without nurse crop. I secured a very good stand and was able to cut the Alfalfa three times, getting over a ton of hay from each cutting. Such a yield surprised me, considering that I sowed the Alfalfa Clover only this spring. C. M. CHAMBERS.

Sheep's Fescue.

English Rye Grass.

**10. HARD FESCUE—Festuca Duriuscula—** It is one of the smaller fescues and of great value on account of its hardiness and drought-resisting qualities, therefore being well adapted for dry hill side pastures and uplands, preferring to grow on light sandy soils. It is well liked by all kinds of stock and its presence in hay indicates a superior quality. After being mown it produces a large quantity of food. It is a hardy perennial, 2 to 3 feet high, flowering in June. **Lb., 15c.; bu. (14 lbs.), $1.50; 100 lbs., $10.75. Lb. postpaid by mail, 25c.**

**11. RED FESCUE — Festuca rubra—** For meadows or pastures on dry, hard or sandy soils this variety is very valuable. It endures severe droughts. The roots go into the ground very deep, and the Grass remains fresh and green while other varieties are apparently dried up. It is very hardy, a true perennial, growing about 1 to 2½ feet high. **Lb., 18c.; bu. (14 lbs.), $2.20; 100 lbs., $14.25. Lb. postpaid by mail, 28c.**

**12. TALL MEADOW OAT GRASS—Avena elatior—** For either hay or a permanent pasture a most valuable Grass, which can be successfully grown in all parts of the country. It will not winter-kill, and will live and endure our cold Northern Minnesota Winters, and can also be successfully grown in parts of the country where it is sometimes very hot and dry. It starts very early in spring, and is a very valuable pasture Grass on this account. It is seldom sown by itself, but mostly with other varieties, as in our Clover Grass Mixtures, where it gives the best results. Succeeds best in deep, rich, sandy soils, and even on clay and heavy dry soil it does well. It is a true perennial, growing 3 to 5 feet high, and flowering in May and June. **Price, Superior Grade: Lb., 20c.; bu. (14 lbs.), $2.50; 100 lbs., $18.00. Lb. by mail, postpaid, 28c.**

H.—Carver Co., Minn., Nov. 12, 1902.—The Bromus Inermis Seed bought of you was sowed alone on well prepared land, and came up thick and nice. Although I had to cut it early on account of the weeds, I was able to cut it again for hay afterwards. The yield as well as the quality of the hay was very good. The Prosperity Corn yielded enormously, but a large per cent is soft corn, as it was caught in the early frost. I shall plant it again, as I consider it the best and most productive corn I ever raised. F. OESTREICH.

E.—Houston Co., Minn., Nov. 10, 1902.—I have sowed your Seeds now for a great many years, and was always perfectly satisfied with them. This last spring I sowed your Mammoth Clover, which yielded 4 tons per acre, and the Yellow Dent Corn 65 bu. per acre of good and well matured corn, while most corn froze here in this section. I shall order some seeds from you again next spring. Be sure and send me a catalogue as soon as ready.

OTTO BUNGE.

Our price on Bromus Inermis Seed is this year lower than ever before, although it is plump and heavy and of the best germination.

Tall Meadow Oat Grass.

**13. RED TOP—Agrostis vulgaris** —This is a very hardy grass and is natural to most every state and predominates on low and marshy ground. It can also be sown together with other grasses on good rich upland soil for either pasture or meadow, where it will make an abundance of good hay or pasture. It is rich in feeding and milk-producing matter.

Red Top is generally sown together with Timothy on low marshes, but the Timothy is usually destroyed by water, while Red Top continues to grow and flourish. For sloughs and very wet ground we advise a combination of Red Top, Tall Fescue, Floating Meadow, Water Spear and Meadow Foxtail Grass.

All of these can withstand overflowing.

Red Top Seed is mostly sold in the chaff, of which we handle two grades. About 14 to 16 lbs. are usually sown per acre.

**13a.** Common Red Top or Chaff Seed. No. 1: Lb., 10c.; 1 lb. prepaid by mail, 18c.; bu., 90c.; 100 lbs., $6.00.

**13b.** Common Red Top No. 2: Lb., 8c.; bu., 70c.; 100 lbs., $5.00.

For description of other valuable Grasses, particularly adapted for sowing on wet, low and marshy ground, see page 5.

Red Top.

**14. FANCY RED TOP—**Clear or Solid Seed—This is the same variety as the above, only that it has been thoroughly recleaned from chaff, and is known as Fancy Red Top. Naturally this is much higher priced than the Common Red Top, but it is the cheapest in the end.

**14a. Fancy Red Top, Best Quality:** Lb., 14c.; bu. (14 lbs.), $1.50; 100 lbs., $9.50.

**14b. Fancy Red Top, No. 2 or Prime:** Bu., $1.25; 100 lbs., $8.75.

**15. RED TOP AND TIMOTHY MIXTURE—**This is generally raised here together around sloughs and such low ground that is not subject to overflow. The seed consists of about one-third of Red Top and two-thirds Timothy, which is about the right proportion to sow. This seed is of the best quality and as they cannot be well separated without a great loss, we offer it at a very low price. About 8 to 10 lbs. of this should be sown per acre. Price: Lb., 10c.; lb. prepaid, 18c.; 10 lbs., 85c.; 25 lbs., $1.95; 50 lbs., $3.80; 100 lbs., $7.50.

**16. ORCHARD GRASS—Dactylis glomerata—**For pasture or hay land a most valuable Grass, and is on account of its earliness very valuable for permanent pastures. It furnishes the first green bite in the spring and the last in the fall, and is quick to recover from close cropping, and even thrives better when it is cropped. When grown for hay, more than one crop can be obtained in one season, and where but one crop is taken the aftergrowth, which is very heavy, gives splendid and rich pasture till late in the fall. It will stand drought, keeping green and growing when other Grasses are dried up, and being very hardy, is of especial value for our Northern States, where it does not winterkill. Its nature is to grow in tufts, and is therefore not adapted for sowing alone; but when sown together with other Grasses, or in our Clover-Grass Mixtures, a close and even sod can be had. It is well suited to shady places, such as orchards and groves. Although it is adapted for a wide range of soil, and will grow on almost all land, it gives best results on deep rich sandy loam or clay soils.

Orchard Grass is of such great value, especially to dairy farmers, that we have selected a special or Orchard Grass Mixture, about which more can be seen on page 11, under C, No. 4.

**16a.** No. 1, or best Northern-Grown Orchard Grass: Lb., 18c.; bu. (14 lbs.), $16.00.

**16b.** No. 2, or Prime to Choice Orchard Grass, the grade as sold by dealers generally. Lb., 17c.; bu., $2.00; 100 lbs., $14.50.

By mail, postpaid, best grade, 25c. per lb.

Tall Fescue.

Orchard Grass.

**17. KENTUCKY BLUE GRASS— Poa pratensis—**The most widely known of all the natural Grasses, which does well everywhere, and can be found in almost every part of our broad country. In some sections it seems to grow singularly well,—for instance in Kentucky,— and this is probably the cause for the name, "Kentucky Blue Grass." It is grown for pasture than for hay, as it is unusually early in spring, and provides good feed already in May and June in our Northwestern States, and again late in the fall until the ground freezes. This grass is very hardy, and is not injured by the cold, and very hard to kill by dry weather, hot sun, the tramping of hoofs or close mowing. It is suited to any variety of soil, and seems to succeed best on moist, rich land. It requires about two years to become well established, and for this reason should be used only where permanent pastures are wanted.

**17a. Fancy Kentucky Blue Grass.** Lb., 15c.; bu. (14 lbs.), $1.70; 100 lbs., $11.50. Pound by mail, postpaid, 24c.

**17b. Prime, Extra, or B Grade:** Lb., 15c.; bu. (14 lbs.), $1.50; 100 lbs., $10.00.

Kentucky Blue Grass.

**18. CANADIAN BLUE GRASS— Poa compressa—**The Canada-grown seed of Blue Grass is sold much cheaper, and is very hardy. We can make the following price on this seed: Lb., 12c.; bu. (14 lbs.), $1.40; 100 lbs., $9.50. Lb. by mail, postpaid, 20c.

**19. TALL FESCUE—Festuca elatior —** This valuable Grass is found throughout Europe and also in this country, where it is highly valued for permanent meadows. Though coarse and robust in habit, it makes a very good quality of hay, which is very nutritious, and is greedily eaten by all stock. Being also very productive, giving larger quantities of hay than many other Grasses, it should be included in all mixtures for permanent meadows for moist and strong soils. It is also a good pasture grass, and in Virginia it furnishes cattle good grazing in midwinter. Not being affected by overflowing and naturally adapted for low lands, where the soil is moist and strong, this is one of the best Grasses to sow in marshes or places which are often under water. It is a perennial, growing from 3 to 5 feet high. Lb., 30c.; bu. (14 lbs.), $3.75; 100 lbs., $25.00. Pound postpaid by mail, 38c.

To secure the best results with Grass Seeds on low and marshy ground, a variety should be sown instead of just one single kind. To enable our friends to make the right sel ction of Grass Seeds we have put up our Clover-Grass Mixtures. On page 9 under A, Nos. 3, 4 and 5, and under B, Nos. 5 and 6, are particularly adapted for Pastures and Meadows on low and very wet soils. Give them a trial and be convinced.

# SLOUGHS AND MARSHES

These are, as a general rule, nothing but waste land and an eye-sore on most farms. If such land is properly utilized it can be made a source of the largest income, as it is apt to produce larger crops than any upland soil, for such soil is always in the highest state of fertility, all the humus matter for years having been supplied from the land surrounding. If the proper kinds of Grass Seeds are sown on such low bottom lands they will soon take a firm hold of the soil and produce enormous crops of the best and most nutritious hay or will make an abundance of pasturage. A variety of grasses properly selected will make a firm sod which allows the harvesting of the hay crop and the pasturing on such low marshes.

To enable our friends to make the proper selection of Grass Seed for low and overflowed land we refer them to our Clover Grass Mixtures on page 9 under A, Nos. 3, 4 and 5, and under B, Nos. 5 and 5, on page 10.

**20. MEADOW FOXTAIL**—Alopecurus pratensis—A fine grass, which is especially well adapted for permanent pastures. It is one of the very first to start growth in the spring, and is of remarkably quick and strong aftergrowth, either when closely cropped or after mowing. It is especially adapted for sowing in low or wet places, in marshes or sloughs, and occasional overflowing for several days does no harm to it. It should be sown in place of Timothy, together with Red Top, Tall Fescue, Floating Meadow, and Water Spear Grass, on low ground and marshes, subjected to occasional overflowing, when very large quantities of fine hay can be had from such otherwise worthless ground. It closely resembles Timothy, but the head is smaller and soft; besides, it is more leafy in character and hardier, starts much earlier in spring, is in blossom and ripe 3 to 4 weeks before Timothy, and springs up again quickly when pastured or mown.

Many are under the impression that this valuable Grass is the same thing as a wild species commonly known as "Foxtail" or "Squirreltail" and are afraid to sow it. If they would read this description carefully they will find that it is not similar to and has nothing to do with this wild Foxtail. Lb., 25c.; bu. (14 lbs.), $3.00; 100 lbs., $20.00. Pound postpaid by mail, 35c.

The seed is very light. One ounce contains 76,000 kernels.

**21. FLOATING MEADOW GRASS**—Glyceria fluitans—A very valuable Grass for improving low and wet meadows, marshes or sloughs. It succeeds best on moist and wet land which is often under water. It will even grow in or under water. It is not well adapted for sowing by itself or alone, but is best sown in a mixture and together with other varieties adapted for low ground, when a large quantity of fine hay can be secured in this way. It is a true perennial Grass, growing about 4 to 5 feet high. Lb., 25c.; bu. (14 lbs.), $2.50; 100 lbs., $17.25. Pound postpaid by mail, 33c.

**22. WATER SPEAR GRASS**—Glyceria aquatica—A variety which prefers low and wet soils, therefore of great value for land which is often overflowed or under water, where other grasses don't succeed, being drowned out. Although it grows coarse and robust, it gives large quantities of very nutritious hay, which is well liked by all kinds of stock. It is a perennial, 4 to 5 feet high. Lb., 30c.; bu. (14 lbs.), $4.15; 100 lbs., $28.00. Pound postpaid by mail, 38c.

**23. FOWL MEADOW**—Poa serotina—A native Grass found in the eastern half of the Northern States, and highly approved of for permanent pastures and meadows. It prefers low and moist lands, and succeeds well in wet meadows, or low places along streams liable to occasional overflow. It is a perennial, 18 to 24 inches high, flowers in July and August. Lb., 15c.; bu. (14 lbs.), $2.40; 100 lbs., $16.00. Pound postpaid by mail, 28c.

**24. MEADOW SOFT GRASS**—Holcus lanatus—This variety is also known as "Honey Grass," "Velvet Grass," "Yorkshire Fog," and "Velvet Mesquite Grass." Although not of high feeding value, it is very valuable for low, soft, spongy places, where other grasses don't succeed. Dr. Phares says: "It has been introduced into Texas, and grows much larger than in the Eastern States or England; and it seems to be more valuable and greatly improved here, It grows 2 to 4 feet high in the South." It is very productive; a hardy perennial, 18 to 20 inches high, flowering in June. Lb., 15c.; bu. (14 lbs.), $1.80; 100 lbs., $13.00. Pound by mail, postpaid, 25c.

**25. RHODE ISLAND BENT**—Agrostis canina—For permanent pastures this is very valuable, but it is more desirable for lawn purposes. It will make beautiful, close, fine sod upon quite sterile soil. It is a very hardy perennial, 1 to 2 feet high, flowering in June and July. Lb. 22c.; bu. (14 lbs.), $2.40; 100 lbs., $16.50. Pound by mail, postpaid, 30c.

**Meadow Foxtail.**

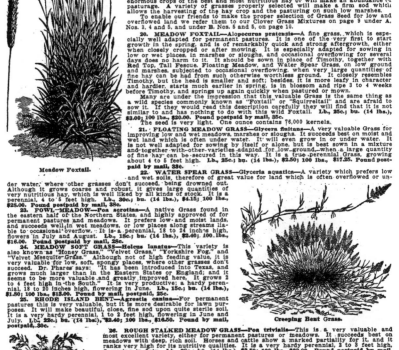

**Creeping Bent Grass.**

**26. ROUGH STALKED MEADOW GRASS**—Poa trivialis—This is a very valuable and most excellent variety, either for permanent pastures or meadows. It succeeds best on meadows with deep, rich soil. Horses and cattle show a marked partiality for it, and it ranks very high for its nutritive qualities. It is a very hardy perennial, 2 to 3 feet high, flowering in July. Lb., 28c.; bu. (14 lbs.), $3.50; 100 lbs., $28.00. Pound postpaid by mail, 35c.

**27. CREEPING BENT**—Agrostis stolonifera—This variety is especially valuable as a pasture Grass, and best adapted for low and moist situations. It starts early and holds out very late in autumn. It prefers deep, rich and moist soils, being very deep rooted, of quick successive growth when cropped close, and of dwarf habit. It is a very hardy perennial, 18 to 24 inches high, flowering in June and July. Lb., 30c.; bu. (14 lbs.), $3.25; 100 lbs., $15.50. Pound postpaid by mail, 38c.

**28. WILD RICE**—Zizania aquatica—The only one of our native plants furnishing food for wild fowl, ducks, geese, etc., which has been made an article of commerce. This seed can be sown on the borders of lakes, ponds and along small streams to great advantage, attracting all of these wild birds from September on. It purifies the water and affords refuge for the small fry from the large fish. It makes a good hay, and in the South two crops can be cut and all cattle are fond of it. Sow in water having a mud bottom. Lb., 15c.; postpaid by mail, 25c.

**29. REED CANARY GRASS**—Phalaris arundinacea—Also offered by dealers under the name of Phalaris Canadensis or Blue Joint, while Blue Joint is known as Calamagrostis Canadensis botanically. Dealers either through ignorance or or the purpose to mislead the buyer, mix up the names.

**Reed Canary Grass.**

Reed Canary Grass is a tall, leafy perennial, 2 to 4 feet or more high, with smooth sheaths and narrow branching panicles 4 to 8 inches long. It is common on low wet grounds and is widely distributed, from New England southward to Tennessee, and extending across the continent to California and Washington. It is a native Grass, also in Europe. It succeeds best on stiff, wet land, and on wet, flooded fields, but will also grow fairly well upon rather dry, sandy soil. It is little affected by either drought or cold, and thrives well in the shade. It will grow on land which is too wet for Red Top, and we can heartily recommend it to sow on low, marshy ground or sloughs, where it will furnish a large amount of hay per acre. If sown on these low lands, it will soon establish itself and drive out the wild or worthless varieties. Lb., 60c.; bu. (14 lbs.), $7.50. Pound postpaid by mail, 68c.

**RED TOP**—One of the most important Grasses for low bottom lands and for moist and wet soil. You will find it fully described on page 4, and also Tall Fescue, which is well adapted for low and moist locations.

**30. WOOD MEADOW GRASS—Poa nemoralis—**This Grass is invaluable for wood pastures or shaded ground, and should be included in all mixtures for permanent pastures, especially in shady places. It grows on almost any soil, succeeding best in moist, shady places, being remarkable for its quick, successive growth when closely cropped. For lawns overshadowed by trees it is particularly valuable, and it produces a very thick growth and a nice even sod. It is a hardy perennial, one and one-half to two feet high, flowering in June. Lb., 35c.; bu. (14 lbs.), $4.20; 100 lbs., $28.00. Pound by mail, postpaid, 43c.

**31. SWEET VERNAL—Anthoxantum odoratum—**Although this variety does not rank as high as some others for nutritive qualities, yet it is very valuable on account of its delicious perfumes, and when included in hay its aroma is imparted to the other Grasses, enhancing the value of the hay, and making it relished by the stock. The odor is more distinguishable when the Grass is drying or dried. We have therefore included it in nearly all our Clover-Grass Mixtures for Meadows. It is a perennial, one to one and one-half feet high, flowering in May and June. Lb., 15c.; bu. (14 lbs.), $1.85; 100 lbs., $12.50. Pound postpaid by mail, 25c.

**32. RESCUE GRASS—Bromus unilioides; also known as Bromus schraderi—**A most valuable and native Grass of the South, and highly valued where it is known. If grazed closely or mowed frequently the roots will live several years like a perennial. It is also known as "Schrader's Brome Grass. "Australian Oats," etc. It makes the best growth during the cooler months, but it resists heat and drought to a remarkable degree. Although it will thrive on any kind of land, it will do best on rich and somewhat damp soil, where it grows three feet high and more, with a large proportion of leaves, which are tender, sweet, and nutritious, and which are renewed very quickly after being eaten down. If sown by itself, about twenty to thirty pounds of seed per acre are used. Lb., 18c.; bu. (14 lbs.), $2.35; 100 lbs., $16.00. Pound postpaid by mail, 28c.

**33. YELLOW OAT GRASS—Avena flavescens—**This variety is particularly well adapted for dry pastures or meadows. It is not so well adapted for sowing by itself or alone, but should be sown in a mixture with other Grasses, adapted for high and dry soils. It is very early, and greedily eaten by cattle, and also makes nice hay, producing a very large aftermath. It is a perennial, flowering in June. Lb., 40c.; bu. (14 lbs.), $3.50; 100 lbs., $36.00.

**34. SOFT BROME GRASS—Bromus mollus—**This variety is very largely used in Europe and is considered a valuable Grass by many. It succeeds best on upland or dry and thin ground, and stands considerable drought. It is not yet used very largely in this country, but should be given a trial. Lb., 15c.; bu. (14 lbs.), $1.65; 100 lbs., $11.00. Pound, postpaid, 25c.

**35. JOHNSON GRASS—Sorghum halpense—**For the Southern States this Grass is of particular value. It is a perennial, the roots penetrate the ground in every direction, and each joint may send up a stem. These are three to six feet high. All kinds of stock are fond of it. It will stand great heat and severe drought, but should be sown alone, on well prepared ground, at the rate of twenty-five pounds per acre. Lb., 11c.; bu. (of 25 lbs.), $2.50; 100 lbs., $9.50.

**36. BERMUDA GRASS—Cynodon dactylon—**For the Southern States particularly this Grass is best adapted, and of great value. It is the chief reliance there for pasture and hay, furnishing rich and green pastures during nine months of the year. On good land it will cut two to four tons of nice hay per acre. It grows wherever corn and cotton grow. Pkt., 5c.; oz., 8c.; ¼ lb., 30c.; lb., $1.00; 4 lbs., $3.75, by mail postpaid.

**The best investment on your farm will be to sow our carefully selected Clover-Grass Mixtures for permanent pastures and meadows. These will furnish you an abundance of the finest nutritious hay, and the most luxuriant pasture. Please read page 13.**

# CLOVER SEED.

No other plant is of such importance to agriculture than clover, and this not only on account of its great value for pasture and for hay, but by far its greatest value comes in as a soil reclaimer, as it restores fertility to the land that has been exhausted by continuous cropping. Clover is the foundation to all successful farming and is unquestionably the most useful plant that can be grown on the farm.

Medium Red Clover.

**37. MINNESOTA GROWN MEDIUM RED CLOVER—**Every farmer is familiar with it, and a field of this knee high means fat cattle, swine and bunchy sheep. In order to keep the farm up, Medium Red Clover should be sown with all spring grain at the rate of 6 to 8 pounds per acre, if for no other purpose than merely for a fertilizer and to keep the weeds down. It will surely prove to be a double benefit, for if pasturage is scarce the cattle can be turned onto it; and if not required for this purpose entirely, our land requires fertilizers of some kind, which barnyard manure alone cannot supply. In a great many farming sections but few cattle are kept on the farm, and in order to maintain the fertility of the soil Clover should be grown, which is the best and the cheapest fertilizer. Good Clover sod turned under gives the best and the biggest yield of Corn, Wheat, Potatoes and Flax.

Our Minnesota Grown Clover Seed, with which we have been supplying our customers, is well known for its hardiness, strong and healthy growth and its wonderful productiveness. In purity and in great vitality it is unsurpassed, for which reason it is always in great demand for export, for which purpose seeds of the highest quality only can be used.

It will pay you to buy our true Minnesota Grown Clover, as it is the cheapest in the end; for you will not run the risk of getting seed that will not grow at all or get your land full of foul seeds, as you undoubtedly would if you order your Clover from dealers in the larger cities, who are obliged to buy commission-house seed, shipped in by everybody and from everywhere, which is sometimes held for years for speculation regardless of spoiling its vitality and germination.

We shall be glad to mail you samples of our Minnesota Grown Clover Seed to compare with others and convince yourselves.

Good and fresh Clover Seed of high quality is very scarce this year, and most dealers in the East or South cannot supply this, while the Clover crop here in this section has been very good, and we are glad that we can offer our customers Clover of the highest quality.

We advise you to send us your order for Clover early, as good Clover Seed is going to be scarce and high-priced before next spring.

**37a.** Price of our Minnesota Grown Clover Seed: Lb., 15c.; peck, $1.90; bu., $7.25; 2½ bu., $18.00; 100 lbs., $12.10. Sacks, 16c. each. Pound by mail, postpaid, 25c.

**37b. COMMON CLOVER—**As a good many want cheaper seed, we offer another grade, which is as good and equal to the grade sold by seedsmen or dealers as Prime, Fair or Good. Peck, $1.75; bu., $6.75; 2½ bu., $16.80; 100 lbs., $11.25. Sacks, 16c. each.

**PLEASE NOTE—**Prices of Clover and Timothy are subject to fluctuations of the market, and we reserve the right to fill orders as quoted above as long as the market permits us to do so. Should the market be higher or lower, then we send seeds to the full value of the money remitted. Buyers of large quantities should write for firm and lowest prices before buying, which we quote by return mail. Then there is sure to be no misunderstanding.

**39a. MAMMOTH RED CLOVER**—Well known in many parts of the country, and highly valued for its enormous yield and for reclaiming exhausted land. For hog pasture and as a hog fattener it has no equal, and is far superior to the common Red or June Clover. Where permanent hog pastures are wanted our Minnesota Grown Mammoth Red Clover has given the best results, as it is very permanent, and does not freeze out as easily as the common Red Clover, and is, therefore, better adapted for fall sowing than this. It will make very large crops of hay, yielding from 3 to 4 tons per acre. As a fertilizer to plow under green it has no equal. Our seed has been grown here and our customers can depend upon getting seed true to name when they send their orders to us.

Price of our Minnesota Grown Mammoth Clover: Lb., 15c.; peck, $2.00; bu., $7.50; 2½ bu., $18.50; 100 lbs., $12.50. Sacks, 16c. each. Pound, by mail, postpaid, 20c.

**38b.** Common Seed: Peck, $1.80; bu., $6.75. Sacks, 16c. each.

**39. CRIMSON CLOVER**—Trifolium incarnatum—Also called scarlet, Giant Incarnate, or German Mammoth Clover. Remarkable for its quick growth, and the only Clover which yields a full and heavy crop the first year. Sown in March or April, it is ready to cut in June or July, yielding a heavy crop of fine hay, and will grow up again from the roots in a short time and furnish good pasture for the rest of the season. We found the Crimson Clover valuable as a sort of catch crop when short of early pasture or where the new seeding was hurt by drought or otherwise, and the hay crop and pasture would be short. Crimson Clover mixed with the quick-growing Italian Rye Grass will make a good and full crop when sown in early spring and make up for the shortage. We have prepared a special Clover-Grass Mixture for this purpose (see page 11, under C), and this has given entire satisfaction for the past few years. For hog pastures Crimson Clover is invaluable, where quick results are wanted, and we refer here to our Clover-Grass Mixtures for hog pastures, as found on page 11.

Crimson Clover will grow on almost any soil. From 10 to 12 pounds of seed are sown per acre. Its average height is about 2 feet; it stools heavily, covering the ground completely with a heavy and thick growth of foliage. It is usually ready to cut for hay in about 8 weeks from the time of sowing, and after mowing can in a short time be pastured until late in the fall. Lb., 10c. Pound postpaid by mail, 18c. Peck, $1.00; bu., $3.85; 2½ bu., $9.60; 100 lbs., $6.40. Sacks, 16c. each extra.

**40a. WHITE CLOVER**—Trifolium repens—Of particular value in mixtures for permanent pastures and lawns, and will grow on almost any kind of soil, except wet or very moist ground. Being very hardy and of creeping habit, it will also prevent the ground from being washed by heavy rains. The seed is very fine, and if sown by itself about 5 pounds are sufficient for one acre; but it is never sown alone, but used mainly for sowing with other Grass seed, especially Blue Grass, to obtain permanent pastures. Minnesota Grown: Lb., 28c.; peck, $3.85; bu., $15.00; 100 lbs., $25.00; sacks, 16c. each. Pound by mail, postpaid, 35c.

**40b. COMMON WHITE CLOVER**—Equal to the grades sold as Prime, Wisconsin-Grown, etc. Peck, $3.65; bu., $14.00; sacks, 16c. each.

The price of Clover Seed is subject to the changes of the market.

Crimson Clover.

Alfalfa or Luzerne.

We have been fortunate enough to secure a fine lot of true Turkestan Alfalfa directly from a grower in Europe, which we are enabled to offer at a reasonable price, and urge all our brother farmers who failed, for some reason, to secure a stand with Luzerne or Alfalfa, to give it at least a trial. Considering that you will be able to save a high feed bill for bran and shorts entirely if Alfalfa succeeds on your farm, this is such an important factor that it should not be overlooked. For a description of the Turkestan Alfalfa see top of next page.

**42. ALFALFA OR LUZERNE**—Medicago sativa—Of all the different kinds of Clover Alfalfa is the hardiest and the most productive. During long protracted droughts it will flourish and yield abundantly when all other vegetation dies.

The taproots descend to great depths wherever the soil is loose and permeable, often averaging 10 to 12 feet. It has been recorded of sending its roots to a depth of 50 and 66 feet, and it is believed that under especially favorable circumstances they may even go deeper. It grows best in a sandy rich loam underlaid by a loose and permeable subsoil. It should not be understood, however, that it requires necessarily sandy soil for growing Alfalfa, for it can be raised on most any kind of soil, even on stiff clay land. The prime condition for its success is that the land be naturally well drained. The subsoil should not be heavy and stiff and impervious to water, but loose enough to drain off all superfluous moisture.

Alfalfa hay when well cured is of the greatest feeding value and is greatly relished by all kinds of stock. It is very rich in protein; that is, in the albuminoids and similar nitrogenous compounds which, when fed to cattle, are transformed into blood, muscle, tendon and bone. It is, therefore, a substitute for wheat, bran and cottonseed meal, usually purchased by the farmer to help to make a balanced ration, with Timothy hay and cornfodder, and since it can be grown on the farm, there is a great saving in the cost of producing beef, pork and mutton. Alfalfa hay can be fed profitably to all kinds of live stock, and is especially valuable for young and growing cattle, horses and sheep.

As a milk producer Alfalfa has no equal and no dairy farmer should be without a field of it, which can be either pastured, or fed green from the field, and a large quantity should be put up for hay. One acre of Alfalfa will furnish forage for 15 to 25 hogs per season. There is no cheaper and better way of producing pork than to allow growing pigs to run in a field of Alfalfa.

It is also the greatest soil renovator, as it takes nitrogen directly from the air and stores it in the soil. By raising Alfalfa you not only provide an excellent quality as well as a large quantity of forage for your domestic stock, but at the same time enrich your fields with a fertilizer, which if purchased in the market would cost you a great deal of money.

To make the best Alfalfa hay the field should be cut when the first flowers commence to appear, as, if cut when in full bloom or even later, the stems might become woody and hard. When grown on the most suitable soils, namely, those which are rich and well drained, and which abound in lime, potash, phosphoric acid and magnesium, and with the stimulus of heat and moisture, Alfalfa yields with ordinary care and cultivation from 1 to 2 tons of rich, nutritious hay every four to six weeks and can be cut, according to location and circumstances, from three to eight times a season.

Luzerne or Alfalfa is easily cultivated and is sown early in the spring on well prepared soil at the rate of 12 to 15 lbs. per acre. It can be sown either by itself or with grain as nurse crop.

It will make a fair growth the first season already, but this depends a great deal upon the circumstances. Some of our customers have cut their Alfalfa fields twice the same year it was sowed, cutting from one to two tons of hay in each instance.

**41a.** Minnesota Grown Alfalfa or Luzerne: Lb., 20c.; peck, $2.35; bu. (60 lbs.), $9.00; 2½ bu., $22.25; 100 lbs., $14.90. Lb. by mail, postpaid, 28c.

**41b.** No. 2 or Common Alfalfa—Kansas or Nebraska grown Seed: Bu., $8.00.

**Alsyke. Clover.**

**42. TURKESTAN ALFALFA**—This has recently been introduced into cultivation by our Agricultural Department. It was found growing on the high tablelands of Asia, and is especially adapted to the sudden changes of temperature that prevail there—intense heat at midday and very often frost at night, even in midsummer. It resembles the ordinary cultivated Alfalfa described on the previous page, excepting that the leaves are shorter and are sparsely clothed with short hairs. Its cultivation has been quite successful in the arid regions of the West, and under conditions where Alfalfa or Luzerne fails the Turkestan Alfalfa will prove to be of the greatest value.

As all of this seed has to be imported, it is rather high priced yet, but all those who failed to obtain good results with the common Alfalfa should give the Turkestan at least a trial, as success is very certain in most every instance. We have imported the true Turkestan Alfalfa directly from Europe, which is of the best quality. There was a great demand for the Turkestan Alfalfa last year, and much of the common Luzerne was doped off to innocent purchasers by unscrupulous dealers. That our patrons may be able to distinguish these two kinds, we will mention here that the Turkestan Alfalfa Seed is not quite as elongated as the common, and that its color has also a purplish hue to it.
Price: Lb., 25c.; lb. prepaid by mail, 35c.; peck, $3.50; bu., $12.50.

**43. SAND LUCERNE**—Medicago media—a variety of Lucerne especially adapted for very dry, sandy land, where it will yield heavy crops. Is very long lived, and will grow in all climates. Pound postpaid by mail, 30c. By express or freight, lb., 25c.; peck, $2.20; bu., $8.00.

**44. ALSYKE or SWEDISH CLOVER**—Trifolium hybridum—The advantages which the Alsyke Clover has over Red Clover and other varieties are its hardiness and true perennial character. It will adapt itself to a great variety of soils, growing on the edge of a stream or in a swamp and on low ground, and yet flourish on dry and stubborn stiff clays and upland soils. It is capable of resisting the extremes of drought and wet alike, and is well liked by all stock either green in pasture or cured for hay. Horses, cows and sheep prefer it to Red Clover. It makes finer and better hay, as the stalks are not so thick and woody as those of Red Clover. It is very sweet and fragrant, and liked by bees. Grows 15 to 24 inches high, heads are round, flesh colored. It can, with advantage, be sown together with Timothy, as both will grow on low ground and moist soil and mature and ripen together at about the same time. If grown for seed, this is taken from the first cutting. When sown by itself or alone, 6 lbs. of seed are required per acre.
Price of our Minnesota grown Alsyke Clover: Lb., 20c.; peck, $2.60; bu., $10.00; 100 lbs., $16.65. Sacks, 16c each. Pound y mail, postpaid, 28c.

**COMMON ALSYKE**—Equal to what dealers sell for Prime, Fair, Good or Choice. Peck, $2.40; bu., $9.00.
For Alsyke Clover and Timothy Mixture, the cheapest for pasture and meadow, see page 2.

**45. KIDNEY VETCH**—Anthyllis vulneraria—a variety of Clover but little known in this country. The seed is about the same shape and size as Red Clover, but the kernels are green on one end. It is grown in Europe on light or sandy land and furnishes good pasturage as well as hay. It is not affected by severe drought, and several years ago, when grown by the Experiment Station at Garden City, Kan., withstood severe drought quite well. It can be sown in July or August, like Crimson Clover, when it will give a large yield early next spring or can be plowed under green. It is ahead of Crimson Clover, as it will not winter-kill so easily. Its yield is from 5 to 8 bushels of seed per acre and is a profitable crop to grow. About 10 to 15 pounds of seed are required for one acre. Lb., 25c.; 15 lbs., 3.00. Pound by mail, 30c.

**46. SAINFOIN or ESPARCETTE CLOVER**—Onobrichis sativa—Another very excellent, but unfortunately little known, fodder plant for light, dry, sandy, gravelly limestone, or chalky soils. It flourishes during long droughts, for, like Lucerne, Esparcette is very deep-rooted, going down 15 to 20 feet into the ground, succeeding where many other grasses will fail. It is cut twice every year, and mostly used for hay; is very nutritious, and when fed to milch cows, improves the quality of the milk. The seeds are large, and are best sown broadcast in spring, under a light (about half crop) seeding of oats or barley, at the rate of 30 to 40 pounds per acre, and covered the same depth as barley. It will thrive and crop from 8 to 12 years according to the nature of the soil. Lb., postpaid, by mail, 20c.; by express or freight, lb., 10c; 30 lbs. (for one acre), $2.70; 50 lbs., $4.25; 100 lbs., $8.00.

**47. YELLOW TREFOIL**—Medicago lupulina—On very light, dry, or poor ground this variety is valuable for a sheep pasture, and can be sown alone or with other Grasses. It grows rapidly and is very productive. Lb., 15c.; lb. (60 lbs.), $7.50. Pound, by mail, 25c.

**48. BOKHARA SWEET or BEE CLOVER**—Melilotus alba—This Clover is especially adapted for bee pasture, and whoever keeps bees should not fail to put in at least half an acre to an acre of it. It is greatly relished by bees, and the honey from it is nice and clear as crystal. It grows on poor and sandy soil and also on land that is as solid as a rock; its strong roots will just penetrate the soil. The value of the Bokhara Clover as a fertilizer was not known at all until recently several experiment stations published articles on it. On account of its quick and vigorous growth and its thick mass of roots that it sends through the soil it possesses better qualities to enrichen the ground when plowed under green than any other Clover, and no matter what the condition of the soil is, dry and sandy or hard clay, it can be improved by turning under a crop of Bokhara Clover. Price: Lb., 20c.; 10 lbs., $1.50; bu. (60 lbs.), $8.50.

## Permanent Pastures and Meadows.

It has become an established fact that Stock Raising and Dairy Farming are the most profitable of all agricultural pursuits, and as this industry increases, more and better grasses for pastures and meadows are required. How to obtain these is the most important question with many farmers. We have made this grass question our special study for a great many years already, and among the many seed firms in this country we were the first to bring this so important a subject of more grass and better permanent pastures and meadows to the notice of the farmers of this country. Others now realize the great importance of this and many seed dealers not only try to imitate us, but copy our Clover-Grass Mixtures word for word. They lack the experience, however, and their grass seeds will never equal that which we offer to our patrons. Having been brought up on a dairy and truck farm in close proximity of Chicago, where land is valued at $125.00 to $200.00 an acre and every foot of ground has to be utilized to best advantage, we have experimented in our boyhood already with all the different kinds of imported grass and clover seeds then available, trying to pasture as many cattle as possible and to raise the largest crops of hay from an acre. We are still carrying on extensive experiments with Grasses and Clover on our own farms, and these are not garden plot trials, but sometimes we devote from five to twenty acres to single varieties. From a field that we sowed to Meadow Fescue in 1894 we harvested seed this year yet and the same we can say in regard to Bromus Inermis.

Besides our own experience with our Grass and Clover Seed and Clover-Grass Mixtures for Permanent Pastures and Meadows we have given the experience of some of our old customers who have sown our Seeds and Clover-Grass Mixtures, and these letters contain facts of actual results just when you want to know. We have devoted only a limited space in our catalogue to these letters, but anybody interested should write us for testimonials in regard to Clover-Grass Mixtures and can then correspond with these parties directly.

Why are our Clover Grass Mixtures best adapted for Permanent Pastures and Meadows and how can these be best obtained?

It is a well established fact that a judiciously selected mixture of several varieties of Grass and Clover Seeds will produce a much larger yield—generally again as much per acre than can be obtained with only one or two kinds sown alone. In sowing a larger variety you are not running the risk of not securing a stand at all, as you would sowing one or two kinds only, for in a larger variety there must best least several kinds of grasses adapted to your soil, while if you sow only one kind this may not be at all adapted and consequently no result. A pasture with a variety of grasses and clover is again as productive and earlier than if but one kind of grass is used, and can also be pastured throughout the season, as most grasses used are deeprooted and are extremely drought-resisting.

Many varieties sown together for a meadow or for hay cover the ground very closely and a larger yield of hay of much better quality can always be obtained from a mixed meadow. What we have said above in regard to grasses being deep-rooted and drought-resisting also applies to the grasses we use for permanent meadows.

In a great many parts of the country only one or two kinds of grasses are known and mostly sown, and these are Timothy and Clover. While Timothy is a splendid Grass, and Clover the foundation of all successful farming, both are not permanent, and not well adapted for pasturing alone, as they are easily affected by drought or frost, thereby making it necessary to re-sow every year or two,—a rather expensive method. In our carefully selected Clover-Grass mixtures several varieties of the Natural Grasses are sown together, and these, will cover the ground very closely and make three spans of Grass grow where formerly but one grew; besides, these Clover-Grass Mixtures will stand various climatic and soil conditions better, will last longer or be permanent, and yield heavily or double the quantity of hay that is secured from ordinary fields sown with Timothy and Clover.

# When and How to Sow These Clover-Grass Mixtures.

The most rapid way to obtain a pasture or a meadow is to sow the Grass Seed alone, without any grain or nurse crop, early in spring. Generally, a full crop of hay or a good close pasture can be obtained the first year already. Most farmers sow with grain, because they do not like to sacrifice this crop for one year, while the fact is, they lose their Grass Seeds sown with the grain almost one year after another, besides all the extra labor, and disappointment of not being able to obtain a stand.

We contend that it is almost as easy to secure a good catch of grasses for either pasture or meadow, with our Clover-Grass Mixtures, if these are sown alone, as it is to obtain a good stand of grain, which is nearly always most certain. Many suppose that the grasses will be protected by being shaded by the grain, and that to a certain extent the young plants will be benefited, which, however, is not the case, because the young plants growing in the shade and being crowded by the grain, are quite feeble and not well rooted. The consequence generally is as soon as the grain is cut and the grasses are exposed to the hot sun, they will commence to wilt and will disappear in a short time. The grain will not give the grasses a chance to take a firm hold of the soil; especially is this the case in droughty seasons, as grain roots deepen from the start and take all the moisture and nourishment for themselves. When the grass seed is sown for itself it will have just as much chance to grow as if you sow grain, and will generally take care of itself. If the ground should be weedy then a mower should be run over the field once or twice to check them, and to prevent their going to seed.

After the ground is carefully prepared, the seed is sown broadcast, which can be nicely and evenly done also very quickly with the little hand seeders, described on page 13. As Grass Seed is very fine it should not be covered too deep, running the harrow over the ground is generally sufficient; however, it is best and more certain if this is followed by a roller to bring the fine seeds in direct contact with the soil.

The prices of our Clover-Grass Mixtures we have always made as low as possible in accordance with the market prices of the seeds, using these best quality of seed only, with which these excellent results have been obtained such as our customers everywhere report, and this is at the same time the best proof that our Clover-Grass Mixtures are carefully selected. It costs but very little, if any, more to sow our carefully selected Clover-Grass Mixtures than to sow Clover or Timothy alone, and when permanent results are considered, the Clover-Grass Mixtures are the cheapest by several times.

## A.—Clover-Grass Mixtures for Permanent Meadows.

The question of what grasses to use in a meadow or hay mixture is, for all those who have had no experience with the different varieties of natural grasses, hard to answer. There are so many valuable grasses and so many different kinds of soil, that it is a difficult matter for a great many to make the proper selection for the purpose required.

For a meadow we must combine those grasses and clovers which blossom and mature at about the same time. Grasses of a bunchy growing habit should be intermingled with those of a spreading nature, so as to fill the spaces and make a compact and even growth of herbage. We also use such kinds as will make a rapid growth after each cutting. As Clover and Grass Seeds sown together will not only increase the quantity, but also the quality, of the hay, we have added Clover to all the Clover-Grass Mixtures intended for such soils that are apt to produce clover of some kind. All kinds of farm stock enjoy a varied ration, and the hay will be relished more and prove more nutritious and milk-producing when the meadow consists of several sorts instead of a single kind.

**A. No. 1.** For dry and high ground, light or medium soils:

| | Sow per Acre |
|---|---|
| Red Fescue ... | |
| Crested Dogstail ... | |
| Hard Fescue ... | |
| English Rye Grass... | 20 lbs. @ 11c..$2.20 |
| Meadow Fescue .... | |
| Bromus Inermis ... | |
| Timothy .......... | 50 lbs.......$5.25 |
| Sweet Vernal ...... | 100 lbs.......10.00 |
| Red Clover ........ | |
| Lucerne .......... | |

**A. No. 2.** For dry and high ground, heavy or strong soil:

| | Sow per Acre |
|---|---|
| Tall Meadow Oat... | |
| Hard Fescue ... | |
| English Rye Grass.. | |
| Meadow Fescue ... | 20 lbs. @ 11c..$2.20 |
| Bromus Inermis ... | |
| Red Top Grass .... | |
| Sweet Vernal ..... | 50 lbs.......$5.25 |
| Timothy .......... | 100 lbs.......10.00 |
| Red Clover ....... | |
| Alsyke Clover .... | |

**A. No. 3.** For moist ground and rich soils:

| | Sow per Acre |
|---|---|
| Meadow Foxtail ... | |
| Meadow Fescue .... | |
| Tall Meadow Oat ... | |
| Italian Rye Grass.. | 18 lbs. @ 11c..$1.98 |
| Timothy .......... | |
| Red Top .......... | 50 lbs.......$5.25 |
| Bromus Inermis ... | 100 lbs.......10.00 |
| Sweet Vernal ..... | |
| Alsyke Clover .... | |

**A. No. 4.** For moist ground, which is overflowed occasionally:

| | Sow per Acre |
|---|---|
| Tall Fescue ... | |
| Meadow Fescue ... | |
| Red Top Grass .... | 16 lbs. @ 11c..$1.76 |
| Meadow Foxtail ... | |
| Timothy .......... | 50 lbs.......$5.25 |
| Alsyke Clover .... | 100 lbs.......10.00 |

**A. No. 5.** For top seeding on marshes and swamps occasionally overflowed, the following mixture is especially adapted:

| | Sow per Acre |
|---|---|
| Water Spear Grass.. | |
| Floating Meadow Grass ........... | 19 lbs. @ 11c..$1.10 |
| Red Top Grass.... | |
| Tall Fescue Grass.. | 50 lbs.......$5.25 |
| Meadow Foxtail ... | 100 lbs.......10.00 |

**A. No. 6.** For peaty and boggy swamps, which as a general rule are so dry during the summer that no vegetation will grow in them:

| | Sow per Acre |
|---|---|
| Meadow Soft Grass.. | |
| Bromus Inermis ... | 16 lbs. @ 12c..$1.80 |
| Timothy .......... | |
| Soft Brome Grass... | 50 lbs.......$5.75 |
| Bromus Erectus ... | 100 lbs.......11.00 |

A meadow in Ohio sown with our Clover-Grass Mixture 8 years ago is just as good as ever and yielded big crops every year during that time even in years of severe drought.

This is what Mr. Schuh, Galion, Ohio, says about our Clover-Grass Mixtures: "My meadow is now 8 years old and is just as good as ever. The yield on 12 acres this year (1897) I value at $203. This Clover-Grass Mixture does not exhaust the soil, does not heave out with frost in winter, withstands drought, and the quality of the Grass for hay and pasture is A No. 1. Your Clover-Grass Mixture is the best all-around Grass that I ever saw. GRASS IS KING, especially if you have the right kind such as you can furnish." Mr. Schuh has been so kind to write us nearly every year in regard to the results, but to print these letters here would take up too much space, but those having our 1898 Catalogue can read them there on page 18.

Mr. L. R. Walker, of Princeton, Iowa, writes us: At what price will you furnish me 500 lbs. of your Clover-Grass Mixture A No. 4 for moist ground which overflows occasionally? I seeded 60 acres with this same Clover-Grass Mixture in 1897, and 35 acres in 1898, and now I want to seed 30 acres more. This Clover-Grass Mixture of yours can't be beat. I had 65 head of cattle on the 60 acres all season and they came out in good shape.

Mr. H. Gakemeier, Murdock, Neb., sowed 40 acres with our Clover-Grass Mixtures in 1892, and during these seven years had splendid crops from it even in the seasons of severe drought during this time. At the time of sending us a large order on Feb. 7, 1902, he writes that the results have even been better the last two years than at first.

# B.—CLOVER-GRASS MIXTURES FOR PERMANENT PASTURES.

For a pasture mixture the chief requisite is that the grasses be early, medium and late, and not to mature all at the same time, so as to furnish continuous grazing throughout the entire season. Tufted grasses must be used only in small proportion for pastures. Their places must be taken by the turf formers with their interlacing mat of underground runners.

### No. 1. For high and dry ground, light soils:

| | Sow per Acre |
|---|---|
| Hard Fescue | |
| Red Fescue | |
| Red Top Grass | |
| Bromus Inermis | |
| Meadow Fescue | 22 lbs. @ 11 cts.. $2.42 |
| English Rye Grass | |
| Crested Dogstail | |
| Yellow Oat Grass | 50 lbs........... 5.25 |
| Lucerne | 100 lbs............10.00 |
| Red Clover | |
| White Clover | |

### No. 2. For high and dry ground, heavy or clay soils:

| | Sow per Acre |
|---|---|
| Meadow Fescue | |
| Orchard Grass | |
| English Rye Grass | |
| Tall Meadow Oat | |
| Blue Grass | 22 lbs. @ 11c.....$2.42 |
| Bromus Inermis | |
| Italian Rye Grass | |
| Timothy | 50 lbs...........$5.25 |
| Red Fescue | 100 lbs............10.00 |
| Alsyke Clover | |
| Red Clover | |

### B No. 4. Specially adapted for wood pastures; also adapted for orchards and shady places:

| | |
|---|---|
| Wood Meadow Grass | |
| Orchard Grass | For top seeding |
| Blue Grass | |
| Tall Meadow Oat | Sow per Acre |
| Meadow Foxtail | |
| Sweet Vernal | 10 lbs. @ 11 cts..$ 1.10 |
| White Clover | |
| Alsyke Clover | 50 lbs........... 5.25 |
| Timothy | 100 lbs........... 10.00 |

### B No. 6. For low bottom lands, sloughs or marshes:

During the summer or early in fall such ground is generally dry enough to allow working it with a team, when it should either be plowed or thoroughly disked and then harrowed. After the grass-mixture as described below is sowed it should be harrowed again to cover the seed.

| | Sow per Acre |
|---|---|
| Meadow Foxtail | |
| Water Spear Grass | |
| Floating Meadow | 15 lbs. @ 12c....$ 1.80 |
| Meadow Soft Grass | |
| Creeping Bent Grass | |
| Meadow Fescue | 50 lbs........... 5.50 |
| Red Top | 100 lbs............10.50 |

### No. 7. Specially selected for sheep pasture on light, sandy soils or dry uplands and hillsides:

| | Sow per Acre |
|---|---|
| Sheep's Fescue | |
| Hard Fescue | |
| Crested Dogstail | 22 lbs. @ 11c...$2.42 |
| Sweet Vernal | |
| Bromus Erectus | 50 lbs...........$5.25 |
| Meadow Fescue | 100 lbs............10.00 |
| White Clover | |

### No. 3. For moist ground and rich soils:

| | Sow per Acre |
|---|---|
| White Clover | |
| Meadow Foxtail | |
| Blue Grass | |
| Fowl Meadow | |
| Meadow Fescue | 20 lbs. @ 11c.....$2.20 |
| Orchard Grass | |
| English Rye Grass | |
| Italian Rye Grass | |
| Timothy | 50 lbs...........$5.2. |
| Red Top Grass | 100 lbs............10.00 |
| Red Clover | |
| Alsyke Clover | |
| White Clover | |

### B No. 5. For top seeding to improve a pasture on low, rich ground or marshes:

| | Sow per Acre |
|---|---|
| Fowl Meadow | |
| Creeping Bent | 10 lbs. @ 11c....$1.10 |
| Red Top Grass | |
| Tall Fescue | 50 lbs...........$5.25 |
| Alsyke Clover | 100 lbs............10.00 |

# C.—Clover-Grass Mixtures for Particular Purposes.

**No. 1.** We call this our Standard Clover-Grass Mixture. It can be sown anywhere on ground which will produce a crop of corn or wheat on good rich prairie soil. It can be mown early and will produce a good heavy crop of hay and the quick and successful after-growth will furnish good pasturage until late in the fall. For a good many years, and in all parts of the country, this, our C No. 1 Clover-Grass Mixture, has given the best results with our brother farmers, so we can earnestly recommend it, and it should be more largely sown.

| | Sow per Acre |
|---|---|
| Meadow Fescue | |
| Tall Meadow Oat | |
| Meadow Foxtail | |
| Orchard Grass | |
| English Rye Grass | |
| Italian Rye Grass | 20 lbs. @ 11c.$2.20 |
| Timothy | |
| Rough Stalked Meadow | |
| Creeping Bent | |
| Blue Grass | 50 lbs........$5.25 |
| Red Top Grass | 100 lbs.......10.00 |
| Sweet Vernal | |
| Red Clover | |
| Alsyke Clover | |

**No. 2.** We have selected this Clover-Grass Mixture with a view to suit the conditions in the Western and extreme Northwestern states, and for similar conditions elsewhere, also in sections of the country where Timothy or Clover are uncertain and don't succeed well when sown alone. We include these, however, as we have found that where they are uncertain when sown alone, they are more apt to succeed when sown with other varieties, and should they fail, the other grasses take their place, and so an entire failure is avoided. This Clover-Grass Mixture is adapted to sow on land that will produce a crop of Wheat, Oats, etc., and is selected with a view to produce a crop of hay and pasture afterwards, or can be pastured entirely.

| | Sow per Acre |
|---|---|
| Bromus Inermis | |
| Meadow Fescue | |
| Tall Meadow Oat | |
| Orchard Grass | 20 lbs. @ 12c.$2.40 |
| Timothy | |
| Blue Grass | |
| Red Top Grass | 50 lbs........$5.75 |
| Alsyke Clover | 100 lbs.......11.00 |
| White Clover | |
| Red Clover | |

**No. 3.** Quite often we hear from farmers that it is impossible to get a stand of tame Grass started in their locality, as everything failed that was tried before. Now, with the large variety of natural Grasses we have, which are adapted to the most widely different conditions of soil and climate, it is easy to obtain a stand of Grass anywhere, and we would advise those who have failed before, and where the conditions of soil and climate are unusually severe, to sow the following Clover-Grass Mixture, and we are certain that the results will be satisfactory:

| | Sow per Acre |
|---|---|
| Bromus Erectus | |
| Meadow Fescue | |
| Bromus Inermis | |
| Hard Fescue | 25 lbs. @ 12c.$3.00 |
| Sheep's Fescue | |
| Rescue Grass | |
| Blue Grass | 50 lbs........$5.75 |
| Red Top Grass | 100 lbs.......11.00 |
| Alfalfa | |
| White Clover | |

## C.—Clover Grass Mixtures for Particular Purposes.—Continued.

**C. NO. 4. DAIRY FARMERS' OR ORCHARD CLOVER-GRASS MIXTURE**—We have selected only the earliest, hardiest, best and quickest growing varieties for this Clover-Grass Mixture. Dairy farmers want to cut a crop of hay very early and have pasture for the rest of the season, or make two crops of hay in a season; and this especially selected Clover-Grass Mixture is admirably adapted for this purpose. It is adapted for good or medium soils which will produce a good crop of corn or wheat, and can be sown anywhere in any part of the country.

| | |
|---|---|
| Orchard Grass ............... | |
| Tall Meadow Oat ........... | |
| English Rye Grass ........... | **Sow per Acre.** |
| Italian Rye Grass ........... | |
| Meadow Foxtail ............. | 20 lbs. @ 11 cts........$2.20 |
| Meadow Fescue ............. | |
| Red Clover ................. | 50 lbs.................. 5.25 |
| Alsyke Clover .............. | 100 lbs..................10.00 |
| Timothy ................... | |

**C. NO. 5. For light, sandy and gravelly soils.**

| | |
|---|---|
| Rescue Grass ............... | |
| Hard Fescue ............... | |
| Sheep's Fescue ............. | **Sow per Acre.** |
| Meadow Brome Grass........ | 20 lbs. @ 11c........$2.20 |
| Soft Brome Grass........... | |
| Bromus Inermis ........... | 100 lbs..................10.00 |
| Red Top Grass ............. | 50 lbs..................$5.25 |
| White Clover ............... | |

**C. NO. 6.** This is our Special Alfalfa, or Lucerne Clover-Grass Mixture, and consists mainly of Alfalfa, Bromus Inermis and such varieties of grass as will stand drought and flourish on poor soils and give large yields in the driest summers, after once being established. The quantity required per acre is 15 pounds. Lb., 11c.; 15 lbs., $1.60; 50 lbs., $5.25; 100 lbs., $10.25.

**PLEASE NOTICE.**—These Clover-Grass Mixtures can be ordered by the number, from either A, B or C, and, in ordering, not only the numbers should be given, but also the letter at the heading of the desired Clover-Grass Mixture.

Bags are included in the prices quoted above.

Our Clover-Grass Mixtures are a success. Read what our customers who have used them say about it. In a few letters we have printed on the enclosed circular you will find convincing proofs of the superiority of our seeds.

**C. No. 7. Trial Clover-Grass Mixture.** We have selected this Clover-Grass Mixture with a view to have those who have never sown it before give it a trial this spring. It is made up of about 15 different varieties of Grasses and Clovers, and can be sown on almost any kind of soil where oats, corn, rye or wheat will grow, and can be used for either meadow or pasture. About 20 to 25 pounds should be sown per acre, according to the land; sowing the last-named amount (25 pounds) on poor soil. 20 lbs., $2.20; 50 lbs., $5.25; 100 lbs., $10.00.

**C. No. 8. Crimson Clover-Grass Mixture, or Special Renovating Clover-Grass Mixture, or Quick Return Mixture.**—We selected and made this up for rapid growth with a view to use for either alternate husbandry or as a catch crop. When sown in early spring, March or April, it will give a full crop of hay in July and pasture for the rest of the year. It can also be sown in fields where the Clover or Grass has mostly been winter-killed, or otherwise injured, and where bare spots are in the spring, when it will be ready to cut with the other Grass or Clover, and a full crop from such a field with bare spots can thereby be secured.

| | |
|---|---|
| Crimson Clover ............. | |
| Italian Rye Grass .......... | **Sow per Acre.** |
| English Rye Grass .......... | 16 lbs. @ 11c...........$1.76 |
| Tall Meadow Oat .......... | |
| Timothy ................... | 50 lbs..................$5.25 |
| Red Clover ................. | 100 lbs..................10.00 |

When used for sowing in fields where there is some Grass or Clover already, the quantity to be sown per acre must be according to the stand of Grass or Clover. Usually five to ten pounds per acre are sufficient.

## Our Specially Selected Clover-Grass Mixture for Hog Pastures.

It is a well-known fact that hogs can be raised more profitably on Grass or Clover than on Corn only, and many farmers have paid very dearly for this bit of experience, when hog cholera and similar diseases caused terrible losses to them, especially in the Corn States. Land that will produce a crop of Corn will grow a fine crop of Grass and Clover easily, and it is just as easy and certainly more convenient to provide Clover and Grasses as Corn, as the pigs will do the work themselves and will make an average gain of a pound a day on a good Clover-Grass pasture, besides keeping healthy and strong. Quick results and a full crop and use of the pasture can be had the first summer from the properly selected mixture. We have given special attention to the selection of the varieties and to the making up of the Clover-Grass Mixtures for Hog pastures, and have arranged them so as to get quick results and a full crop the first year, as well as to obtain permanent hog pastures and have the use of these the first year.

**A. HOG PASTURE CLOVER-GRASS MIXTURE FOR QUICK RESULTS AND A FULL CROP THE FIRST YEAR** —When sown early in spring, the heavy and luxuriant growth of the Grasses and Clovers will furnish rich and succulent food through the summer. Crimson Clover, used in the right proportion with other Grasses and Clovers, and this "A" Hog Pasture Clover-Grass Mixture will bring the best results. Sow 12 lbs. per acre. Lb., 11c.; 12 lbs. (for one acre), $1.30; 50 lbs., $5.25; 100 lbs., $10.00.
Please write for special prices when large quantities are wanted.

**B. CLOVER-GRASS MIXTURE FOR A PERMANENT HOG PASTURE,** as well as the full use of it the first year. The following varieties we have found giving the most satisfactory results for this, and can be sown on good, rich, low ground, or on ordinary Corn land: Crimson Clover, Mammoth Clover, Alsyke Clover, White Clover, Italian Rye Grass, English Rye Grass, Orchard Grass, Creeping Bent Grass, and Timothy. Sow 15 lbs. per acre. Lb., 11c.; 15 lbs. (for one acre), $1.60; 50 lbs., $5.25; 100 lbs., $10.00.

**INCLUDE OUR CLOVER GRASS MIXTURES IN YOUR ROTATION OF CROPS, AS YOU WOULD TIMOTHY AND CLOVER.**

When you sow our Clover Grass Mixtures, you do not sow them necessarily for permanent, but can break up your pasture or meadow at most any time, and you will get more benefit from them than from Clover and Timothy alone, because some quick growing grasses being added to nearly every mixture, you will obtain a pasture or meadow the same year, n ally, you sow the seed. Our Clover Grass Mixtures will make a quick growth and form a close sod in a very short time. Please read what our customers say in regard to them, on the enclosed circular.

The prices quoted by the descriptions of the Grasses and Clovers from pages 1 to 9 for pounds, pecks, bushels or 100 pounds, do not include freight or express charges. We have, however, by nearly all varieties quoted the single pound price postpaid by mail, and we send the seed in one or more pound lots prepaid by mail at the pound price so quoted.

We furnish grain bags for Clover and Timothy at 16c. each, extra. For other Grass Seeds, such as Red Top, Orchard Grass, etc., please add 10c. for each 100 lbs. or less, for sacks, and if grain sacks are preferred, please add 16c. for each sack required.

Weights of Grass Seeds and Clovers: These are now sold and bought by the pound and 100 pounds, but we quote them also in bushel quantities. When Grass Seeds are ordered in bushel lots we send 15 lbs. to the bushel, and the prices quoted in the foregoing are based on 14 lbs. to the bushel, except on a very few kinds where it is noted different. Clovers weigh 60 lbs. and Timothy 45 lbs. per bushel.

# LAWN GRASS MIXTURES.

Nothing adds more to the appearance and attractiveness of a house than if it is surrounded by a nice and well kept lawn, which everybody can afford to have at very little expense.

Lawn Grass can be sown at most any time during the year, as the seed is very hardy. The best time is, however, early in spring, on soil prepared the previous fall.

If the ground intended to be sown for a lawn has to be graded, secure as good ground as you possibly can get, avoiding such as has obnoxious weeds in.

Do not try to improve a lawn that is as solid as a road by simply scattering Lawn Grass Seed over it, as this is unnatural; you should prepare a seed bed by making the ground loose and mellow by digging or hoeing the ground up, and after it is well pulverized, by means of harrowing or raking, it is ready to receive the seed, which should be sown on a quiet day, as the seeds are mostly light and very apt to be carried off by winds.

Three to four bushels of Lawn Grass Seed should be sown per acre, or one pound for every 300 square feet. It is necessary to sow the Grass Seed very thick so as to obtain a close stand, which will prevent the weeds from coming up. A great many lawns have to be sown over again when not enough seed had been used. After sowing the seed it should be harrowed or raked in lightly, which should be followed by a roller so as to bring the seed in direct contact with the soil and insure an immediate sprouting. If a roller is not at hand, firm the ground down by means of a wide board or a plank.

Nothing is more important than a good and proper LAWN GRASS MIXTURE, composed of fine-leaved and deep-rooted Grasses, such as will start to grow early in spring and stay nice and green until late in fall. Under favorable circumstances, common Grasses may do it, but it is best to sow a carefully selected mixture of hardy and deep-rooted Grasses that will withstand drought and severe colds in winter without freezing out.

In the selection of our Grasses for our Lawn Grass Mixture we use the greatest care, and as we are the only seed house making the grass question a specialty, handling large quantities of fancy Grasses, we are in a position and able to prepare the finest Lawn Grass Mixtures, which insure the best results.

Lawns can be made at most any time from early in spring until fall, as long as the ground has moisture enough to enable the sprouting of the seeds.

The Lawn.

**PARK MIXTURE —** This will make a very even and close turf in a few weeks' time. It roots deeply, withstanding severe droughts without turning brown, and will not stool or grow in clumps. This mixture is unequaled for parks, tennis or croquet grounds. **Pound postpaid by mail, 28c.; 4 lbs., $1.10. By express or freight, not prepaid: Lb., 20c.; bu. (14 lbs.), $2.40; 50 lbs., $8.00; 100 lbs., $15.00.**

**GARDEN CITY LAWN GRASS—**Where a fine Lawn around a private house is wanted, this Lawn Grass Mixture will be found best adapted. The Grasses used in its combination will give a luxuriant growth in spring, summer and autumn, not being affected by drought very easily, and are always presenting the same green, velvety appearance. **Pound postpaid by mail, 25c.; 4 lbs., 95c. By express or freight, not prepaid: Lb., 15c.; bu. (14 lbs.), $2.00; 50 lbs., $7.00; 100 lbs., $13.50.**

**SPECIAL MIXTURES—**We are at all times glad to make up Special Mixtures of Lawn Grass to meet the requirements of existing conditions. Where combinations of Grasses for terraces, shady places, exposed situations, etc., are wanted we have been very successful.

**SPECIAL GOLF LINK AND TENNIS COURT MIXTURE—**Our special mixture for this purpose is composed of fine, hardy Grasses of low and creeping habit that will form a firm and close sod in a very short time, which will withstand any amount of wear upon it without suffering. Nearly all of the selected Grasses being deep-rooted the golf and tennis grounds established can withstand drought and heat without suffering. As some of the varieties of Grasses of which these mixtures are composed are imported, our Golf Ground and Tennis Court Mixture comes a little higher than ordinary Lawn Grass Mixture. If prepaid by mail, 35c. **Price: Lb., 25c.; bu. of 14 lbs., $3.25; 5 bu., $14.50.**

## OUR SPECIAL OFFER.

Most of our old customers and friends are acquainted with the high merits of our Clover Grass Mixtures for permanent pastures and meadows already, and as a special inducement to those that have not tried them yet and to those that wish to order more we offer the following liberal premiums.

With an order for $20.00 worth of our Clover Grass Mixtures at catalogue prices, selected from pages 9, 10 and 11 only, we agree to send either a Little Giant or a Cyclone Seeder, valued at $1.50, for premium; or we will send you a handsome mantel clock finished in bronze and valued also at $1.50. You can make your selection of these three. A great many of our friends may have a seeder already and would prefer something else that is practical and useful, and will be surely delighted with such a handsome timepiece, which is sure to be an ornament to your parlor or sitting room. This clock is made after a very handsome design and represents the "Liberty Bell." You will find it more fully described on page 40 of this book on the pages for "Novelties and Specialties." It is a correct timekeeper, and you will find it as useful as ornamental.

For description and illustration of seeders, see page 13.

All of our patrons cannot use $20.00 worth of Clover Grass Mixtures, and to enable those who order less to get the clock or one of the seeders for premium we make the following suggestions: If your order should amount to only $10.00, then send 75 cents, or one-half the value of the mantel clock and seeders, extra; if $15.00 worth is ordered, then add 38 cents extra, or 7½ cents for every dollar short on $20.00 worth of seed.

Besides the premiums offered above we give agricultural books of your selection from our book list under the same conditions as to seeds as stated before, as follows:

With an order for $15.00, a book or books from our list to the value of $1.00, and a $10.00 order for the same seeds is entitled to a book or books worth from 50 to 75 cents. Seeds to be ordered at catalogue prices from pages 9, 10 and 11. Please note therefore that this offer does not apply to Timothy and Clover Seeds or Seeds described on pages 1-8.

Topeka, Kan., Dec. 5, 1901—With the Lawn Grass Mixture I bought of you last spring, I had the best success. The ground was well prepared like garden land, before I sowed the seed. The seed came up in a very short time and formed a firm and even mat of grasses in a very short time. The grasses are of such pretty dark green, velvety color. Although my lawn is only established since last spring, it is one of the best ones in the city. If people only knew how comparatively easy it is to make a lawn with your Lawn Grass Mixtures they would not think of laying sods, which, although so expensive, is so uncertain.      H. C. BIRCH.

# PREMIUMS AND SPECIALTIES.

Every farmer needs one of these handy little implements for sowing Clover, Timothy and other Grass Seeds. Even if you have an extra attachment for your Grain Seeder or Drill you should have one of these little hand Seeders, as you cannot sow light kinds of Grass Seeds such as Meadow Fescue, Bromus Inermis, Red Top, etc., with these attachments, but only Timothy, Clover and solid Seeds.

When farming is carried on on a small scale there is no need of buying an expensive broadcast Seeder, as these little machines meet all the requirements, sowing all kinds of Grain, Flax and Grass Seeds perfectly.

**The Cyclone Seeder.**

**Gem Seeder.**

**Portable Platform Scale.**

**THE CYCLONE SEEDER**—A machine which should be on every farm. It is so simple in construction that a boy can use it; it is light, strong and durable, and with ordinary care will last a lifetime. It will sow Timothy, Clover, Millet, Hungarian, Grass Seeds of all kinds, as well as Flax, Wheat, Oats, Rye, Buckwheat, Turnips, Corn, Bone Dust, and all other grain or seeds, perfectly even and any desired amount to the acre. Any desired quantity, from one quart to three bushels, can be sown per acre by following the simple directions on every machine. Price only $1.50; 3 in one order, $4.25.

**FARMER SEED CO.'S GEM SEEDER**—This is a Seeder that we had expressly manufactured for us, and is a machine which is perfect in every respect. All the material used in it is first-class, making it therefore absolutely impossible to get out of order from ordinary usage. Holds ½ bushel of seed. Runs so easily and smoothly that the weight of the handle will run it. The distributor is superior to all others and not used on any other machine. Handsome in appearance, durable, light in weight, guaranteed to work to perfection and be first-class in every respect. It will sow Wheat, Rye, Oats, Barley, Rice, Flax, Millet, Turnip Seed, Clover and all kinds of grasses; in fact, all seed sown broadcast; also fertilizer, ashes, salt, etc., etc. Price only $1.25; 3 in one order, $4.00.

**THE LITTLE GIANT SEEDER**—This machine is in many ways similar to the Cyclone Seeder, of which we have sold many thousands, and all have given the very best satisfaction. The gearing is rigid, being in an iron frame. It is simple in construction, light, strong and durable; very easy running, and weighing but 3 pounds complete. The hopper or sack holds nearly a bushel of seed. A man walking at the rate of 3 miles per hour will sow 80 acres of wheat or 60 acres of Clover Seed in a day of 10 hours. Man or boy can sow on hilly, stumpy, stony and rough as well as on clean and old ground, perfectly even and any desired quantity per acre from 1 quart to 3 bushels by following the simple instructions and directions. Price only $1.50; 3 in one order, $4.25.

Any one of the above described Seeders can be had as premium with an order for $20.00 worth of Clover-Grass Mixtures, at catalogue prices, selected from pages 9, 10 and 11. On page 11 this is more definitely explained. Please notice that we also offer a fine and highly ornamental mantel clock with $20.00 worth of Clover-Grass Mixtures, instead of the Seeder.

**PORTABLE PLATFORM SCALES ON WHEELS**—The Scales that we offer are manufactured by the Fairbanks Scale Co., whose scales have a world-wide reputation for accuracy and durability, and are acknowledged by everybody as the standard Scales. No farmer should be without a good and reliable scale, and do away with all guesswork on weights, so much practiced.

Our Scales are made of the best material throughout, with finely tempered steel bearings and pivots, where both strength and extreme hardness are required, carefully proportioned iron levers and frame.

Our prices on the different sizes of Scales are as follows:

|  |  |  |
|---|---|---|
| 400 lb. platform, 21x15 | $12.50 |
| 600-lb. platform, 22x16 | 14.00 |
| 1000-lb. platform, 26x17 | 15.50 |
| 1200-lb. platform, 26x17 | 17.00 |
| 1500-lb. platform, 28x20 | 19.00 |

**Portable Platform Scales.**

**Corbin's Dehorning Pencils.**

Farmers, dehorn your calves by using Corbin's Dehorning Pencils. Every pencil warranted to dehorn 50 calves, if used according to directions. It acts without pain or loss of appetite. Calves should be dehorned when 5 to 20 days of age, 5 to 10 preferable. In the first place, to dehorn calves makes them more gentle, and they can be fed in a much smaller space, and it don't take half the room to shed them in the winter, and when you come to sell them they will bring $2 more a head dehorned.

Sawing horns off of cattle is considered barbarous, and should be stopped by dehorning them when young. Warranted to never fail. The manufacturer agrees to forfeit $5.00 for every calf from 5 to 20 days old which his Dehorning Pencil fails to dehorn. Each Pencil will dehorn 40 calves. Price per Pencil, $1.00, 3 for $2.50, prepaid by mail.

**UNION FAMILY SCALE**—

For use in a farm house or in any family this is the best, as the heavier weighing may be obtained by placing loads upon the platform, and the finer ones with the load in the scoop. The Scales have a capacity of ½ oz. to 30 lbs. for finer weighings, and ¼ lb. to 240 lbs. for the coarser weighings. The platform is 10½x13¾ inches. Price of Scale, $3.00.

# MILLET.

Probably there is no other fodder plant more favorably known than Millet, and yet there is not enough attention paid to it. Nothing pays better for a stock raiser and dairy farmer than a few acres in Millet of some kind, for it is of the greatest feeding value and milk-producing quality, and yielding at least again as much of the most delicious hay per acre than Timothy and Clover. It should be sown regularly every year, and not merely as a catch crop. When spring is so unfavorable that other crops fail to grow or when the season is so late and wet that other crops will not mature any more, then there is always the greatest demand for Millet. We will fill all orders at the low prices quoted below as long as our large stock lasts, and reserve the right to change to market prices when it is exhausted

**HUGARIAN MILLET**—No other variety is so well known and so much grown for hay as the Hungarian Millet. It is so valuable because it takes such a short season to make a fine crop of the most nourishing and milk-producing hay. On this account it is the best catch crop when other crops, already put in, for some reason fail to grow. If sown as late as the 15th of July to the 1st of August good results can be expected, if the chances are favorable. In the neighborhood of larger cities, where early potatoes are extensively grown for the market. Hungarian Millet is generally sown as soon as the potatoes are dug, and thus two crops are harvested in one year from the same piece of ground. Hungarian will not grow as coarse as many other Millet varieties, but still it yields quite heavy, three to four tons of hay per acre is considered an ordinary crop. The hay is very leafy and of the very best quality, being greedily eaten by all kinds of stock. Weight of seed, 48 lbs. per bushel. For hay, sow 3 pecks per acre, while to grow seed from 2 pecks is sufficient. Price: Bu., $1.40; 2½ bu., $3.40; grain sacks 16c. each extra.

**THE HOG MILLET**—This Millet has been grown for several years here in Minnesota and the Dakotas, and within the last few years has been put on the market under various names, such as "Manitoba" or "Russian Millet," "Broom Corn Millet," etc. The name HOG MILLET has been selected on account of its great value for feeding stock, ESPECIALLY HOGS. It is of great value in sections where corn cannot be cheaply and safely grown, and in such localities the Hog Millet solves the problem as to the profitable raising of swine. In 50 to 60 days from the time the seed is sown it is ready to harvest. The seed ripens while the fodder is yet green, hence it can be cut and used for both hay and seed with equally good success. When wanted for the seed and hay from 30 to 60 bushels of seed can be raised per acre, besides the fodder or hay. It is unlike the German or Common Millet and Hungarian in habit of growth, having a branching head, and in the appearance of the seed, which is much larger. Peck, 50c.; 1 bu., $1.35; 2½ bu., $3.25; grain sacks extra, at 16c. each.

**EARLY FORTUNE MILLET**—A new and entirely distinct variety of Millet. The seed is 3 or 4 times the size of German Millet and of a beautiful mahogany color. The great advantage this Early Fortune Millet has over other varieties are its extreme earliness, as it heads in from 25 to 30 days, and 2 crops can be easily raised on the same ground the same season, even here in the northwest where the seasons are short. It yields very heavy, both Seed and Fodder. One most valuable feature about this Millet is that the hay can be fed to horses and other stock without any danger of bad results from feeding the whole seed when it is allowed to ripen. We have only a limited quantity of it and advise our brother farmers to order at least enough of it to get a start, as we are certain that you will all be well pleased with it. Large Packet, 5c.; lb., 25c.; 4 lbs., 85c., postpaid by mail. By express or freight not prepaid, lb., 15c.; peck, 50c.; bu., $1.35; grain sacks extra, at 16c. each.

**GERMAN** or **GOLDEN MILLET**—This grows very rank and is one of the best varieties for hay or fodder. On good, rich soil it will make a growth from 4 to 5 feet high, and although the hay may seem coarse, yet it is so tender, if cut at the right stage, which is when in full bloom, that even hogs will eat the cured hay quite greedily. A yield of five tons of hay per acre is nothing unusual. Peck, 50c.; bu., $1.40; 2½ bu., $3.40.

**New Hog Millet.**              **Hungarian.**

German or Golden Millet.

**COMMON MILLET**—This does best on dry, light, rich soil and grows 2½ to 4 feet high, with a fine bulk of stalks and leaves, and is excellent for forage. About 3 pecks of seed is sown per acre. Peck, 35c.; bu., $1.20; 2½ bu., $2.85; grain sacks extra, at 16c. each.

**JAPANESE BARNYARD MILLET**—A variety of Millet which was first grown here in this country by Professor Brooks, of the Massachusetts Agricultural College, who

**Japanese Barnyard Millet** brought it from Japan. It has proven to be very valuable and is highly recommended for the following reasons. It will grow 6 to 8 feet in height and yield 15 to 25 tons per acre. It may be siloed, fed green or cured into hay, and its feeding quality is superior to Fodder Corn. It can be sown at any time from the middle of May to the end of July, either broadcast at the rate of 12½ pounds per acre or in drills, using 8 pounds of seed per acre. The seed so far has been scarce and high priced, but we can offer it at a less price than usual. Large Packet, 5c.; lb., 20c.; 4 lbs., 75c., postpaid by mail. By express or freight not prepaid, lb., 10c.; 15 lbs., $1.00; 50 lbs., $3.25.

Japanese Barnyard Millet is also offered by a certain seed dealer here in the Northwest as the Billion Dollar

**NEW SIBERIAN MILLET**—A good Millet, introduced several years ago from Russia, and is an entirely distinct variety, the seed being of an almost orange color, but the heads are about the same as of the Common Millet. It stools quite heavy and the joints being so close together the plants are just covered with blades. It is a heavy yielder, and the hay is of very fine quality. It will yield from 50 to 70 bushels of seed per acre. Being an introduction from the extreme north it is very hardy, and will prosper under conditions when other varieties fail. Large Packet, 5c.; lb., 22c., postpaid by mail. By express or freight, not prepaid, lb., 10c.; peck, 50c.; bu., $1.35; grain sacks extra, at 16c. each.

If in need of larger quantities of Millet and Hungarian, write us for special prices, which we quote by return mail.

**New Siberian Millet.**

**DWARF ESSEX RAPE.**—Throughout a large portion of the United States farmers and stockraisers could advantageously grow of this so succulent and nourishing a forage crop for feeding stock during the summer and autumn months, when the supply of grasses and clovers is often limited. Dwarf Essex Rape can be grown to good advantage on land that has already produced an early maturing crop of some sort, such as oats, rye or winter wheat. Of how great a value rape is as a pasture or fodder plant has been fully realized by a great many farmers and stockraisers here in the Northwest during the two severe droughty years of 1900 and 1901; and everybody who is acquainted with its high feeding value would not be without it for another year.

Dwarf Essex Rape is a pasture plant for all kinds of live stock—sheep, cows and swine; for fattening sheep it is most valuable. To provide for an early pasture for sheep and swine it should be sown early in spring, and as it is a remarkably fast grower, it will be ready to be eaten off in five weeks from the time of sowing. Unlike other plants it can be sown at any time during spring and summer, and you can have a good pasture just when you need it.

Dwarf Essex Rape is very nourishing, and nothing will get sheep and hogs sooner and better ready for market than this. It is an easy matter to bring spring pigs up to 200 pounds in weight when six months old if fed on Rape.

Late in the fall when most pastures are barren Dwarf Essex Rape yields a splendid feed, as frost will not hurt it any, and it is so well relished by all stock, sheep, hogs and cows alike, that as long as there is anything left of the plants they will eat it. Rape can be sown with grain, using 3 pounds per acre, to provide for pasture for sheep after harvest. It can also be sown in corn when this is cultivated the last time. Good results are generally obtained for late fall pasture when Dwarf Essex Rape is sown after the spring grain has been harvested. When Rape is sown broadcast, 5 to 6 lbs. should be sown per acre. We handle only the genuine Dwarf Essex Rape, which has proven to be the only satisfactory kind, and offer it at a reasonable price. Other dealers may quote lower prices, but they cannot sell the genuine Dwarf Essex for less; they must offer inferior seed. **Large pkt., Lb.; 20c.; postpaid by mail. By express or freight: Lb., 10c.; 5 lbs., 40c.; 10 lbs., 75c.; 25 lbs., $1.65; 50 lbs., $3.00; 100 lbs., $5.50; 200 lbs., at $5.35.**

DWARF ESSEX RAPE

To mislead the farmers one seed firm brags up **Dwarf Victoria Rape**, and offers this at a higher price, claiming that this is the only good Rape, while it is authentically known that there is no rape under this name produced in all England, from where all Rape Seed is imported.

Louriston, Minn., June 5th, 1899.—When you quoted me on my list of seeds last spring I thought your prices for the Rape were too high, so I bought that elsewhere, and mixed it with my oats to get fall pasture, and now the oats are full of plants with yellow flowers, and I think it is mustard. How can I get rid of it? The Clover Grass Mixture and other seeds I bought of you last spring are doing nicely and all your seeds have proven satisfactory.　　ANDREW ENGBERG.

**EARLY AMBER SUGAR CANE.**—This is the only variety of Cane that makes a fine syrup, clear as crystal. Cane syrup made from our Early Amber Cane grown right here in Rice County has become famous, as it took first premiums at the State Fairs in four different states. The syrup has a very delicious flavor, and all that have used it prefer it to the New Orleans Molasses. There is nothing like a home product on your table, for you know that it is a pure article.

Dairy farmers say that this is the most valuable fodder plant in existence for their use. Notwithstanding its great adaptability as a food for live stock, it is only quite recently that the real value of sorghum (or sugar cane) has attracted general attention. Its great merit is now beginning to be appreciated, and the demand is increasing about tenfold every year. It is profitably grown anywhere from Manitoba to Mexico, on any good corn ground, and does not appear to be affected by drought. As a fodder plant it is the most economical plant in existence, and of the very best quality, being sweet, tender, nutritious, and greedily eaten by cattle, horses and hogs. Dairymen find that the cows will give more and richer milk from its use, and it is claimed that as high as 50 tons of the green fodder have been grown per acre. It can be cut several times during the season if not allowed to get too high, and makes a good, sweet hay. Sow 100 lbs. per acre for best results. It is a profitable crop also to grow for the seed, which is excellent for feeding poultry, and is frequently ground and substituted for buckwheat flour. **Lb., 15c.; 3 lbs., 45c., prepaid by mail. By freight: Lb., 6c.; 10 lbs., 45c.; 25 lbs., 90c.; 50 lbs., $1.50; 100 lbs., $2.75.**

The Best

Milk Producer

**Early Amber Sugar Cane.**

**KAFFIR CORN**—An excellent fodder plant, yielding two crops of fodder during a season. It grows from four to five feet high, making a straight, upright growth. The stem or stalk bears numerous wide leaves. The stalks keep green and are brittle and juicy, not hardening like other varieties of sorghum, and making excellent fodder, either green or dried, which is highly relished by cattle, horses and mules. The seed crop is also heavy, sometimes yielding sixty bushels to the acre. For the grain sow in rows three feet apart, three to five pounds of seed to the acre. For fodder sow one-half bushel to one bushel, either broadcast or in drills. **Pkt., 5c.; lb., 20c.; 3 lbs., 50c. By freight: Pkt., 50c.; lb. (50 lbs.), $1.50; 2 bu. or more @ $1.40.**

**JERUSALEM CORN**—Claimed by many to be an improvement on Kaffir Corn, as it is a surer crop in unfavorable seasons. Produces a large crop of fodder which is of very good quality. Seed white and nearly flat. Yields a good grain crop also. Five to six pounds will plant an acre in drills, 40 to 50 lbs. broadcast. **Pkt., 5c.; lb., 25c.; 3 lbs., 60c. By freight: Per pkt., 75c.; bu. (50 lbs.), $2.50; 2 bu. or more @ 2.25.**

**BRAZILIAN FLOUR CORN**—The kernels are pure white, and when ground into flour, it is considered equal to the best wheat flour. It will ripen where other Corn does, and is cultivated the same; plant 5 to 6 quarts per acre. **Large pkt., 5c.; pint, 15c.; qt., 30c., postpaid. By express or freight: Qt., 15c.; 4 qts., 50c.; peck, 90c.**

**BRANCHING DOURA (Yellow Milo Maize)**—Highly valuable because of its certainty to produce heavy crops on poor dry soil. The quantity of seed for fodder, for which stock shows a marked partiality, is enormous. The seed heads grow very large, producing a large quantity of grain, which is superior food for fowls. Cultivate same as corn; plant 4 to 6 lbs. per acre. **Large pkt., 5c.; lb., 20c.; postpaid. Lb., 10c.; 10 lbs., 80c.**

**SERADELLA or CULTIVATED BIRDSFOOT**—For light, poor, or sandy soils Seradella is one of the best fodder plants. We know its great value, and have urged our brother farmers for several years to give this valuable forage plant more attention. It is sown at the rate of 10 to 15 lbs. per acre by itself, or it can be sown in Winter Wheat or Rye in early spring, and after the grain is cut it begins to grow rapidly. It is very remarkable for its drought-resisting qualities and dense, close and thick growth, covering the ground completely and choking out all weeds; also, very desirable as a catch crop. It is not a perennial, but can be cut twice and gives good pasture in one year. **Price, prepaid by mail. Oz., 5c.; lb., 20c.; 4 lbs., 70c. By express or freight, not prepaid: Lb., 10c.; 15 lbs. (for 1 acre), $1.35; 25 lbs., $2.25; 50 lbs., $4.40; 100 lbs., $8.35.**

**Write for special Prices on Larger Quantities of Rape and Sorghum.**

**Kaffir Corn.**

# VETCHES.

**SAND OR WINTER VETCH, HAIRY VETCH—Vicia Villosa**—Among the various leguminous plants introduced during recent years with such manifest advantage to farmers there is not one of greater value than the Hairy Vetch. As a soil reclaimer and forage crop it has no equal and it is only to be regretted that it is not more universally sown. It is an annual plant, similar in growth to a very slender and straggling pea vine, the vines often reaching 10 to 12 feet in length, and covering the ground with a dense mat of forage 2 feet in depth. Stock of all kinds eat it greedily, both in pastures and when cut for hay. It bears our heaviest frosts without injury, and is one of the few plants which can be grown during the winter for green manuring. Whilst it does not make a very vigorous growth during the winter, it yet lives and grows, and is ready to push into quick and luxuriant growth as soon as ever the mild days of spring set in. When once this growth starts, it continues through wet and drought, and the quantity of forage made is wonderful. It has made as high as 45,000 pounds of green feed to the acre, and this feed is of the most nutritious character. It is much richer in protein (the muscle and growth producing element) than Red Clover, or than the Cow Pea, whilst in fat-producing matter it is nearly the equal of those plants. As a soil improver it is richer in nitrogen, phosphoric acid and potash than any of the Clovers or the Cow Pea. If intended for forage or hay, it should be sown at the rate of 30 or 40 pounds to the acre, with a light seeding of winter oats, wheat or rye. This will hold up the vines, and make it easier to cut and harvest the crop. If intended for pasture or a soil improver, sow alone at the rate of 40 or 50 pounds to the acre. Sow early in spring or in August and September, on well prepared land. When sown alone it will make a perfect mat all over the field, which will continue to increase in thickness all through the spring and summer, as the vines fall down and grow through again. When plowed down the soil will be found to be as mellow and full of vegetable matter as possible, and when consolidated with the roller will be in the finest condition for the production of wheat, oats, grass crop, or a crop of potatoes. Lb. postpaid, 23c. 25 lbs., $2.75; 50 lbs., $5.00; 100 lbs., $9.50, by freight or express.

**SPRING VETCHES or TARES—Vicia sativa**—A very productive and highly nutritious fodder plant; is grown very extensively in England, also Canada. It is either cut green for soiling, or made into hay; is well liked and greatly relished by cattle. It is sown broadcast in spring, at the rate of one bushel per acre. **Per lb., 10c.; 50 lbs. (1 bu.), $3.00, by express or freight.. Lb. postpaid, 18c.**

**Teosinte.**

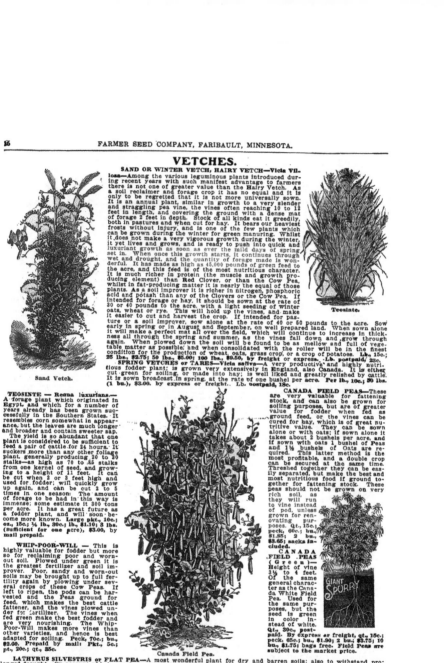

**Canada Field Pea.**

**TEOSINTE — Reana luxurians.**—A forage plant which originated in Egypt, and which for a number of years already has been grown successfully in the Southern States. It resembles corn somewhat in appearance, but the leaves are much longer and broader and contain sweeter sap.

The yield is so abundant that one plant is considered to be sufficient to feed a pair of cattle for 24 hours. It suckers more than any other foliage plant, generally producing 20 to 30 stalks—as high as 70 to 85 stalks from one kernel of seed, and growing to a height of 11 feet. It can be cut when 2 or 3 feet high and used for fodder; will quickly grow up again, and can be cut 2 to 5 times in one season. The amount of forage to be had in this way is immense; some estimate it 300 tons per acre. It has a great future as a fodder plant, and will soon become more known. Large pkt., 10c.; oz., 15c.; ¼ lb., 30c.; lb., $1.10; 3 lbs. (sufficient for one acre), $3.00, by mail prepaid.

**WHIP-POOR-WILL** — This is highly valuable for fodder but more so for reclaiming poor and worn-out soil. Plowed under green it is the greatest fertilizer and soil improver. Poor, sandy and worn-out soils may be brought up to full fertility again by plowing under several crops of these Cow Peas. If left to ripen, the pods can be harvested and the Peas ground for feed, which makes the best cattle fattener, and the vines plowed under for fertilizer. The vines when fed green make the best fodder and are very nourishing. The Whip-Poor-Will makes more vines than other varieties, and hence is best adapted for soiling. Peck, 70c.; bu., $2.00. Prepaid by mail: Pkt., 5c.; pt., 20c.; qt., 35c.

**CANADA FIELD PEAS**—These are very valuable for fattening stock, and can also be grown for soiling purposes, but are of greater value for fodder when fed as ground feed, or the vines can be cured for hay, which is of great nutritive value. They can be sown alone or with oats; if sown alone it takes about 2 bushels per acre, and if sown with oats 1 bushel of Peas and 1½ bushels of Oats are required. This latter method is the most profitable, and a double crop can be secured at the same time. Threshed together they can be easily separated, but make the best and most nutritious food if ground together for fattening stock. These peas should not be grown on very rich soil, as they will run to vine instead of pod, unless grown for renovating purposes. Qt., 15c.; peck, 60c.; bu., $1.85; 2 bu., $3.65; sacks included.

**CANADA FIELD PEAS (Green)**—Height of vine 3½ to 4 feet. Of the same general character as the Canada White Field Pea. Used for the same purposes, but the seed is green in color instead of white. Qt., 30c. postpaid. By express or freight, qt., 15c.; peck, 65c.; bu., $1.90; 2 bu., $3.75; 10 bu., $1.75; bags free. Field Peas are subject to the market price.

**LATHYRUS SILVESTRIS or FLAT PEA**—A most wonderful plant for dry and barren soils; also to withstand prolonged drought. On account of being so deep rooted it is extremely hardy and is not injured by severe frost in the winter or in spring. Two or three cuttings can be made in one season and a large amount of very rich hay can be made on a comparatively small area. It is as excellent for pasture as it is for hay, and according to chemical analysis is twice as rich for feeding stock as Clover or Alfalfa. Packet, 5c.; 3 packets, 12c.; oz., 15c.; ¼ lb., 50c.; lb., $1.20, prepaid by mail.

**GIANT SPURRY**—Spurry is of great value for light or thin ground, and several years' experimenting at the Michigan Agricultural College has proven that it is the only plant which can be grown on poor, sandy, dry soil, that will surely return a paying yield. Dr. Manley Stiles, of Lansing, Mich., calls it the clover of sandy soils, yielding 7,700 pounds per acre; and in another report to the Michigan Agricultural Station, he says: "The Spurry has shown wonderful productiveness. Its value as a manurial plant on light sands is pronounced. It seems to enrich the soil more rapidly than other plants. It is readily eaten by cows, sheep and cattle."

Price, prepaid by mail: Oz., 8c.; lb., 22c. By express or freight: Lb., 12c.; 10 lbs. (for 1 acre), $1.00; 50 lbs., $4.75.

**Sand Vetch.**

## AUSTRALIAN SALT BUSH.

The many thousands of acres of alkali lands of the West may be made productive and profitable by planting Salt Bush. Cattle, Horses, Sheep and Swine eat it and thrive on it. This plant is not an experiment, it is a demonstrated success. It flourishes where grasses and other forage plants will not grow, and furnishes enormous quantities of nutritive food for stock, and remains green all winter. Single plants grown on the worst alkali lands have reached a diameter of 16 feet in one season. It succeeds everywhere, and there seems to be no question but that it will in time eliminate alkali from the ground, rendering it suitable for other crops. Prof. Tower states that its nutritive strength is nearly equal to that of Alfalfa. Large pkt., 5c.; oz., 20c.; lb., $1.25.

EARLY SOJA BEANS (Coffee Berry.)—During recent years this has been largely sold under the name of German Coffee Berry at extremely high prices, but we prefer to offer it under its correct name. The berries ripen in about three or four months from the time of planting, producing a crop of twenty to forty bushels to the acre and are as easily grown as other beans. When roasted and ground it closely resembles coffee and tastes quite similar. Some mix half and half with coffee when using and claim it is superior. Its great value to the farmer lies in the fact that when ground it makes one of the most valuable crops for feeding stock and adds greatly to the milk production. Claimed also to be much superior to clover for fertilizing soil and for pasturing, or feeding the green fodder, of which it frequently yields from eight to twelve tons per acre. Plant in drills two or three feet apart and one foot between plants. Pkt., 5c.; ¼ lb., 15c.; lb., 30c.; 3 lbs., 80c.; postpaid. Pk., $1.00; bu., $3.50.

## FIELD BEANS.

NAVY BEAN—The Navy Bean is grown very extensively for field culture. We can supply a very high grade of this standard bean. Peck, 80c.; bu., $3.25; sacks included.

CALIFORNIA WONDER BEAN—Price: Peck, $1.00; bu., $3.50. See page 43 for full description of this valuable variety, the best for field culture.

BURLINGAME MEDIUM—Beans pearly white, rust proof, and the heaviest yielders. Qt., 18c.; peck, 90c.; bu., $3.25.

WHITE MARROWFAT—Standard variety for field culture: Early, productive, and of excellent quality, green and when cooked. Qt., 18c.; peck, $1.00; bu., $3.50.

NEW EVERGREEN BROOM CORN

During recent years the whole Broom Corn product has been controlled by a broom corn trust, and a great many farmers have cleared as much as $100 off an acre. Get our book on Broom Corn and Brooms,—a treatise on raising Broom Corn and making brooms on a small or large scale. Illustrated. Cloth, 50c., prepaid.

NEW EVERGREEN BROOM CORN—The best variety for general cultivation on account of color and quality of brush; brush of good length, and always of green appearance when ripe, never gets red and has no center stalk, which is a most desirable point to broom corn raisers and manufacturers. Large pkt., 5c.; lb., 20c.; 3 lb., 50c.; postpaid. By express or freight: 10 lb., 50c.; 25 lb., $1.10; 50 lb., $2.00.

NEW JAPANESE BROOM CORN—The earliest Broom Corn known; matures in about 75 days; can therefore sometimes be planted as a catch crop or even after wheat. Brush is fine and long, without center stalk. Large pkt., 5c.; lb., 20c.; postpaid. By express or freight: 10 lbs., 50c.; 25 lbs., $1.00; 50 lbs., $2.35; 100 lbs., $4.50.

NEW RUSSIAN FLAX—More attention should be paid to good and clean Flax Seed, as it is such an important item. While you raise Flax you might just as well raise the very best, so you will not have to stand a dockage of 10 to 15 lbs. per bushel for foul seeds, such as wild mustard, barn weed and wild buckwheat, so commonly found in Flax. We offer good, clean and healthy seed for a very reasonable price. Peck, 65c.; bu., $1.75; 2 bu., $3.40; grain sacks 16c. each extra. Price of Flax is subject to the market. Write us for definite prices.

SPRING RYE—This is mostly sown for a forage crop, together with Vetches and Oats, but it can well be sown by itself, and is especially valuable as a catch crop when winter grain has been killed out. Peck, 40c.; bu., $1.35; 2 bu., $2.60; sacks included. For prices on larger quantities please write us.

LUPINS—One of the best plants known for reclaiming poor and particularly sandy and old, worn-out land; by plowing in the Lupins such land can be made very valuable. It is so highly valued in Germany that it is called the "Gold of the Desert" or "Desert Reclaimer." When dried for fodder it is very good for sheep. Lb., 20c., postpaid. By express or freight: Lb., 10c.; 10 lbs., 90c.; 100 lbs., $8.00.

EXACT SIZE OF SEEDS

WHITE BEAUTY SUNFLOWER.

WHITE BEAUTY SUN FLOWER—A mammoth single-head Sunflower with pure, snow-white seeds. This strikingly distinct new sort is not only the most beautiful, the most vigorous, the most valuable for stock and poultry feeding, and for oil production, but owing to the fact that all its powers are expended in producing one mammoth head, it is simply a marvel for productiveness, outyielding the old sorts almost two to one, 3,000 pounds per acre being no unusual yield. Pkt., 6c.; ¼ lb., 20c.; lb., 35c.; postpaid by mail.

MAMMOTH RUSSIAN SUNFLOWER—A more profitable or important crop can hardly be raised, especially by prairie farmers. The seed is highly valued by farmers and poultry breeders who have tried it. The hens will fatten on it and lay more eggs than on any other food. Single heads measure from 12 to 22 inches in diameter, and contain a lot of seed, which makes it a cheap food for fowls. Next comes the great value as fuel; when dried, the stalks will make a good hot fire, while the seed-heads, with the seed in, will make a better fire than the best hard coal. One acre at least should be planted and used for either fuel or the seed for poultry. Four quarts will plant one acre. By mail, postpaid: Pkt., 3c.; qt., 20c. By express or freight: Qt., 10c.; 4 qts., 30c.; ¼ bu., 45c.; bu., $1.50.

NEW JAPANESE BUCKWHEAT—This is a brown or almost dark variety, and is very early, about a week earlier than the Silver Hull. It is a vigorous grower of both vines and seed, and yields quite heavily. The flour made from it is of the best quality. It will not require as thick seeding as other Buckwheat, as it branches out so much. It is perfectly hardy and will grow in the extreme north. Peck, 40c.; bu., $1.45; 2 bu., $2.75; sacks included.

NEW SILVER HULL BUCKWHEAT—This is a very thin-shelled Buckwheat of gray silvery color; the kernels are of medium size and very solid. It is a prolific grower and the heaviest yielder yet introduced, and will make first-class Buckwheat Flour. It continues longer in bloom than common Buckwheat and is most excellent for bees. Peck, 40c.; bu., $1.45; 2 bu., $2.75; sacks included.

We shall be pleased to quote lowest prices on Flax, Buckwheat and other Seeds in larger quantities upon inquiry.

NATURAL SIZE

Silver Hull Buckwheat.

# IMPROVED, HARDY NORTHERN GROWN SEED GRAIN.

WHY IT IS NECESSARY TO CHANGE SEED GRAIN—To keep the farm up means not only that it is kept in a high state of fertility, but the largest possible yields should be obtained from it, and this can only be accomplished by using the best seed obtainable. While most of our wide-awake farmers are well aware of this fact, a great many hesitate to make a change in their Seed Grain, because they have an idea that their land will not produce as much as in former years, while the decrease in their crops rests mainly with the seed stock sown. All such grain that was badly affected by rust and smut, and consequently so weakened that it yielded but a small crop of shrunken and shriveled grain, should be discarded and not be used for Seed Grain. Such grain is lacking in vitality, and will produce but a feeble sprout, and no matter how favorable the circumstances are it is not apt to produce much of a crop.

All the Seed Grain that we offer is full of vigor and vitality, and is therefore not easily affected by smut, rust, drought and other unfavorable circumstances. It is an established fact that our Improved Northern Grown varieties of Seed Grain are unsurpassed in vitality and productiveness. Its yield is generally again as large as that of common varieties or such grain that has been raised year in and year out on the same land.

Our Seed Grain has all been raised on the best and the cleanest ground, which is free from foul weeds, and besides we have the most perfect cleaning machinery and can make the most particular separations.

The reason that you should send us your orders is because we are FARMERS and Seed GROWERS ourselves, using the utmost pains to produce the best seed grain obtainable, and offer these true to name. Besides, we are located in the best farming country of the Northwest, and the greatest variety of soil, from the richest prairie soil, heavy timber land, to the rich sandy bottom lands of the Cannon and Straight Rivers, are at our disposal. If you send us your order we are certain that you will be satisfied with the results and that you will order from us again when in need of Seeds.

Macaroni Wheat.

MACARONI WHEAT—Triticum durum—This was introduced several years ago by our Department of Agriculture, and has been thoroughly tested in many sections of the United States, with the most gratifying results. It is an introduction from Russia, and belongs to the durum group (family of hard wheats). In Europe it is simply called hard wheat, and correctly so, since the hardest bread-wheats of the world are really soft compared with it. In the Volga River region the most excellent bread and macaroni are made from it in large quantities, and many of our American flour mills are grinding macaroni wheat this year. Millers who have ground it prefer it to ordinary wheat, as it makes better and more flour than this. The only drawback is that not enough of it is raised so far, as the Macaroni Wheat is too hard to be ground together with common wheat. The grains are very hard and glossy, often translucent, yellowish white in color, occasionally inclining to reddish, and rather large. In the field Macaroni Wheat is often mistaken for barley, as it resembles this very much. It grows rather tall, and the leaves are broad and smooth, and have a peculiar whitish color. The heads are compactly formed and are bearded. This wheat is hardy and not attacked by smut or rust, and is a sure crop, averaging from 50 to 100 per cent more than any other wheat. It is extremely resistant to drought and other unfavorable circumstances. In our Northern and Northwestern States Macaroni should be sown in spring. Where the winters are mild, however, as they are south of the thirty-fifth parallel of this country (Kansas and further south), it can be grown to best advantage as winter wheat. The grain is very large, and as it does not stool very heavily, one and a half to two bushels are required per acre.

Price: Lb., 10c.; peck, 50c.; bu., $1.50; 2½ bu, $3.50; 5 bu, $6.75; sacks included.

PEDIGREE BLUE STEM WHEAT—This is the hardiest as well as the most productive variety of Spring Wheat ever introduced, as it is not so easily affected by unfavorable circumstances, such as drought, rust and blight, and even the chinch-bugs, than other varieties, as it is a robust grower, rooting and stooling quite heavily, and the heads are well protected by its chaff so that the grain is well enclosed. For a full description of this wheat we refer to the last cover page. Price: Peck, 50c.; bu., $1.50; 2½ bu., $3.50; 5 bu., $6.75; 10 bu., $13.00; sacks included.

VELVET CHAFF or BLUE STEM—This is the old, well-known and reliable Hard Spring Wheat. For milling purposes it is equal to Fife Wheat, but yields considerably more per acre than this. Being a very old variety, it is not as pure as the Pedigree Blue Stem offered above. Year in and year out the offered above. The main Wheat crop raised

The following is an extract from the "Pioneer Press" of St. Paul: old Velvet Chaff or Blue Stem Wheat has been the most reliable; when other varieties fail this will always produce a sure crop. Peck, 35c.; bu., $1.25; 2½ bu., $3.00; 5 bu., $5.75; sacks included.

The following is an extract from the Pioneer Press of St. Paul:

Woman Professor of Domestic Science Makes Macaroni Bread.

Pierre, S. D., Special, Nov. 21, 1902.—The Experiment Station at the State Agricultural College has been working on macaroni wheat and flour from that grain to find the adaptability of this grain to Dakota conditions and its worth in case a crop can be secured. Alice Dynes Feuling, the professor of domestic science at the college, has been experimenting upon the bread qualities of this wheat, and is meeting with success. She sent a loaf of the macaroni bread to Gov. Herreld, who pronounces it to be excellent. So far as is known this is the first effort made in the United States to test the breadmaking qualities of this wheat, and the lady in charge of the work is pleased both with her success in this line of experimenting and the fact that she has the honor of making the first tests in this country.

**MINNESOTA NO. 163 FIFE WHEAT**—Our brother farmers, especially in the Spring Wheat growing sections, making a specialty of Wheat growing, are undoubtedly greatly interested in this new Wheat. Professor Hays, of the State University at St. Anthony Park, Minn., originated this Wheat, and a special bulletin issued by the Experiment Station on Seed Wheat gives a full description and the history of it. In comparison with the old standard varieties of Wheat the Minnesota No. 163 is far ahead in every respect, in yield as well as in quality. It is a Wheat with new life, vigor and vitality, growing heads almost again as long as the old, common Fife Wheat, which, on account of being run out and mixed with other kinds, is not as good a yielder any more as it used to be.

The Minnesota No. 163 yields well, grades well, weighs well and, on account of being such a vigorous grower, is less subject to rust and blight than other varieties. It grows a stiffer straw than other kinds and stands up well, when other varieties lodge on account of unfavorable conditions.

Its gluten is of great strength and rather large in amount. We secured our original seed stock from the Experiment Station directly, and have taken special pains to keep it clean and pure, so that our Seed Wheat that we offer of this new variety is true to name and is sure to please every Wheat grower.

The parent variety of this new Wheat is thought to be a variety of Red Fife Wheat, and the MINNESOTA NO. 163 is a Fife Wheat, with which the Wheat growers here in the Northwest are so familiar. It has become known all over the world as NO. 1 HARD, from which the famous Minnesota Hard Spring Wheat Flour is made.

Unfortunately this old Fife Wheat has become so badly mixed, and is what might be called "run out," that it is hard to find it pure. For this reason alone this new Wheat, being pure and unmixed, should be sown, and we are certain that Wheat growers everywhere will appreciate it.

A yield of 35 to 45 bushels per acre is nothing unusual under favorable circumstances.

Price: Peck, 50c.; bu., $1.50; 2½ bu., $3.50; 5 bu., $6.75; sacks included.

Mr. August Hamling, Saginaw Co., Mich., writes us, Oct. 25, 1901: For the good Seed Wheat you sent me I thank you a thousand times, for I harvested 72 bushels of Minnesota 163 Fife from 1¾ acres. I think I beat everybody in yield in the state of Michigan. The Wheat is large and plump in berry and of the best quality.

**SPELT, SPELZ**—Triticum spelta—This grain is largely grown in some parts of Europe, especially in Southern Germany, in Switzerland, Spain, Denmark and Austria. It is closely related to Wheat; the kernels, however, are tightly enclosed in the hulls or husks, and these adhere to the grain when it is threshed. In sections of Germany where Spelt is largely grown, the hulls are separated from the grain by running it through especially constructed cleaning or scouring machinery, and is ground into flour the same as Wheat, and some claim that it will make better flour and bread than Wheat. It has lately found its way into this country, and has been successfully grown here, and is now offered by different seedsmen. Its greatest value here is for feeding purposes, as it is a heavy yielder, and will produce large crops on land where wheat will not do well any more. The straw is very stiff and does not lodge easily, and the grain does not shell out. It can be fed the same as Oats with the hulls. It may later, however, find favor with the millers, when it becomes known, and we recommend it for trial. Price: Pkt., 5c.; lb., 15c., by mail, postpaid. By freight: Peck, 40c.; bu. (40 lbs.), $1.00; 2½ bu., $2.25; sacks included.

**SASKATCHEWAN FIFE SPRING WHEAT**—Is noted for its great productiveness, earliness, vigor, and freedom from smut and all diseases. Its greatest point of excellence is the hard and

Minnesota No. 163 Fife Wheat.

flinty kernels, whereby it is recognized as the best milling Wheat in in every part of this country and Europe, and is known everywhere as the true NO. 1 HARD WHEAT. The Pillsbury-Washburn Flour Milling Co., in Minneapolis, the largest millers in the world, make the celebrated Minnesota Patent Flour, known and exported to every part of the world, from this Wheat, and Mr. C. A. Pillsbury pronounces it to be the best and most valuable milling Wheat in the world. We have carefully grown and selected this Wheat for seed purposes, and our stock is undoubtedly the best of the Hard Fife in existence. Pk., 35c.; bu., $1.30; 2½ bu., $3.00; 5 bu., $5.75; sacks included.

## WINTER WHEAT.

**WINTER WHEAT**—Although Winter Wheat is sown only in the fall of the year, we like to call the attention of our customers to our Hardy Northern Grown varieties. A great many may not be aware of the fact that we can raise big crops of Winter Wheat here in this extreme northern climate, and such kinds of Winter Wheat that prosper here and make large average yields year in and year out, are the ones that can be depended upon as sure croppers in every locality. With common Winter Wheat grown in a milder climate fair crops may be had occasionally, but good average yields cannot be expected from it year in and year out. To insure the best results with Winter Wheat our Hardy Minnesota Grown Seed Wheat should be sown. This can stand 40 and 50 below zero of bare frost without suffering; neither have excessive thawing and freezing any effect on it.

**BEARDED FIFE WINTER WHEAT**—This is the only Winter Wheat which will equal the well known No. 1 Hard Fife Spring Wheat in milling qualities, and commands a premium of several cents per bushel from the millers in Winter Wheat sections where it is known. The kernels of this Winter Wheat are reddish, with a very thin hull, are hard and flinty and very rich in gluten. It is adapted to all sections of the country where Winter Wheat is largely grown, and will not freeze out or winter-kill. It is also a leader on account of its heavy yielding qualities. Our average crop is from 30 to 38 bushels per acre, while our customers report heavier yields, and at the Experiment Station in Indiana the yield was 43 bushels per acre, while at the Experiment Station of Iowa, who also gave it a thorough test, a yield of 55 bushels was obtained per acre. This proves also that under more favorable conditions for growing Winter Wheat than we have here in Minnesota, and under such conditions as usually exist in the so-called Winter Wheat states, a much better yield can be relied upon. Pk., 40c.; bu., $1.20; 2½ bu., $2.85.

**RED TURKISH WINTER WHEAT**—This is an old and well known bearded variety, and closely resembles our Bearded Fife Winter Wheat, described on the previous page. Although it is of the same habit of growth, it falls a little short in hardiness and productiveness, but still it always held its own against all the bald varieties, as it hardly ever winter-kills. Pk., 40c.; bu., $1.20; 2½ bu., $2.85; sacks included.

Spelts.

**MANDSCHEURI BARLEY —** This grand new Barley was introduced from Asia by the Ontario Agricultural College several years ago, and is beyond doubt the most valuable Barley ever introduced into this country, greatly outyielding the justly celebrated Manshury Barley. It is an early 6-rowed variety, maturing in 80 to 90 days from time of sowing; is very strong strawed and stools well, bearing large and well filled heads of plump and well filled grain, possessing malting qualities of the highest order, and is adapted to all kinds of soil and climate. Another important factor is its nice and bright color, which will not turn dull and yellow when exposed to rainy weather during and after ripening, as most of the other varieties do, and on this account it will always be in good demand by the brewers, and command the highest market price. A good malting Barley will always sell for at least 10 to 15 cents more than such as is discolored and can only be used for feeding purposes. By growing the Mandscheuri there can quite easily be a gain of $5.00 to $10.00 per acre.

Professor Henry, of the Wisconsin Experiment Station, is loud in its praises, and hopes that its cultivation will become general throughout all of our Barley-growing states. Mandscheuri, in a comparative test of 37 varieties grown under the same conditions, and with no attempt made at getting above an average crop, easily outdistanced the whole field by an average yield of 15 bushels more per acre. The introduction of the old and well known Manshury Barley is reckoned as having been worth millions of dollars to our farmers, and we are confident from the Agricultural Station reports and from our own experience that this new Barley will eclipse Manshury in size, yield and value of product. Peck, 35c.; bu., 90c.; 2½ bu., $2.10; 5 bu., $4.10; 10 bu., $8.00; sacks included.

**MANSHURY BARLEY—**This is an old, well-known, 6-rowed variety, introduced by Professor Henry, of the Wisconsin Agricultural Experiment Station, 13 or 14 years ago. Since then it has been the standard and most popular Barley ever introduced. It has been worth millions of dollars to farmers in the Barley growing states. It is a Barley of wonderful productiveness, and has no equal as a heavy yielder; its malting qualities are unsurpassed, and on this account always commands the highest market price. It ripens early and has strong, stiff straw, with long and heavy heads, filled with nice plump kernels, which are of a pretty bright color, and will not discolor from wet weather. It is in fact the best Barley to grow either as a Barley to feed or to grow for the market. The Manshury Barley yields here in Minnesota, in ordinary seasons, 60 to 65 bushels per acre, and in favorable seasons has yielded as high as 80 bushels; figuring only 45 to 50 cents per bushel, it is one of the best paying crops. Our stock of this is pure as the original, and will produce as heavy crops as in former years, and we cannot recommend it too highly. Peck, 30c.; bu., 85c.; 2½ bu., $2.00; 5 bu., $3.85; 10 bu., $7.65; sacks included.

**BLACK BARLEY—**How to produce the largest amount of grain from an acre, best adapted for feeding milch cows and for fattening stock, is the most important question with every farmer and dairyman. You will surely not make a miss by sowing Black Barley for this purpose, for it is an extra heavy yielder, yielding from 70 to 80 bushels to the acre, and it is of the greatest feeding value at the same time. No other grain fed as ground feed is so nourishing and milk-producing as Black Barley, and for fattening hogs it is invaluable. It should not be sown on ground that is too rich, as it is apt to lodge, but sow it on ordinary good soil; even on thin and poor soil it will make large crops when other varieties of grain fail entirely. It is not affected by prolonged droughts, and is, therefore, the best grain for drought-stricken countries. The grain is huiless, very plump and heavy, and of a pretty bluish black color. Peck, 50c.; bu., $1.60; 2 bu., $3.00; sacks included.

**WHITE HULLESS-BEARDLESS BARLEY—**Also known as "Ideal Barley" and "Giant White Hulless Barley." It grows very large, and has heavy, well filled heads without beards, and in the field it looks about the same as the "Beardless Barley" (see below), but the kernels shell out without the hulls, like the Black Barley, and are the prettiest and handsomest white berry, plump and oval in shape, that has ever been grown. It is not a malting barley, but can be used for feeding only, and as a fattening feed for hogs it has no equal; it makes sweeter meat and nicer lard than corn. It is a vigorous grower, and can be sowed after all the other grain is sown, and will mature before wheat or oats will. It can also be sown for hay, and if sown early enough can be cut twice, and will make two good crops of hay in one year. Peck, 50c.; bu., $1.75; 2 bu., $3.25; sacks included.

**SUCCESS BEARDLESS BARLEY—**This is a new 6-rowed Barley, and, as the name indicates, without beards, which is the most valuable improvement on barley for years. On account of the long, harsh and objectionable beards, a great many farmers will not grow Barley at all, because it is so disagreeable to handle. It is 6-rowed, like the old Manshury Barley, and the berry is of the same appearance as this. It is a vigorous grower, producing strong short straw, heavy and well filled heads, and is the earliest Barley known, which makes it very convenient during harvest, as you can have the Beardless Barley out of the way before you cut wheat and oats. With good land and season, it has produced 80 to 90 bushels per acre, already. In regard to soil, it is not particular, as you can raise a good crop of Beardless Barley on land that is too poor to produce a crop of wheat or oats. Not getting so easily discolored as other Barley, it is a first-class Barley for malting, and will always bring the highest market price. It should not be mistaken for the Beardless Hulless Barley which is described above, and which is grown for feeding purposes only. Ever since this grand new Barley was introduced, there has been such a demand for it that we were always short supplying our trade, and we anticipate another great rush for it this year. On account of raining almost daily during the ripening season this barley is somewhat off in color, and if you write us for a sample before you order, it would, therefore, be more satisfactory. Pk., 40c.; bu., $1.10; 2½ bu., $2.65; 5 bu., $5.00; sacks included.

Success Beardless Barley.

Yield over 100 Bus. per acre.

FARMER SEED CO'S. GIANT CANADIAN OATS. Introduced 1903

**CANADIAN GIANT.**

These are the kind of oats to grow for sure cropping, heavy plump grains with the largest per cent of meat and a small per cent of hull; stiff straw that will save the crop until harvested. Heads long, heavy and full. Being originated in Canada, they are extremely hardy and of vigorous growth, so that neither drought nor excessive moisture will affect them as much as other varieties. The grain is large, white, plump, with thin hull, weighing 40 lbs. per bu. with ordinary thresher cleaning. On account of the large per cent of meat these oats are of much greater feeding value than most other kinds, and are well suited for oatmeal and other oat products.

Before we offered these elegant oats we have grown them two years in succession to convince ourselves of their superior merits. They will yield under ordinary farm cultivation from 75 to over 100 bushels per acre. We don't ask you to build your hopes on 200 bushels and more per acre for we are farmers ourselves and know that we are dealing with intelligent people who realize that such yields are impossible.

OUR CANADIAN GIANT OATS surpass all others in heavy weight, thin hull, stiffness of straw, and what is the most important, also, in heavy yields. In short, they are the most profitable for farmers to grow and for merchants to handle. They ripen evenly and medium early, and notwithstanding that the straw is of fair length, bearing very large heads, filled completely with the plump grains almost as heavy as wheat, they stand up stiff and straight until fully matured. For extreme hardiness, yield, weight and quality the Canadian Giant Oats are superior to any other variety.

The price is low enough so that you can sow a good field with them. Peck, 40c.; bu., $1.25; 2½ bu., $2.75; 5 bu., $5.25; 10 bu., $10.00; sacks included.

**LINCOLN OATS.**

We consider this one of the best main crop varieties of Oats, and no other kind ever made such a record. It not only equaled, but surpassed all claims made for it, and is pronounced the best, most productive and hardiest Oat ever introduced.

It is early, with heavy, stiff straw, bearing large and heavy heads, with well filled, plump grain. It has very thin and soft hulls and the plump and meaty berry can be slipped out from it by pressing it between the fingers. On this account it is of the greatest feeding value, and for making oatmeal there is no other Oat better adapted. Ever since it was introduced it has taken the lead, not only in quality, but also as the heaviest yielding Oat, producing as much as 174 bushels from one bushel of seed sown, and yielding an average of 116 bushels from one bushel of seed sown in seven different states. They are not like most other Oats, which, when you put them on good, rich ground, they lodge, and sometimes the whole crop is lost, but on account of their strong, stiff straw, will stand up erect and produce a heavy crop of grain. It is more thankful in this respect than other Oats, and this peculiar quality accounts for its heavy yielding. This Oat is never affected by rust, and the grain is always very handsome. It is the best seller on the market, and whoever wants to get an early white oat, either for himself or to raise for the market, it pays best to get the Lincoln.

In every locality where it was grown it has been in the lead, and so far has outyielded all other varieties sown alongside of it, and weighed from 5 to 10 pounds more to the measured bushel. Price: Peck, 25c.; bu., 80c.; sack of 2½ bu., $1.75; 5 bu., $3.35; 10 bu., $6.50; sacks included.

**EARLY CHAMPION OATS.**

This grand new variety, which was introduced in 1898, has given excellent satisfaction to our customers, and it gave the largest yield per acre of any variety in the test at the Iowa Agricultural College, and is highly recommended by them. Has comparatively short straw, matures a week to ten days earlier than other kinds, thus largely escaping the liability to rust. Its greatest value lies in its special adaptability as a nurse crop to sow with grass seed, as it does not stool as freely as some other sorts. Will not lodge on rich land. Henry Wallace, editor Wallace's Farmer, says: "I would rather risk sowing grass seed with them than any other variety I know of." Price per peck, 25c.; bu., 80c.; 2½ bu., $1.75; 5 bu., $3.35; 10 bu., $6.50.

**NEW ZEALAND OATS.**

The original seed of this was sent several years ago from New Zealand to Dallas County, Iowa, and was carefully planted and grown by itself ever since. It proves to be very hardy and a vigorous grower. It averages a trifle higher than other sorts, but has very stiff straw and is never known to lodge. It has a record of yielding 102 bushels per acre, when other varieties in the same field yielded only 45 to 50 bushels. They are about a week later than the common Round Head Oats, thus giving time to harvest the early grain first. We obtained our seed stock direct from the introducer, and it is therefore the genuine. Peck, 30c.; bu., 80c.; 2½ bu., $1.75; 5 bu., $3.35; 10 bu., $6.50; sacks included.

**AMERICAN BANNER OATS.**

This is one of the prettiest and best Pure White Oats, and deserves more attention. It is well adapted to sow on good and rich soil, where it will not lodge on account of its short and stiff straw. In season of excessive rains and on well-manured soil there is no other Oat that will carry its heavy load of grain so well as the American Banner. It will yield well under most all conditions; on ordinary soil a crop of 100 bushels per acre is generally harvested, while on good and rich ground it will even yield heavier, where most other kinds would lodge and fall entirely. The grain is white, large and plump and ripens early. It stools freely and throws up a large number of stems, and for this reason can be sown thinner than other varieties.

These Oats are unsurpassed in quality and yield, and those who are troubled with lodging Oats should try this variety. We have grown it long enough and are convinced that it will please everybody. Better put in a field of them this year and convince yourself of its great merits. It will neither smut, rust nor lodge. We have a fair stock of them which we offer at a reasonable price. Peck, 30c.; bu., 80c.; 2½ bu., $1.75; 5 bu., $3.35; 10 bu., $6.50; sacks included.

**NEGRO WONDER OATS**—This is a heavy yielding black, or rather gray, Oat, and will surely please everybody who gives it a trial. It is a very early Oat, with stiff straw, and nothing short of a cyclone will lodge it. It always yields heavily; 80 to 95 bushels is an average for it here in Minnesota. It is very thin hulled and has a much larger percentage of berry than other Oats, and on this account is of the highest feeding value. On account of their high feeding value, and greater productiveness than White Oats, Black Oats are raised more extensively and are sold more in the market than they were in former years. In fact all Black Oats, being thick and hard shelled, always sold for a cent or two less in the grain market, but Black Oats such as we offer are of greater feeding value, and on account of their sweetness, are even preferred by the stock. A great many farmers have tried in vain to get good Black Oats, and we are sure they will be well satisfied with the Negro Wonder. Peck, 30c; bu., 95c.; 2½ bu., $2.25; 5 bu., $4.25; sacks included.

## WHITE BEAUTY OATS.

We introduced this so valuable Oats to our trade two years ago, and find it fully up to our claims and expectations. All of our patrons who gave it a trial wrote us letters of approval, stating that they are more than pleased with it. It has been grown in most every State of the Union, and is adapted to most every locality. As its name implies, it is a pure white medium early Oats, very productive and the grain quite heavy. It stools quite heavily, and the straw is extra strong and stiff, holding up its load of grain wonderfully. A field of this Oats, with large branching heads, well laden with heavy grain, is a most beautiful sight. The grain is of the very best quality, large, plump and well filled. An average yield of this Oats is from 75 to 100 bu. per acre.

Price: Peck, 40c.; bu., $1.00; 2½ bu., $2.35; 5 bu., $4.50; 10 bu., $8.50; sacks included.

## IMPROVED WHITE RUSSIAN OATS.

This is an old standard variety and hardly needs a description. It is quite distinct from other kinds of oats on account of being a side, or a mane oats. Years ago, when first introduced, this used to be a very late oats, but since it has become thoroughly acclimated it is not more than a week later than our earliest varieties, and is considered one of the best and most productive kinds ever offered. It is very prolific and under ordinary cultivation will yield 100 bushels per acre. It is extremely hardy, enduring the cold, and sometimes rather unfavorable climate of our Northwest without suffering, and is entirely rust and smut proof. In berry it is longer and larger than other varieties and is especially adapted to sow with wheat for succotash, ripening well together with the Blue Stem. On account of its long berry it can be easily separated from wheat. Price, .25c; bushel, 80c; 2½ bushels, $1.75; 5 bushels, $3.35; 10 bushels, $6.50; sacks included.

**SILVER MINE OATS**—This is a very hardy and prolific variety with long but very stiff straw. It can be sowed on very rich and well manured soil without danger of lodging. When a great many oat fields were badly lodged last year by rain storms and excessive wet weather, the Silver Mine stood up without crinkling. The grain is of the clearest white color, and there will never be a dark kernel of grain in it. It will grow and thrive under the most unfavorable conditions of soil and climate and is always a sure crop. Price—Peck, 25c; bushel, 80c; 2½ bushels, $1.75; 5 bushels, $3.35; 10 bushels, $6.50; sacks included.

White Shonen Oats.

**BLACK TYROLIAN OATS**—The increasing demand for Black Oats during the last year has induced us to give it more attention. We have tried a great many kinds of Black Oats, but most of them were of inferior quality. Only two, the Black Tyrolian and Negro Wonder Oats combine all the good qualities required. The Black Tyrolian is a native of Tyrol, Switzerland, and is the blackest of all so-called Black Oats. It is much hardier than other Oats, which enables it to withstand drought and wet weather. The straw is stiff and heavy, and will stand up better than any other Oats. We have grown it on rich, new woodland, but it showed no inclination at all to lodge, although we had plenty of wet weather. The kernels are short and plump, have a fine, soft shell, and are somewhat flattened like the Lincoln Oats. It is a vigorous and strong grower, and is a very early Oat. Peck, 50c.; bu., $1.10; 2½ bu., $2.50; sacks included.

**WHITE SHONEN OATS**—This is by far the handsomest White Oats introduced. The kernels are of pretty white color, plump and heavy, and do not run out to a long point. During the latter years they have come to the front as a big yielder. Prof. W. A. Henry, of the Wisconsin Experiment Station, says of it in Bulletin 16: "For productiveness, stiffness of straw and thinness of hull, the White Shonen stands at the head of the list." We have raised these elegant Oats here in Minnesota now for the past six consecutive years, and have never seen them yield less than at least 80 bushels per acre, although we have had years of severe drought, so that other Oats did not yield more than half a crop, but White Shonen never failed. It surely pays to discard your old, run-out and mixed Oats and get an Oat with new vigor and productiveness. We pay the greatest attention to our Seed Oats, and know that what we offer is the pure and genuine White Shonen. Peck, 30c.; bu., 80c.; sack of 2½ bu., $1.75; 5 bu., $3.35; 10 bu., $6.50; sacks included.

Somerset, Pa.—I am not going to scold you for selling me White Shonen Oats. The season was not very good for Oats, and the very best farmers in this section did not average more than 50 bushels per acre. I had seeded 12 acres with your White Shonen Oats, which yielded 884 bushels, or an average of 73¾ bushels per acre. May you long sell your A. No. 1 Seeds.                    W. B. KEIM.

David City, Neb., 11-27, 1900.—You will probably remember that I bought different kinds of seeds from you last spring. The White Shonen Oats made a very heavy yield, and are the prettiest White Oats that I have seen. They are very stiff in straw and did not rust a particle.                    JOHN MEDINGER.

# True and Reliable Northern Grown Seed Corn.

With no other farm product does the crop depend so much upon the nature of the seed than with Corn. It is not only a matter of germination, but the greatest importance is its vigor and vitality produced by most careful and scientific breeding in a Northern climate. It is an easy matter to produce Seed Corn that will sprout and grow, but it may be a Corn not at all adapted to certain climatic and soil conditions, and will often not mature when circumstances are not just right, as it is not hardy and acclimated, while it is a well-known fact which cannot be denied that our hardy Minnesota Grown Seed Corn insures great vigor and vitality, rapid growth, early ripening and the greatest productiveness. Being located so far North and in the best corn growing section of the Northwest, the Seed Corn that we produce here is thoroughly acclimated and therefore the best Corn for you to grow. Our Corn growing season is but short, but after summer has once set in everything grows with wonderful rapidity, owing to the great fertility of our soil and the peculiar climate. Such varieties of Corn that take 120 days to ripen in the Great Corn Belt can be matured here, after three or four years of careful growing, in at least 20 days less. What a gain of only one or two weeks in the maturing of our Corn crops means a great many farmers and Corn growers have experienced oftentimes. The last two weeks are generally the most critical for our growing Corn crop, and only one week earlier may mean hundreds of dollars ahead sometimes.

All of our Seed Corn is thoroughly tested and none of it sent out of which we are not certain as to the germinating, yet we advise our brother farmers, no matter where they buy their seed corn, to test it before planting. It is but little trouble to try a few kernels in earth, and by so doing the responsibility can be placed where it belongs. It is best to order early and have the seed corn on hand in time for testing and planting.

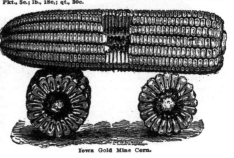

Minnesota Ideal.

**MINNESOTA IDEAL YELLOW DENT CORN**—Finally we have succeeded in producing a Yellow Dent Corn that fills all the requirements of a Corn for our Northwestern States. The Minnesota Ideal is a Corn that matures in 80 days and less, and produces just as large yields as such varieties requiring from 90 to 110 days to ripen. Reliability is stamped upon every feature of this Corn. It is a Corn that will not fail to produce a crop in the worst Corn year, as it is such a strong grower, sending its strong roots deep into the soil, and it will therefore produce a paying crop in most any locality where other varieties would not gather nourishment enough to grow a fair-sized stalk, much less than to mature an ear. The Minnesota Ideal is of a very distinct type, as our cut also indicates, the ears being symmetrically formed, long, straight and tapering to a point at once. The grain is of medium depth, compact and heavy, and ears medium to large, the average ear measuring about 10 to 11 inches. In stalks it grows only seven to eight feet in height, which are short-jointed and produce an abundance of fine fodder. We should like to have every one of our patrons plant at least some of this Corn, for we know it will do them good and secure us a friend and customer. Price: Sample ear, prepaid by mail, 25c.; qt., prepaid 40c.; by freight or express, qt., 25c.; peck, 75c.; bu., $2.25; 2 bu., $4.25; sacks included.

**MINNESOTA GROWN IOWA GOLD MINE CORN**—This is a well-known and standard variety of Corn originated in Iowa about 10 years ago. Since we have raised this elegant variety here in Minnesota for the last seven years, it has become so thoroughly acclimated that it matures here at least two weeks earlier than in Iowa, where it was originated. The Minnesota Grown Iowa Gold Mine is one of the most profitable Dent Corn varieties to grow here in the Northwest. It is early—ripening in 85 to 90 days. The ears are of good size and symmetrical, of a bright golden yellow color, and as handsome as a $20.00 gold coin just from the mint; grain is very deep; cob small and therefore dries out very quickly as soon as ripe. Seventy pounds of ear corn make 60 to 64 lbs. of shell corn, and in hauling to market it weighs 5 bushels more to the wagon load than common varieties in the same size wagon.

Price: Qt., 15c.; peck, 65c.; bu., $2.00; 2 bu., $3.75; sacks included. By mail, postpaid: Pkt., 5c.; lb., 18c.; qt., 30c.

**MINNESOTA LEAMING**—This is the Improved Leaming, introduced years ago by Mr. Leaming, of Ohio. It was always a standard variety, but being run out and mixed somewhat, some undesirable points have been bred off, and a decided improvement on the old well-known Leaming has been made. On good, well manured soil it has yielded as heavy as 134 measured bushels of shelled Corn per acre. It has large size ears, and the kernels are of good depth, and of a yellow orange color, but with a very small red cob. The stalks grow only to a fair size with quite an amount of good fodder. Price: Qt., 15c.; peck, 50c.; bu., $1.75; 2 bu., $3.25; sacks included. Prepaid by mail: Pkt., 5c.; lb., 18c.; qt., 30c.

**MINNESOTA NUMBER THIRTEEN**—An elegant early variety of Yellow Dent Corn, introduced by Professor W. M. Hayes, the well-known agriculturist of our Minnesota Experiment Station. Our original Seed stock was procured from the originator directly, and have raised this Corn now five years in succession, never failing to secure a large crop of good and solid ears. It is a full Yellow Dent Corn, with kernels packed closely upon the cob, and well-filled from tip to tip. This Corn ripens in 85 days, and in even less time if the season is favorable. The Minnesota No. 13 was not caught by frost last year, as it was well matured long before Sept. 13, when Jack Frost paid us his first visit. Although it ripens so extremely early, it is a heavy yielder, producing from 65 to 100 bushels per acre. From our own experience we can recommend this Corn to our brother farmers as the best, nicest and the most productive early Yellow Dent Corn offered. Price, express or freight: Qt., 20c.; peck, 65c.; bu., $2.00; 2 bu., $3.75; sacks included. Prepaid by mail: Pkt., 5c.; lb., 20c.; qt., 35c.

Iowa Gold Mine Corn.

**NEW WHITE CAP YELLOW DENT—** This Corn will be appreciated by those living in droughty sections and by those farmers who have thin, poor soil. The ears are always large, handsome and well filled. The tip ends of the grain are white, the inside yellow, making it a beautiful color. It grows strong, rank and thick, 7 to 8 feet high. It has a large number of rows on the cob, making it a great yielder, and is sure to mature in from 90 to 95 days. Price: Qt., 15c.; peck, 65c.; bu., $1.85; 2 bu., $3.50. By mail, postpaid: Pkt., 5c.; lb., 18c.; qt., 30c.

MINNESOTA KING CORN — This is the best early Dent Corn to plant here in the Northwest, as it has never been caught by frost, for it matures extremely early and is one of the few varieties of Corn that yielded a full crop of well-matured ears last year. For description and price see last cover page.

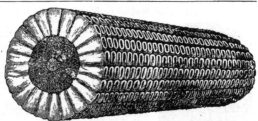

**Minnesota White Dent Corn.**

This is an extra early White Dent Corn, maturing just as early as the Pride of the North, but yields almost again as much as this on the open prairie and on poor and thin soils. It makes very good sized ears, with long and deep kernels growing very compact around it. This is the best pure white Dent Corn adapted for a Northern climate, like that of Minnesota, Wisconsin and the Dakotas. We have grown it here in Minnesota now for several years, and it has always made sure and good crops, yielding considerably more, and being earlier than other kinds. It is a vigorous grower, taking strong hold in the ground, and averaging about 7 feet in height, producing good-sized ears, which are well filled to the extreme end of the cob. We recommend it to all who wish a large eared, heavy yielding, white Dent Corn. Qt., 15c.; peck, 65c.; bu., $2.00; 2 bu., $3.75; sacks included. Prepaid by mail: Pkt., 5c.; lb., 18c.; qt., 30c.

## New Field Corn—Murdock Golden Dent

An enormous Golden Dent variety, so early that it can be grown in the Northern States, and out-yields any other sort. It originated in Wisconsin, and is the finest Field Corn we have ever seen. Ears very large and handsome, 24 rows of deep kernels. It is enormously prolific, producing over 125 bushels to the acre in very dry seasons. In hills four feet apart each way, and with ordinary cultivation. Its great vigor enables it to stand dry weather remarkably and give a good crop when other sorts fail from drought. It is not a tall growing variety, and large sized ears are borne by each stalk, which run as uniform as though they were all made in the same mold and they are as perfect and handsome as though they were made of wax. No other variety of Corn can approach this, and it is bound, when known, to be more extensively grown than all other kinds put together. Owing to its extreme earliness it may be harvested earlier than most other Dent Corn varieties, even when planted much later. It is earlier by several weeks than Iowa Silver Mine, Legal Tender and Learning, and will mature with PRIDE OF THE NORTH and Minnesota No. 13. It is seldom one sees anything bred up to such perfection as is this new Corn. Pkt., 5c.; lb., 20c.; qt., 35c. By express or freight: Peck, 75c.; bu., $2.00; 2 bu., $3.75.

## Prosperity Corn.

This is a very large-eared, full yellow Dent Corn, maturing in 90 days here in Minnesota. We offered this Corn to our brother farmers two years ago for the first time, and it has met with such approval by all those who have tried it that we feel confident it will become the "standard" or the leading Corn variety here in the Northwest. What every farmer wants and needs is a Corn that will mature a well formed and good-sized ear inside of 90 to 95 days, and such a Corn we offer in our Prosperity. This has more solid, meat than any other variety, for it ripens early, maturing in at least 90 to 95 days; and is, therefore, a sure Corn to plant here in the Northwest. It grows larger ears than the Iowa Gold Mine and the Early Mastodon Corn, which are well filled from tip to tip, and will yield as much, if not more, than the heaviest yielders in the main Corn-growing belt. Under ordinary circumstances, it has yielded with us 125 bu. from an acre. It is deep-rooted and therefore a great drought resister. The ears are large and handsome, with medium deep grain of golden yellow color and red cobs. This Corn has so much vigor that it will very often make two ears to a stalk. It husks and shells very easily. It is not only a great producer of grain, but also of fodder, the stalks being of fair size, which are short-jointed, and therefore very leafy. This is another great merit of this Corn, for who is not in need of Corn fodder? Good and well cured Corn fodder is just as nourishing and even better for producing a good flow of milk than hay.
Price: Qt., 30c.; pk., 65c.; bu., $2.00; 2 bu., $3.75. By mail, postpaid: Pkt., 10c.; lb., 25c.; qt., 45c.

We give the "Independent," of Hutchinson, Minnesota, credit for the following:
"Mr. Peter Morten, one of our best and most observing farmers, says: 'Prosperity Corn is the biggest eared, soundest and most prolific I have come across. I got thirty pounds of the seed last spring from the Farmer Seed Co., of Faribault, Minnesota, and harvested 335 baskets full of ears.' The specimens shown are all he claims for it."

**Murdock Golden Dent.**

Mr. J. H. Anderson (M.), Blue Earth Co., Minn., wrote us Sept 20th, 1902: "Thanks to you people. I raised a good crop of well-matured Corn from the Prosperity Corn I bought of you last spring. This fine field of Corn is attracting much attention, as it is the only Corn in this locality that is fit for seed. I have a great many offers from farmers even now already of $1.25 per bu. to go into the field and pick it themselves. I have tried 7 different kinds of Corn during the last ten years and your Prosperity Corn is the best that I ever came across."

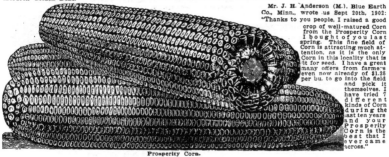

**Prosperity Corn.**

# ABUNDANCE.

### THE MOST PRODUCTIVE, LARGE EARED, YELLOW CORN IN EXISTENCE.

#### Ripens in Less than 100 Days.

The Abundance, which is now offered by us for the first time, was originated by the same grower to whom we owe so many meritorious kinds, like, for instance, the Iowa Silver Mine, which has a record of producing over 200 bushels from one acre.

We claim that the Abundance has the longest grain and the largest ears of any 100 day corns in cultivation and that it will outyield and outweigh any corn in the world.

The Abundance is very much the same corn as the Iowa Silver Mine, except that it is Yellow and earlier. Stalks grow to a height of about 7 to 8 feet, set the ears about 3½ to 4 feet from the ground. Ears solid, very uniform in size and shape, measuring from 10 to 12 inches in length and weighing about 1 to 1½ pounds. There are usually 18 to 20 rows to the ear of very deep kernels, which have a rich golden yellow color and fill out the ear well over the tip. Cobs are very small. Seventy pounds in ear will make sixty-four pounds shelled; that is, only six pounds of cob to a bushel. It is the earliest large-eared variety of yellow corn, and in the Northern States fully matures in 90 to 95 days.

The Corn is very hardy and resists drought wonderfully. It can be grown successfully everywhere except in too Northern states where the season for ripening is too short, like Northern Minnesota and North Dakota. For these sections our Minnesota Ideal is the best Corn.

¼ lb. packet, 10c.; 1 lb., 25c.; qt., 40c., prepaid by mail. By express or freight: Qt., 20c.; peck, 75c.; bu., $2.50; 2 bu., $4.75; sacks included.

**PRIDE OF THE NORTH, or QUEEN OF THE PRAIRIE.**
Although this is an old standard variety, having been originated here in the Northwest over twenty years ago, it is a difficult matter to replace it by other early maturing kinds, as it is the earliest of all Yellow Dent Corns, maturing here in Minnesota in 80 days, and matures in this northern latitude if planted the 1st of June. The ears are 8 to 10 inches long, with small cob and a very long and deep kernel. Seventy pounds of ears will make 60 pounds of shelled corn. Color bright orange and very uniform. The stalks grow only to a medium height, and are very leafy. The ears, which are of medium size, are of a very distinct type, and the deep kernels are packed closely on the cob.

Price, express or freight: Qt., 15c.; peck, 65c.; bu., $1.75; 2 bu., $3.35; sacks included. Prepaid by mail: Pkt., 5c.; 1b., 18c.; qt., 30c.

**SNOW WHITE DENT CORN**—This is the latest introduction of J. C. Suffern, the well known Illinois Corn breeder, and is in fact a novelty, it being the whitest large Dent Corn ever offered. It is a large, uniform, hard, smooth-kerneled Corn, which is as nearly snow white as possible. This Corn has been bred to the point where it combines large size, denseness, uniformity, smoothness and a very white color of grain, with sure maturity at any point south of the 43d parallel of latitude. It is free from dry rot, smut and barrenness, and for making the desired quality of brewers' grits, corn meal, hominy, corn flour and the various other corn products, the Snow White is the only Corn.

Ears of "Snow White Dent Corn" average 10½ inches long, 7½ inches in diameter, and grow low, upon a short, thick, wide-bladed, deeply-rooted stalk, which has been bred to the point where it concentrates its energies in the production of but one good ear. This Corn matures in about 110 days. Cobs are medium-sized, and all white. 100 bushels per acre a very common yield. Worth 5 to 10 cents per bushel more for milling.

Price: ¼ lb. packet, 10c.; 1 lb., 25c.; qt., 45c., prepaid by mail. By freight or express: 1 lb., 15c.; qt., 25c.; peck, 75c.; bu., $2.50.

**IOWA SILVER MINE**—A standard variety of White Dent Corn, which is remarkable for its large yields. Two hundred and fifteen bushels shelled Corn were grown on one acre in Scott county, Iowa, besides heavy yields wherever planted. It is the largest eared 100-day White Dent Corn. Stalk grows to a height of about 7 or 8 feet and sets the ears about 3½ to 4 feet from the ground, just the right height for easy picking.

Abundance.

The ears are very uniform in size and shape, with 16 to 20 rows of pure white kernels set on a small white cob, and the ears are well filled out over the tip. The cob dries out rapidly, so that it is ready for market earlier than any white Field Corn in existence. Seventy pounds of Corn in the ear will make 62 pounds shelled. It has not a large growth of fodder, having been bred essentially for grain, though it has plenty of blades to support the growth and is as well rooted as any Corn grown. It is hardy, a great drought resister and a Corn which will give satisfaction wherever planted. Price: Qt., 15c.; peck, 65c.; bu., $1.85; 2 bu., $3.50. By mail, postpaid: Pkt., 5c.; 1b., 18c.; qt., 30c.

## EARLY FLINT CORN VARIETIES.

(Continued on Next Page.)

Iowa Silver Mine.

**EARLY LONGFELLOW DENT CORN**—This matures even earlier than the well-known Pride of the North, and yields much more than this, without regard to the conditions of the soil. The stalks yield an elegant fodder, and can also be recommended as an early fodder corn. For farmers here in the Northwest this Corn is of the greatest value, for it will grow and mature wherever Corn can be grown, and is always a sure cropper. The ears are long and the kernels small, but the size of the ears makes up for this. Price: Qt., 15c.; peck, 50c.; bu., $1.65; 2 bu., $3.25. Prepaid by mail: Pkt., 5c.; 1b., 18c.; qt., 30c.

**IMPROVED KING PHILIP**—(Extra Early Red Flint.) An old time New England favorite perfected by us. Extremely hardy. One of the best and most reliable very early sorts. Ears 8 to 10 inches long. Quart, 20c.; peck, 75c.; bu., $2.25; 2 bu., $4.00. Bags free. Postpaid by mail: 1 lb., 18c.; qt., 35c.

**COMPTON EARLY FLINT**—The best variety of Corn for northern latitudes, and the longest-eared flint Corn in the country we believe. Ears measure 10 to 16 inches long, 8 broad rows making a most attractive appearance. The stalk grows to medium size, and many of them bear two ears. Very leafy and is a valuable variety for ensilage. We expect all our northern customers to order this Corp; while we also recommend it very highly to plant on thin ground in any latitude and for late planting. Price by mail: 1 lb., 18c.; qt., 35c. Freight or express: Qt., 35c.; peck, 75c.; bu., $2.25; 2 bu., $4.00; sacks included.

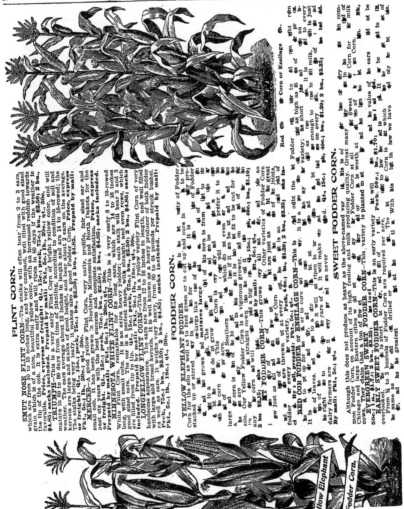

# FLINT CORN.

**SMUT NOSE FLINT CORN.**—The stalks will often bear from 2 to 3 ears, which are from 2 to a nice, beautiful yellow color, with an increase if the weather is grain which are from a nice, beautiful yellow color, with an increase if the weather is favorable. Price, express or freight: Qt., 15c.; peck, 75c.; bu., $2.50; 2 bu., $4.50. Prepaid by mail: Pkt., 5c.; lb., 20c.; qt., 30c.

**TRIUMPH.**—This is a very early Flint Corn of bright yellow color, and will mature in 80 to 90 days from time of planting, according to condition of soil and weather. The ears and stalks of good height, and bear about 2 ears on the stalk. The stalks being very leafy, it makes also a good Fodder Corn. Price, express or freight: Qt., 15c.; peck, 75c.; bu., $2.50; 2 bu., $4.50. Prepaid by mail: Pkt., 5c.; lb., 20c.; qt., 30c.

**MERCER.**—A good yellow Flint Corn, very early, profitic, fair sized ear and small cob. It has been grown in Northern Minnesota and North Dakota for the past six years with the best success and complete satisfaction. Price, express or freight: Qt., 15c.; peck, 75c.; bu., $2.50; 2 bu., $4.50; sacks included. Prepaid by mail: Pkt., 5c.; lb., 20c.; qt., 30c.

**MINNESOTA WHITE FLINT CORN.**—This is a very early 8 to 10-rowed White Flint Corn, remarkable for its long ears, which are 14 to 16 inches long, with small cobs. It is an extra heavy yielder; each stalk will bear 2 and 3 good sized ears. The ear is of a perfect shape. Price, express or freight: Qt., 15c.; peck, 75c.; bu., $2.50; 2 bu., $4.50; sacks included. Prepaid by mail: Pkt., 5c.; lb., 20c.; qt., 30c.

**LONGFELLOW FLINT CORN.**—This is a yellow variety Flint Corn of very handsome and broad kernels. It is well known as a heavy yielder and good fodder corn and will bear from 12 to 16 inches in length, and well filled with 14 to 64 pounds per struck bushel. Price, express or freight: Qt., 15c.; peck, 75c.; bu., $2.50; 2 bu., $4.50; sacks included. Prepaid by mail: Pkt., 5c.; lb., 20c.; qt., 30c.

# FODDER CORN.

**YELLOW ELEPHANT FODDER** ... to feed green or to cut up and cure in the silo ... stacked up or stored ... grows ...

**RED COB FODDER or ENSILAGE CORN.**—This is ...

**SWEET FODDER CORN.**

**EVERGREEN SWEET FODDER CORN.**—This is an early variety ...

**EARLY SWEET FODDER CORN.**—This is short in the ... overlooked ... From ½ to 2 bushels of ... are required per acre ...

Yellow Elephant  Fodder Corn.

# Northern Grown Seed Potatoes.

In order to secure the largest possible yields combined with the best quality a change in Seed Potatoes is more essential than with any other seed. If our Selected Northern Grown Seed Potatoes are planted 400 to 500 bushels can be as easily grown per acre as 100 to 150 bushels of scrub stock. To raise a good and large crop of healthy tubers will not cost any more than to grow a small crop of poor Potatoes, which are hardly marketable.

Our Northern Grown Seed Potatoes insure a vigorous growth, an early maturity and the largest crops obtainable.

We ship our Potatoes in the spring as soon as danger of freezing is over, so that they will arrive in good time for planting. All orders for Potatoes are acknowledged as soon as received and forwarded as soon as possible.

Our customers can select a barrel of any three different varieties at the barrel price of each variety, and we will pack them separate in one barrel.

**EXTRA EARLY OHIO SEED POTATOES—**This grand old and reliable Potato is too well known to require a lengthy description. Almost every farmer and potato grower has at least given it a trial and where the true and genuine stock was secured, it has always given the best satisfaction. No matter how many new early varieties are introduced, the Early hio is still the leading market Potato, and as such we place it at the head of our Potato list. Carloads of this standard early variety are shipped every year to Southern States for Seed Potatoes, and the product thereof shipped back again to our largest Potato markets in the Eastern and Northern States, where it naturally spoils the market for the home-grown Potatoes. The Southern Potato grower realizes that by planting our extreme Northern Grown Early Ohio, he will have his crop at least from 10 days to 2 weeks earlier ready for the market than if he would plant his own or more Southern grown stock. Our Northern Grown Early Ohio are vigorous and healthy and will naturally produce the largest crops and mature almost 2 weeks earlier than such as are bought up by seed dealers in the larger cities who pick them up in the open market, and as long as they have a reddish color and an oblong to an oval form, call them "Early Ohio. We have harvested a good crop of good and genuine Early Ohio Potatoes, and offer them at a reasonable price. Peck, 4 0c.; bu., $1.20 bbl., $3.25.

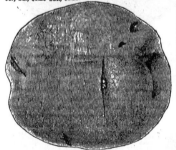

Bliss' Triumph.

**BLISS' TRIUMPH—**This new, splendid early market Potato was originated several years ago in the state of New York, and from there introduced first in the Southern states, where it is now one of the leading early market Potatoes, and always sells from 10c. to 30c. per bushel above the market price. It is claimed to be at least a week earlier than the Early Rose and the Early Ohio. The tubers are of a very handsome appearance, being almost round and most uniform in shape and size, with eyes slightly depressed, which are mostly on the seed end. Its color is of a pretty light red. Its beautiful appearance, wonderful productiveness, and superior table qualities make it a favorite as an early market Potato wherever introduced. Being planted in the same field with other early varieties, it out-yielded them by far, although the tubers never grow over large. It produces at least from 12 to 15 tubers per hill, all of marketable size. It is a vigorous grower. Blight and potato bugs wil not hurt it much, and it is entirely scab proof. Its flesh is of the purest white color, both raw and when cooked. We cannot recommend this new elegant Potato too highly, and everybody who does not give it a trial this year will find it to be to his disadvantage. Peck, 40c.; bu., $1.20; bbl., $3.25.

**ACME—**A splendid new variety of the Early Ohio class, originated several years ago. The tubers have the peculiar markings of the Early Ohio, but still are quite distinct from that variety. It is several days earlier in ripening than the Early Ohio, and can be marketed long before they are matured When they are small yet, like walnuts, they will cook nice and mealy, and are of the finest flavor.

The tubers grow fair to large, and are very uniform both in form and size, both seed and stem ends are round and full; skin is of a light pink to flesh color, with specks peculiar to the Ohio class, and the eyes flush with the surface. Although an extra early kind, it is an excellent keeper. For early eating and an early market Potato this splendid variety cannot be too highly recommended. Peck, 40c.; bu., $1.20; bbl., $3.25.

Acme.

# PEARL OF CANNON VALLEY.

**Pearl of Cannon Valley.**

Cannon Valley is the most fertile sandy bottom land along Cannon River, which crosses our beautiful city, Faribault. This is the result of planting 75 Seed Balls procured from Germany six years ago, and we are glad to say that we have produced a potato that is well worth the trouble and expense that we have undergone on account of the great many tests and experiments with such a large collection. Only one of the many varieties of potatoes, the Pearl of Cannon Valley (named in honor of the soil it was produced in), possessed all the requirements of a choice market as well as fine table potato in the highest degree. It surpasses such choice table varieties like the Freeman and Snow Flake potatoes, well known to most everybody, by far, and saying that it yields three times as much as these would not be giving it full credit, for it is a most prolific grower, yielding immensely, and is not particular as to the conditions of the soil and weather. The Pearl of Cannon Valley tubers grow from medium to large and very large, with hardly ever any small ones that are not marketable. The potatoes are of a handsome oblong form nearly oval and are of the most uniform shape and size of all potatoes so far introduced. Its russety skin is of light cream color, and eyes are few, flushing with the surface. It is a very robust grower, and is neither affected by drought nor by excessive moisture, as the last three- or four years of extreme seasons have fully proven, for during the droughty season of 1900 we harvested at the rate of 275 bu. per acre, and this last year when we had such excessive moisture it yielded over 300 bu. per acre. During the growing season not any of the vines showed signs of blight, nor rot when dug to be stored away, while a great many kinds did not yield back the seed planted on account of rotting. The potato cooks up nice and floury, and when done it is entirely done and not only the outside. The very type of it expresses choice table quality, and the appearance of a plate of the fine potatoes is inviting. Whoever gives them a trial will not be disappointed. **Price, postpaid: 1 lb., 25c.; 3 lbs., 60c.; by freight or express: Lb., 15c.; ½ peck, 40c.; peck, 70c.; bu., $1.55; bbl., $4.75.**

**CARMAN NO. 3 POTATO**—For a main crop and late market Potato the Carman No. 3 cannot me recommended too highly. It combines all the good qualities required of such a Potato. Like Carman No. 1, it is a seedling from seedlings, and resembles this kind in having few and shallow eyes. This potato is the heaviest cropper ever introduced. It seems as though blight, drought and the ravages of potato bugs have no effect upon it at all. Farmers and potato growers for the Eastern and larger potato markets are always striving to have the very best and the most perfect they can get to grow for main crop, and in order to make growing Potatoes for the market pay they have to get such kinds that yield the most and at the same time be of the best quality obtainable. After giving Carman No. 3 a trial you will be convinced that this Potato will meet these demands in every respect. The tubers grow large to very large, and are of a regular oblong form, with few and shallow eyes, creamy white color, and its flesh is of extreme whiteness, both raw and when cooked. It boils nice and floury, like the Snow Flake and Freeman, and in flavor it ranks just as high as any of these. Although the tubers grow very large, they have neither hollow hearts nor dark parts, as generally found in large and coarse-growing varieties, but will boil nice and mealy all through. It is the most perfect keeper, and will keep until late in the spring without sprouting. The tubers set while the vines are small, but do not ripen until late. This giving it such a long season, and yielding such heavy crops. **Peck, 40c.; bu., $1.15; bbl., $3.00.**

**Sir Walter Raleigh.**

**SIR WALTER RALEIGH**—One of Mr. Carman's latest and best—a seedling of the Rural New Yorker No. 2. It must be acknowledged that Mr. Carman has originated some of the most popular varieties now grown, notably the Rural New Yorker No. 2 and Carman No. 3. It resembles the Rural New Yorker No. 2 in shape, but a little more buff in color. The flesh is whiter and of better quality. It is from four to six days earlier than the Rural. It is more uniform and yields practically no small tubers—every one of marketable size. Whitest flesh and finest grained Potato, exceeding even the Snowflake. It is unquestionably the best of its type, and will soon supersede all others of this class. It has the advantage of developing such large tubers. At the Rural grounds it proved the best and heaviest cropper of forty-nine varieties; it not only being the finest eating Potato but also the heaviest yielder. This is also a Potato with new blood and new vigor and will outyield all other varieties. Our Seed Potatoes of this variety were raised of the best seed obtainable, and are true and genuine. **Peck, 40c.; bu., $1.15; bbl., $3.00.**

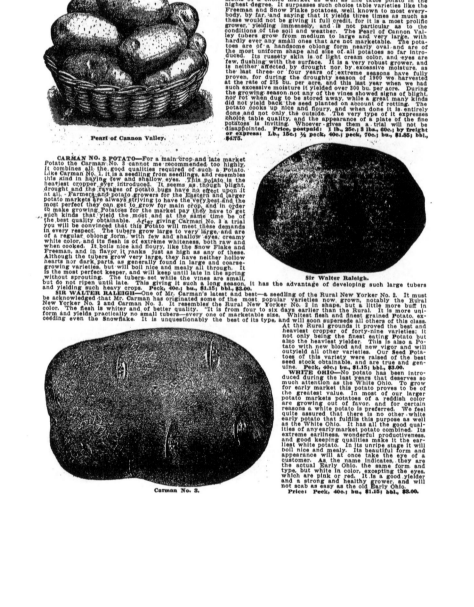

**Carman No. 3.**

**WHITE OHIO**—No potato has been introduced during the last years that deserves so much attention as the White Ohio. To grow for early market this potato proves to be of the greatest value. In most of our larger potato markets potatoes of a reddish color are growing out of favor, and for certain reasons a white potato is preferred. We feel quite assured that there is no other white early potato that fulfills this purpose as well as the White Ohio. It has all the good qualities of any early market potato combined. Its extreme earliness, wonderful productiveness, and good keeping qualities make it the earliest white potato. In its unripe stage it will boil nice and mealy. Its beautiful form and appearance will at once take the eye of a customer. As the name indicates, they are the actual Early Ohio, the same form and type, but white in color, excepting the eyes, which are pink or red. It is a good yielder and a strong and healthy grower, and will not scab as easy as the old Early Ohio. **Price: Peck, 40c.; bu., $1.15; bbl., $3.00.**

## FREEMAN.

It was overlooked to grow enough of these last year, and on account of planting them on a low piece of ground those planted did not turn out well. All of the first grade stock was sold out last fall already and we offer second-sized Freeman at the following prices: **Peck, 30c.; bu., $1.00; bbl. $2.60.** As our stock of these is not large, those ordering second size Freeman should name their second choice.

**ARCADIA POTATO**—There is hardly another kind of potato grown which is as handsome and uniform in size and shape as the Arcadia. The tubers are of an oval shape, somewhat flattened, with few and shallow eyes that a almost flush with the surface, and is the smoothest and most attractive potato ever offered. The potatoes grow from large to very large and are of a nice and clear white color. It is a potato that will never scab, no matter if it is grown on an old and heavy manured soil. In maturing it is medium late and the tubers are of the most regular shape and size, with no small ones that are not marketable. In table quality it is equal to the Freeman and Snow Flake, and in yield it exceeds most all other varieties. This potato originated in Newfoundland, from where we secured our seed stock several years ago. **Price: Peck, 30c.; bu., $1.00; bbl., $2.60.**

**RURAL NEW YORKER NO. 2**—Is a large, white-skinned variety, oval in form, and rather flatish; flesh is white and close grained, solid and of the very best quality, it cooking dry and floury; eyes are few and shallow. The tubers are large and the smoothest and cleanest of all potatoes grown. In fact, there is no other Potato of such handsome appearance as the Rural New Yorker. Although it is a large yielder, it grows but few and small vines. It is very hardy and will stand the heaviest manuring without getting scabby or spotted. For this reason it is one of the most desirable varieties for farmers and Potato growers near larger cities to grow for a main crop Potato for the market. Under ordinary circumstances they will yield from 300 to 400 bushels per acre, and by heavy manuring this yield can almost be doubled. **Peck, 30c.; bu., 90c.; bbl., $2.50.**

**EARLY MINNESOTA ROSE**—Besides the Early Ohio no other potato had a better run in former years than the grand old Early Rose. Years ago, when first originated, and quite a number of years afterwards, it used to be the standard of all the early market varieties; and for an early market potato nobody would hardly think of planting anything else but Early Rose. But as a general rule when people have a good thing, they are not aware of it, and so it was with the Early Rose. By careless growing it gradually weakened and was finally so run out that it would produce only slim yields, and the tubers would be of very irregular shape, and long and spindly. We offer this grand old Early Rose again with new blood, in its old time purity and productiveness, and claim that it is the same potato that it was years ago when first originated. They are of a handsome oblong form, very uniform in shape, and of a pretty pinkish color, and cannot be compared with the old run out Early Rose of irregular shape and faded reddish color. The table and market qualities of this grand old potato are unexcelled. **Peck, 30c.; bu., 90c.; bbl., $2.40.**

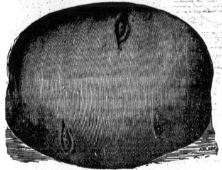

**CARMAN NO. 1**—Is a seedling from seedlings raised through several generations with the object of developing good and suppressing undesirable qualities. It resembles the Rural New Yorker very much in form and in having few and shallow eyes. The tubers grow very large, and will produce small ones only in unfavorable seasons. The Carman No. 1 proves to be an enormous producer of handsome and well-shaped tubers which are of the best table qualities. Skin is of a yellowish white color; flesh white and fine grained and cooks very even throughout, and dry and mealy. Like the Rural New Yorker, it will stand heavy manuring without getting scabby or spotted. The tubers will always be nice and clean and free from disease. We recommend Carman No. 1 very highly as the Potato to grow for profit; in fact, there could be no better Potato to grow for the market, it being of such good and uniform size and shape, and of such choice table qualities. It will always sell itself wherever shown, and all those who have tested it will surely want it again. It is medium late in ripening. **Peck, 40c.; bu., $1.10; bbl., $2.85.**

Lakeside Champion.

**Early Minnesota Rose.**

**LAKESIDE CHAMPION**—Is a large and handsome potato, the tubers having a nice form, oblong to long; skin is of a nice pink color and eyes are prominent, though not deep; the flesh is fine white, both raw and when cooked, is of the most excellent flavor. This elegant Potato being originated in the extreme North, is perfectly hardy and will yield heavy crops under the most unfavorable circumstances, and will not be easily affected by blight, and not at all by potato scab or rot. It is intermediate in season, and for a good market Potato and Potato for late keeping it has no equal. **Peck, 30c.; bu., 90c.; bbl., $2.40.**

**PINGREE POTATO**—This is a new variety, introduced only lately, and is a very productive main crop Potato. In choice table and long-keeping qualities it is unsurpassed, and whoever gives them a trial would not like to be without them again. The introducers describe them as follows: "The PINGREE is a main crop Potato; is productive to an extraordinary degree. The tubers are bunched closely in growing, which materially lessens the labor of harvesting. The Potato itself is of the size and shape best liked in the leading markets. The skin is of a bright, light russet color. Eyes are few and nearly flush with the surface. In quality nothing can surpass it. In fact, in this particular we know of no sort that equals it. Its snowy whiteness when cooked, together with its dry and floury nature, has made it a favorite on every table where it has been tried."

It is intermediate in ripening, and is not affected by Potato blight, as most other varieties. **Price: Peck, 30c.; bu., 95c.; bbl., $2.50.**

**Thoroughbred.**

**THOROUGHBRED**—This is an elegant new potato of the Early Rose type, and in every respect just as good, if not better, than this when first originated. The skin is of a beautiful pink color, shape oblong to long and very regular; the eyes, although large, are even with the surface. It is a rank and free grower of vines and tubers, with so much vitality and vigor that it is certain to make a good crop even in seasons of severe droughts. The tubers grow large to very large, and are of handsome appearance, and the table qualities are of the very best. It is a seedling of the Early Rose and claimed to be 10 days earlier than this. Besides being so early it is an enormous yielder and, in fact, all who have tried it consider it a perfect potato for early marketing; being of such extreme earliness, very large size and handsome form, they will always sell at first sight on the market. **Peck, 35c.; bu., $1.10; bbl., $2.75.**

**KING OF THE EARLIEST**—This excellent new Potato, introduced by a Potato grower in the Northwest, is indeed a marvelous Potato. Its originator claims for it extreme earliness, claims it to be earlier than any early Potato introduced heretofore. Hundreds have tested it last year and reported good eating Potatoes in 28 to 35 days after planting. It is a seedling of the Early Ohio, of better quality and far more productive. It resembles the Early Ohio, in type and form, but is lighter in color. As an early market potato for farmers and gardeners this excellent Potato is of inestimable value on account of its extreme earliness and productiveness. **Peck, 40c.; bu., $1.20; bbl., $3.15.**

### SECOND SIZED SEED POTATOES.

Before our Seed Potatoes are stored away in our cellars they are carefully assorted as to size and quality. We make two grades, a Choice and Selected Seed Stock and Second Sized Seed Potatoes. The latter are just as pure and true to name as the first grade, they being taken from the same stock and consist of the small and medium sized tubers. The very small ones, however, are discarded.

Last year we had such an unusual large demand for Second Sized Seed Potatoes that we were unable to fill all orders. We would therefore advise those of our patrons and customers who order of these to specify at the same time the kind they want of First Sized Potatoes in case Second Sized Stock should be sold out when their order reaches us.

In case, however, when Second Sized Potatoes are ordered and we should be sold out we reserve the right to send the money's worth in First Grade Potatoes of the varieties ordered, unless otherwise specified as mentioned above.

Of the following varieties we have Second Sized Seed Potatoes at the prices stated:

**King of the Earliest.**

| | Price per bu. | Price per bbl. | | Price per bu. | Price per bbl. |
|---|---|---|---|---|---|
| Early Ohio | $ .90 | $2.40 | Carman No. 3 | $ .90 | $2.40 |
| Pride of the South | .90 | 2.25 | Carman No. 1 | .85 | 2.25 |
| Pearl of Cannon Valley | 1.35 | 3.00 | Rural New Yorker | .75 | 2.00 |
| Early Rose | .70 | 1.75 | Sir Walter Raleigh | .85 | 2.25 |
| Thoroughbred | .85 | 2.30 | Freeman | 1.00 | 2.65 |
| Bliss Triumph | .90 | 2.40 | Arcadia | .85 | 2.00 |
| Pingree | .75 | 1.75 | King of the Earliest | .85 | 2.50 |
| | | | Lake Side Champion | .60 | 1.50 |

We offer Second Sized Seed Potatoes only in bushel and barrel quantities, and will not fill orders for peck quantities. Our potato Collections, described below, refer to First Grade Seed Stock only.

**POTATO COLLECTIONS**—Our patrons ordering Seed Potatoes can select any 3 varieties at barrel price of each variety, and we will pack them separate in a barrel. And for the advantage and convenience of those that wish to try small quantities of our standard sorts we have put up our collections, each of which is composed of an extra early, a medium early and a late Potato, and in each collection the Potatoes are again different from the others, so that whoever orders all 3 of the Potato Collections gets 9 different kinds.

**COLLECTION NO. 1.**

| | | |
|---|---|---|
| Early Ohio | 4 packs | |
| Carman No. 3 | 3 packs | 1 Bbl., 11 Pecks, |
| Thoroughbred | 3 packs | for only $2.85. |

**COLLECTION NO. 3**

| | | |
|---|---|---|
| Early Minnesota R | 4 packs | |
| Lake Side Champi | 4 packs | 1 Bbl., 11 Pecks, |
| Sir Walter Raleigh | 3 packs | for only $2.85. |

**COLLECTION NO. 2.**

| | | |
|---|---|---|
| Acme | 4 packs | |
| Carman No. 1 | 4 packs | 1 Bbl., 11 Pecks, |
| Bliss Triumph | 3 packs | for only $2.85. |

With every one of these collections we will put in one pound of any new or old variety of Potatoes that you may select from our Catalogue.

## SEED POTATOES BY MAIL.

Many seed dealers make it a practice to send Potato eyes by mail. From actual experience, however, we have learned, that a better and more satisfactory method is to send whole tubers by mail. Potato eyes soon after being cut lose a great share of their vitality, by wilting and drying up, and those that are not spoiled before planting time make only a feeble growth. We send medium sized tubers by mail of which 3 to 6 Potatoes will make a pound with about 50 to 80 eyes. These Potatoes can be cut any time when ready for planting, and the whole vitality is thus saved. **Price for all varieties of Seed Potatoes, except when noted, prepaid by mail: Lb., 20c.; 3 lbs., 50c.**

## PREMIUM

With an order for six barrels or more of Seed Potatoes we give the Acme Hand Potato Planter for premium.

**THE ACME HAND POTATO PLANTER**—It is considered a good work for a man to plant three-quarters of an acre of potatoes in a day, and with this Planter a man can plant two acres in a day of ten hours and do it easier and better. The secret of the success of the Acme Hand Potato Planter is that IT MAKES THE HOLES, DROPS AND COVERS AT ONE OPERATION. "Almost as easy as walking," is the remark of many who have used it.

The Acme is the Pioneer Implement of this kind; it is the lightest (weighs but 2½ lbs.), strongest and most durable Hand Potato Planter made. Be sure and buy only the ACME Planter. **Price, $1.00.**

# MANGEL-WURZELS.
### For Feeding Stock,

The value of Mangel-Wurzels for feeding stock cannot be overestimated. No one who keeps horses, sheep or cattle should be without these roots for fall and winter feeding. The results from their use are wonderful, as is clearly shown in the improved health and condition of animals, the increased yield of milk in cows and the great saving in hay. They can be raised at very trifling cost, and yield immense crops per acre, if the ground is rich.

**Five or Six Pounds of Seed Required per Acre.**

**CULTURE.**—Sow in drills 2 feet apart and about 2 inches apart in drills, thinning to 12 or 15 inches in the row. Long varieties are best suited to deep soil; globe sorts succeed better than long ones on sandy soil. They make a heavy growth, and if large quantities are grown it is best to have the rows wide enough apart to use a horse in cultivation.

**THE IMPROVED MAMMOTH LONG RED MANGEL**—This is the best Long Red Mangel. It is enormously productive, yielding from 50 to 60 tons per acre, a single root often weighing from 25 to 35 pounds and more. They are of good and massive shape, of very fine texture and good quality, and though growing to immense size, are not coarse. They are easily harvested, as they grow well over the ground. We select only the largest roots of true type, and produce a superior strain of this valuable Mangel. Price, postpaid by mail: Pkt., 4c.; oz., 7c.; ¼ lb., 12c.; lb., 30c.; 4 lbs., $1.10. By express or freight: Lb., 22c.; 5 lbs., $1.00; 10 lbs., $1.80.

**NEW GATE POST MANGEL**—We have found this a valuable new Mangel, and consider it a standard and main crop variety. We call the attention of growers of Mangels to it, and ask them to give it a trial this year. It is a yellow, Tankard-shaped variety, and very massive and solid. Price, postpaid by mail: Pkt., 4c.; oz., 7c.; ¼ lb., 12c.; lb., 30c. By express or freight: Lb., 22c.; 5 lbs., $1.00.

**RED GLOBE MANGEL**—An early variety, producing smooth globe-shaped roots; adapted to grow on shallow soil. Price, postpaid by mail: Pkt., 4c.; oz., 8c.; ¼ lb., 15c.; lb., 32c. By express or freight: Lb., 24c.; 5 lbs., $1.10.

**CHAMPION YELLOW GLOBE**—For growing in shallow soil this is especially adapted. The roots are round or of globular form, and grow to a large size. It is very productive, easily pulled, and an excellent keeper. Price, postpaid by mail: Pkt., 4c.; oz., 8c.; ¼ lb., 15c.; lb., 32c. By express or freight: Lb., 24c.; 5 lbs., $1.10.

**Mammoth Long Red.**

**NEW GIANT YELLOW INTERMEDIATE**—Grows more than half above the ground, with fine neck and large root. Enormously productive, easily pulled; an excellent keeper. This being a hybrid of a Mangel and a Sugar Beet, it is of the highest feeding value, and therefore preferable to Mangels for stock, while for sugar the below described varieties are best adapted. Pkt., 4c.; oz., 8c.; ¼ lb., 15c.; 1 lb., 35c., prepaid by mail. Pound, 27c.; 5 lbs., $1.25, express or freight.

# SUGAR BEETS.
### For Sugar-Making.

Although the yield of Sugar Beets is not as large as that of the Mangel's they are of a superior quality, containing a large amount of saccharine matter. There is no crop where the quality of the seed used is of more importance than this. We have grown for us in the most skillful scientific way, seed of the Vilmorin's Improved and Klein Wanzleben, the two leading varieties now in cultivation in this country. It is only by the use of the best seed procurable, and with good culture, that beet sugar making is profitable.

**KLEIN WANZLEBEN**—Probably more widely grown than any other, and undoubtedly the best sort for general cultivation. It produces from 14 to 18 tons to the acre, and contains from 15 to 18 per cent of sugar. The root grows below the surface. Easier grown than any other variety. Pkt., 4c.; oz., 8c.; ¼ lb., 15c.; lb., 35c. prepaid by mail. By express or freight: 1 lb., 27c.; 5 lbs., $1.20.

**VILMORIN'S IMPROVED**—Although not quite so large as the Klein Wanzleben, it contains fully as large a percentage of sugar. The green leaves are smooth-edged and spreading. The root grows below the surface. Pkt., 4c.; oz., 8c.; ¼ lb., 15c.; 1 lb., 35c. prepaid by mail. By express or freight: Lb., 27c.; 5 lbs., $1.25.

**Write for special prices on larger quantities of Mangel and Sugar Beet Seed.**

Guide Rock, Neb.—All seeds I bought of you last spring were very good. The Mangel-wurzel seed especially has done splendid, for most of the Mangels weighed from 20 to 30 pounds each.

# MINNESOTA TANKARD MANGEL.

The Golden Tankard is considered the best Mangel grown, and our selected strain of this is superior to the Golden Tankard, and unequaled for yielding and feeding qualities. It is remarkable for its milk producing qualities, and for the rich, deep yellow color of the flesh; contains considerable sugar, and is very nutritious. Taking it altogether, our strain of this Mangel is a superior root, growing nice and even in shape. The growth is vigorous. It is easily lifted and produces enormous crops, and is an excellent keeper. With no specially selected ground and good average cultivation the yield will average 45 tons per acre, while with a little extra care in selecting and preparing the seed bed and careful cultivation it will yield 60 to 70 tons per acre. Price, postpaid by mail: Pkt., 4c.; oz., 5c.; ¼ lb., 15c.; 1 lb., 38c.; 4 lbs., $1.40. By express or freight: Lb., 30c.; 5 lbs., $1.25.

Hamilton, Mont.—The seed I purchased from you was all right in every respect. I think every seed germinated, especially the Minnesota Tankard Mangel - Wurzel. From the ¼ pound of seed I harvested 11 wagon loads of roots, some of them measuring 16 to 18 inches in diameter. For stock feeding purposes they are nearly equal to the Sugar Beet, and for dairy cows I think they are the cheapest feed that can be grown. The Minnesota Tankard would be a leader for you in this country if you could get it properly introduced. Its shape makes it so easy to harvest; it is an immense yielder and a first-class keeper, and in quality it is at least one-third better than the Improved Long Red, and for irrigating it requires only half the water that Sugar Beets and other roots do. Yours truly, W. A. STEWART.

**Klein Wanzleben Sugar Beet.**

# "PLANET JR." FARM AND GARDEN TOOLS.

Space will not permit our showing and describing all of the "Planet Jr." tools, but we will send a fully illustrated catalogue free for the asking to any who desire it, and we can supply promptly anything ordered. "Planet Jr.," goods are standard machines, the best on the market. In sending your orders to us, you can rely on getting bottom prices.

### Planet Jr. No. 3, Hill and Drill Seeder.

This seeder is the lastest and most perfect development of the hand seed drill. It sows evenly in drills, and also drops in hills, at 4, 6, 8, 12 or 24 inches apart. No time is lost; no seed is wasted. It is quickly set to sow different kinds of seed in the thickness desired.

**Price $10.50.**

The accurate hill - dropping drill, which gives a regular stand of plants with the least seed, saves its cost over and over in seed alone. We guarantee this drill to be more accurate than any other made, and to give satisfaction in every respect.

### Planet Jr. No. 4, Combined Hill and Drill Seeder, Single Wheel Hoe, Cultivator and Plow.

This admirable tool combines in a single implement a capital hill dropping seeder, a perfect drill seeder, a single wheel hoe, a cultivator, and a plow. It holds two quarts and as a seeder is like the No. 3, sowing in continuous rows, or dropping in hills at five different distances. The drill is detached and the tool frame substituted by removing but one bolt. It is useful almost every day of the season, at every stage of garden work.

**Price, Complete, $10.50, as a Drill only $8.50**

### Planet Jr. No. 25, Combined Hill and Drill Seeder and Double Wheel Hoe.

This new combined machine is intended for a class of gardeners who have a large enough acreage in crops for a Double Wheel Hoe to be used to good advantage, and yet prefer not to buy a separate Wheel Hoe.

As a Drill it is almost identical with the "Planet Jr." No. 4 Drill; will sow in drills or hills, 4, 6, 8, 12 or 24 inches apart. **Price, $13.50.**

As a Wheel Hoe it is identical with the "Planet Jr." No. 12 Double Wheel Hoe, the very best machine on the market. The change from Drill to Wheel Hoe takes but a moment, and the entire combination is one we can heartily recommend and guarantee satisfactory.

### Planet Jr. 12 Tooth Cultivator.

**$8.25; Without Pulverizer, $6.55.**
This tool has rapidly grown into favor with farmers, market gardeners and strawberry growers. It has a high frame and the chisel-shape teeth cut an

**inch wide each,** and cultivate deep without throwing earth upon the plants.

### No. 12 Double Wheel Hoe.

This perfect wheel hoe is invaluable for use in all small crops. Its variety of work is almost incredible. Changes and adjustments of the tools are made with the greatest quickness. It has 11-inch wheels, which can be set at four different distances apart; the frame is malleable, with ample room for tool adjustment and can be set three different heights.

**Price, $7.00.**

### No. 13 Double Wheel Hoe. Price $4.75.

This tool is the No. 11, with 6-inch hoes only, these being the tools that are most generally useful. Any or all of the other tools shown with No. 11 may be added at any time.

### No. 1 Combined Drill Seeder and Wheel Hoe.

This has long been the most popular combined tool made. From a drill it is changed to its other uses by removing two bolts, when hoes, etc., can be quickly attached. It is an excellent seed sower, a first-class double and single wheel hoe. It is an every-day time and labor-saving machine and a remedy for backache. **Price, $9.50.**

### No. 16 Single Wheel Hoe.

This latest and best single-wheel hoe has a very full set of tools, several of them being of new design, such as have been found to work in the very best manner. It has 11-inch wheel, with broad face; is very light, strong and easy running.

**Price $5.85.**

### No. 17½ Single Wheel Hoe, Price $4.50.

This machine is similar to No. 16, except it has no plow or rakes. Thousands of them are sold annually for cultivating sugar beets and onions.

### Planet Jr. No. 8 Horse Hoe.

Probably no other cultivating machine is so widely known as the "Planet Jr." Combined Horse Hoe and Cultivator, for it is in use throughout the civilized world. It is so strongly built as to withstand incredible strain, yet it is light and easy to handle.

**Price, $8.50.**

Every part is perfected to make the tool acceptable to the intelligent farmer, the cheapest. Without Depth Regulator (order as No. 7).

# The Farmer Seed Co.'s Novelty and Specialty List for 1903.

In presenting this list of novelties to our friends and customers, we feel confident that all will be well repaid in giving a part, if not all, of these grand new varieties a trial. A few of the varieties herein mentioned were listed in our catalogue last year and we are very thankful for the very many flattering reports received. It is indeed cheering to know that our efforts are rewarded by satisfied customers.

**EARLY WHITE MAY RADISH**—This is not only the earliest White Radish, but the earliest of any color, good sized Radishes having been pulled in from 15 to 18 days after sowing. The Radishes are pure white, oblong, crisp and tender. The tops are small, which renders them suitable for forcing and admits of close planting. Very desirable. Pkt., 5c.; oz., 15c.; ¼-lb., 35c.; lb., $1.25.

### EARLY WHITE MAY RADISHES.

**NOTT'S EXCELSIOR PEA**—This is a fine new Extra Early Dwarf Green Wrinkled Pea. In earliness it equals American Wonder; in height about 15 inches. In quality equal to Premium Gem, and as a cropper it excels either. In a comparative test with above, side by side, the Nott's Excelsior yielded one-quarter more pods by measure, and by weight one-third more, which shows conclusively that the pods of Nott's Excelsior are more compactly filled with peas; a great yielder, because it can be planted so much closer than tall growing sorts. Price by mail, postpaid: Pkt., 5c.; ½ pint, 15c.; pint, 25c.; qt., 45c. By express or freight, not prepaid: Qt., 30c.; 4 qts., $1.00; peck, $1.75.

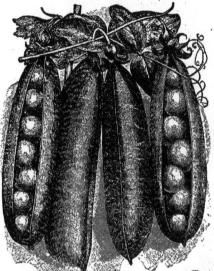

### NOTT'S EXCELSIOR PEA.

**PEEP O' DAY SWEET CORN**—New last year. Described as the "EARLIEST ON EARTH." Originated in Minnesota. Offered in Minneapolis markets 5 to 7 days earlier than any other well known extra earlies. Five inches long, perfectly formed, well filled. Tender and sweet.

Pkt., 5c.; ½ pint, 12c.; pint, 20c.; qt., 35c.; prepaid; peck, $2.00, not prepaid.

### PEEP O'DAY SWEET CORN.

### VALENTINE GIANT STRINGLESS BEAN.

(See cut). This valuable variety, which is of recent origin, has proven to be superior to any other green podded bean ever offered and will be prized by all who grow for home or market use. It possesses the following points of superiority over the old Red Valentine and other sorts: 1—It is ready for market fully a week earlier. 2—The pods average 1-3 larger, being from 5 to 6 inches in length. 3—They are always absolutely stringless, round, full and fleshy. 4—It is more prolific, producing from 20 to 30 per cent more pods. 5—Its quality is unsurpassed, being most deliciously flavored. It is beyond question the most profitable bean to grow for the early market, as its enormous yields, its earliness and its good quality all combine to render it very popular and much sought after. Give it a trial this year and you will forever plant it afterward. Pkt., 10c.; pt., 25c.; qt., 45c., prepaid; pk., $1.50; bu., $4.50, not prepaid.

**HOUSER CABBAGE.**

HOUSER CABBAGE—A new and entirely distinct round late Cabbage, the largest, hardest-heading, fine grained variety known. Originated by Mr. Houser, one of the most successful market gardeners in the east. The heads are large, weighing on an average 18 to 20 pounds. They grow so compact and free from spreading leaves that fully 500 more heads can be obtained to the acre than with other late sorts, and in solidity it cannot be excelled even by the Danish Ball Head. Heads measuring 36 inches in circumference had hearts measuring only two inches. This late Cabbage is perfect in every respect as to size, weight, quality, sure heading, smallness of heart and long keeping.

**OUR CLAIMS.**

FIRST, LATENESS—It is the latest of all large Cabbages, being at least two weeks later than any strain of the Late Flat Dutch type.

SECOND, SOLIDITY—It cannot be excelled in this particular, even by the Danish Ball Head. It is very compact, each leaf well overlapping the head.

THIRD, SIZE—It is fully as large as any of the late varieties, the heads averaging 18 to 20 pounds; many specimens have been grown to weigh 25 to 30 pounds.

FOURTH, SHAPE—The heads are round and deep through, and should any of the heads crack it is always at the stem end, which does not destroy its use for market. The heart extends only 2 to 2½ inches into head (see illustration).

FIFTH, YIELD—By reason of its compact habit of growth, and its freedom from loose leaves fully 500 to 300 more heads can be grown to the acre. Fully 95 per cent in an ordinary season will make merchantable heads. DO NOT FAIL TO GIVE THE HOUSER A TRIAL. Pkt., 10c.; oz., 40c.; ¼ lb., $1.40.

FARMER SEED CO'S EARLIEST—This grand new Cabbage of the Wakefield type will become a leader when farmers and gardeners become acquainted with its superior points; grows one-third larger than the Wakefield and is at least five days earlier. Heads uniform, solid, and it is a remarkably short stumped variety. By all means give this new Cabbage a trial, and our word for it, you will not be disappointed. Pkt., 8c.; oz., 30c.; ¼ lb., $1.00; lb., $3.50.

**FARMER SEED CO'S. EARLIEST.**

EARLY SPRING CABBAGE—An extra early flat headed variety, coming in with the Wakefield, and yielding a third more than any of the other extra early sorts. It has all the merits of the Early Summer. Has only 4 or 5 outside leaves, so that it may be successfully planted 21 inches apart or about 14,000 to the acre. It is wonderfully uniform in shape and almost entirely edible. Very fine grained and has the peculiarity of heading firmly at an early stage in its growth so that though small, with its remarkable solidity, it can be cut long before maturity. Its compact form, good quality and earliness, together with a large yield per acre, renders it valuable for market gardeners as well as the private garden. Pkt., 8c.; oz., 30c.; ¼ lb., $1.00; lb., $3.50.

MARBLEHEAD MAMMOTH CABBAGE—This is the largest variety of the Cabbage family in the WORLD; heads have been grown so large that they could not be got into a two-bushel basket, having a diameter two inches greater; 30 and 40 lbs. is no uncommon weight for the Mammoth, and in some instances weighed over 90 lbs. Pkt., 8c.; oz., 25c.; ¼ lb., 55c.; lb., $2.00.

**EARLY SPRING CABBAGE.**

**Cucumber, Yokohama Climbing.**

YOKOHAMA CLIMBING—A most beautiful late sort; the foliage never suffers from disease. The fruits are cylindrical, bright green and very slightly spined or prickly. Later, if ripe, they turn brighter, almost into wax color. Flesh white, of finest flavor and never bitter. It bears its fine large fruits in the greatest profusion. Pkt., 10c.; oz., 25c.

EARLY CYCLONE CUCUMBER

EARLY CYCLONE CUCUMBER—It is very hardy, and probably the most prolific of all varieties. In addition to being so wonderfully prolific, it is very early, and the Cucumbers retain their beautiful green color longer than any other sort. It is one of the very best varieties for slicing, as it is very crisp and of good quality, and as it produces fruits of medium size it is likely to be of much value for pickling purposes. Pkt., 5c.; oz., 10c.; ¼ lb., 20c.; lb., 55c.

## F. S. CO.'S
## NEW ICE LETTUCE.

The heads are of enormous size, extremely tender and of the finest flavor, the color of the leaves is of a tender green changing into yellow toward the center. It is wonderfully well closed, and even in great heat the plant runs only slowly to seed. Heads are as solid as the firmest cabbage. This wonderful variety is the finest Cabbage Lettuce yet introduced. Pkt., 10c.; oz., 30c.

The vine is handsome and exceedingly luxuriant. One hill will cover a trellis at least 10 feet square with a solid sheet of dark green, through which the sun cannot penetrate. It is the fruit, however, which is the most curious and distinct in feature. It averages, when mature, about 4 inches long by 2½ inches in diameter, and is covered with strong protruding points or horns. The skin is perfectly smooth and of a very deep dark green, except around the base of the horns, where minute white dots form circles in curious mossic patterns. When the fruits ripen they turn a brilliant orange and yellow, in speckled and clouded effects, and are then highly ornamental.

HORNED AFRICAN CUCUMBER

These ripe fruits are of great value for decorative purposes as they will keep sound and perfect for weeks. The young fruits make most excellent pickles, and from this state up to their full size they can be eaten green, the same as ordinary Cucumbers, and are tender and delicious. It cannot be too highly commended, and everybody should grow it where ordinary Cucumbers fail.
Pkt., 10c.; 3 for 25c.

**Cumberland Cucumber.**

CUMBERLAND CUCUMBER—We believe this to be the best pickling Cucumber ever produced. The variety is of the hardy White Spine type, is a rapid, strong and vigorous grower and very prolific in fruit. The pickles differ from all other hardy sorts in being thickly set with fine spines over the entire surface, except the extreme stem-end; and during the whole period of growth, from the time they first set until fully grown, the form is exceptionally straight and symmetrical, thus being as choice for a slicing variety as it is for pickles. The flesh is firm, but very crisp and tender at all stages. Price: Pkt., 10c.; oz., 25c.; ¼ lb., 75c.

**Farmer Seed Co.'s New Ice Lettuce.**

**Sunflower Globs of Gold.**

"Globes of Gold" Double Dwarf Branching Sunflower. A new double dwarf Sunflower, forming a well-branched plant, 3 to 3½ ft. in height. Each of the numerous branches carries a large, densely double, globe-shaped flower of deep, rich, golden yellow color. (See cut.) 10.

**CRYSTAL WHITE**—The best variety ever introduced for table use. Flesh is solid, crisp, fine grained and sweet. In all our experience in the growing and testing of various varieties of Turnips for table purposes we have never found any that equaled Crystal White. It grows rapidly, and, as shown in our illustration, is a pure white variety and almost round in shape, although at times the Turnips are a trifle more oblong than picture indicates. The flesh is white, solid, crisp, and when cooked is of most delicious quality imaginable. In ordinary seasons it will mature in five or six weeks, and while the bulbs are not quite so large as some sorts, they more than make up in quality what they lack in size. **If you wish a splendid table Turnip you will find CRYSTAL WHITE all that can be desired. Pkt., 10c.; oz., 25c.; ¼ lb., 60c.; lb., $1.75.**

**NEW RADISH TRIUMPH**—This novelty is both unique and useful. It is very early, being a "Twenty Day" Radish, of globular form and its tops are very short, which makes it valuable for cultivation under glass. The flesh is very crisp and solid and of mild flavor. Its most distinctive feature, however, is the unique color of the skin. The ground color is pure white, striped horizontally with bright scarlet. It is a most attractive ornament for the table, and market gardeners will find ready sale for it. Some of the roots may come in solid color, the strain not being quite "fixed" yet. **Pkt., 10c.; 3 pkts., 25c.**

**NEW "HEART O'GOLD" SQUASH**—A very distinct and beautiful new Squash. The vines are strong, vigorous and healthy, which enables it to resist the ravages of borers successfully. It is also very prolific, owing to its strong growth and freedom in setting fruit. The color of the fruit is a rich reddish orange, and the shape is not only attractive, but economical in cutting, there being little or no waste. The flesh is very deep, with small seed cavity, of excellent quality, either for pies or as a vegetable. **Pkt., 10c.; ½ oz., 30c.; oz., 50c.**

"HEART O'GOLD" SQUASH

**New Radish Triumph.**

**Icicle Radish.**

**NEW "ICICLE" RADISH**—Entirely distinct; long, slender, pure white; very early; much the earliest and finest long white. It is ready for use fully as early as the Long Scarlet Short Top, with less foliage, rendering it most desirable for forcing. In the open ground the roots continue brittle, crisp and mild, until they are fully as large as those of the Long Cardinal. It is ready for use following the olive-shaped Earliest White, and is destined to become a leading variety. **Pkt., 5c.; oz., 10c.; ¼ lb., 35c.; lb., $1.15.**

**GIANT TREE TOMATO**—This wonderful variety is bound to spring into general favor wherever grown; it has been thoroughly tested, and should be in every garden. It grows from 10 to 15 feet in height, and if planted early will begin to ripen by July 10th and bears its heavy loads of luscious fruit until killed by frost. The flesh is firm and solid, almost seedless; fine grained, and of a most delicious flavor. It is the largest tomato we have ever grown. The fruit weighs from 16 to 24 ounces, and specimens have been grown weighing 3 pounds; one well developed plant will produce enough fruit for a small family the entire season. The

**Giant Tree Tomato.**
originator spent 20 years in experimenting with this fruit before success crowned his efforts. **Pkt., 10c.; ½ oz., 20c.**

**THE NEW CENTURY TOMATO—** Best extra early Tomato in existence. This is a distinct variety; the fruits are of uniform size and form, very large and apple-shaped, almost round, of a beautiful bright scarlet color, as smooth as glass, and always free from cracks. They have only small seed cavities with comparatively few seeds. The solidity and firmness of the flesh makes them ONE OF THE BEST VARIETIES FOR SHIPPING, they are also WONDERFUL KEEPERS. The flavor is excellent and free from acidity. The fruits ripen very early, fully as early as the Atlantic Prize, and are borne in large clusters in great abundance and continuously until killed by frost. THIS IS ONE OF THE HEAVIEST CROPPERS. Vines are large with quite large dark green leaves; they are of very vigorous and healthy growth, and drought or blight do not effect them. The NEW CENTURY is the BEST family Tomato FOR THE HOME GARDEN, the BEST kind to grow FOR THE MARKET and is ADMIRABLY ADAPTED TO CANNER'S USE. Price: Pkt., 15c.; 2 pkts. for 25c.; ½ oz., 35c.; oz., 60c.

**MINNESOTA PERFECTION.** (See cut.) The largest of all the Musk Melons. Often weighs 25 lbs. This is the grandest Musk Melon ever introduced, grows to an enormous size, frequently weighing 25 lbs. The flesh, which is exceedingly sweet, is of a light green shade. The rind is tough, and stands shipping better than any variety we have ever grown. In productiveness it excels all have tried Perfection will use no other kind. Pkt., 10c.; oz., 15c.; ¼ lb., 40c.; lb., $1.00.

## WATER MELON.

**BLACK DIAMOND—** A cross between Kolb's Gem and Hoosier King. All that could be said of the Kolb's Gem as to good shipping qualities can be truthfully stated in a higher degree of the Black Diamond. All the praise of high quality bestowed on the Sweetheart can be repeated of our new Melon; but its prominent point of merit is its EXTREME SIZE—No Melon ever yet produced anything like so uniformly large fruit nor approached it in productiveness. Melons weighing from 75 to 90 pounds are frequent. Pkt., 5c.; oz., 10c.; ¼ lb., 25c.; lb., 75c.; 5 lbs., $3.25.

## MUSK MELON.

**GOLDEN TRIUMPH—** We have as yet to find a melon that surpasses it in flavor, and that is what is really most desirable in melons for home use. Good size, flesh sweet and tender, very prolific. Should be grown extensively for the restaurants, as it always brings the highest prices on account of its beautiful color when sliced. The flesh is thick, sweet and juicy; color a deep pinkish orange, and very handsome. Every one who has a small garden, and wants a fine musk melon, will do well to try our Golden Triumph. Pkt., 10c.; oz., 25c.; ¼ lb., 65c.

other sorts, and many growers who

**CRIMSON GLOBE BEET—** This Beet is remarkable for its smooth skin and fine shape. We have been growing it on our trial grounds for several years, and could not help noting its many desirable qualities. It is a second early variety, does not grow large and coarse, the matured beets being medium in size and rather oblong in shape. The flesh and skin are both very dark and quality fine, being sweet and tender. The tops are small and dark in color. We are confident that this Beet will please all who plant it. Pkt., 5c.; oz., 15c.; ¼ lb., 35c.; lb., $1.00.

Early White Milan Turnip.

Kleckley's Sweet Water Melon.

**KLECKLEY'S SWEET WATER MELON—** Large oblong Melon, 20 inches in length by 10 to 12 inches in diameter, somewhat tapering at the ends. The skin is dark green, flesh bright scarlet, ripening to the close skin, the rind being only about one-half inch in thickness. Seeds white, lying close to the rind, leaving a large solid heart which does not crack open when ripe. The scarlet flesh is sweet and sugary and is of such texture that it leaves no strings of pulp whatever in eating. The Melon is better for home use than for shipping, and we believe it is THE BEST TABLE MELON TO-DAY. Monte Cristo is very much like it. Pkt., 5c.; oz., 10c.; ¼ lb., 25c.; lb., 85c.

**EARLY WHITE MILAN TURNIP—** As early as the Early Purple Top Milan, and possesses all of its good qualities. The entire bulb, inside and out, is clear ivory white in color; the outer surface is perfectly smooth. It grows so quickly that even the outer surface of the bulb is quite tender.

It will undoubtedly find a welcome in our markets, as, in addition to the heavy crop assured by its adaptability for close planting, it will be found to be fit for use at least a week earlier than any other white variety in cultivation. (See cut.) 10c. pkt., 15c. oz., 40c. ¼ lb., $1.25 lb.

**BISMARCK APPLE —** This wonderful new dwarf apple is said to come from New Zealand. Its chief value is its early fruiting, color, appearance and perfect hardiness. A little tree not over a foot high has been known to bear a large apple a few months after planting. The apples are of very large size and beautiful rich golden yellow color, and of the most distinct and delicious flavor. Fine for planting in boxes or in the garden. 30c. each, three for 75c.

## HYBRIDIZED POTATO SEED.

Hybridized Potato Seed.

We have the pleasure of offering a very choice strain of Potato Seed—the product of numerous hybridizations between many of the best new and old varieties in cultivation. Growing new sorts from the seed-ball seed is a very interesting employment for old or young. There is the widest range of difference in color, shape and general characteristics between the different seedlings; every one is more or less unlike every other. Great success has already attended the attempt to improve this valuable esculent, and the end is not yet—many varieties will yet be found which will bring a golden harvest to the fortunate growers, and prove of inestimable value to the world. Directions for planting, cultivating, etc., on each pkt. Price, 10c. per pkt.; 3 for 25c.; 7 for 50c.

Arctotis Grandis.

**ARCTOTIS GRANDIS—**
A remarkably handsome new annual from Southwest Africa, growing luxuriantly and forming profusely branched bushes of about 2 to 2½ feet in height and breadth. The leaves are soft and whitish. Its flower-heads, borne on long stems and rising well above the foliage, are large and showy, from 2½ to 3 inches across; the ray florets being pure white on the upper surface, are embellished by a narrow yellow zone at their base; reverse of petals pale lilac. Being of very easy culture, the plants produce their splendid flowers most abundantly and in constant succession from early summer to the autumn. Magnificent and prominent novelty. Pkt., 20c.; 3 for 50c.

Poppy Rosy Morn.

**NEW GIANT FRAGRANT CENTAUREA—**
Centaurea Imperialis—This new Centaurea, a cross between C. Mosthata and Margaret, represents the best that has been produced in these beautiful summer-blooming plants. The bushes are about 4 feet high, of enormous dimensions and are COVERED WITH LARGE, BEAUTIFUL FLOWERS of the form and fragrance of Centaurea Margaret. WILL KEEP OVER A WEEK in water, if cut just when they are about to open.

**PURE WHITE—**Large, sweet and beautiful.
**ARMIDA—**Very delicate color, pink with white tinge.
**FAVORITA. —** Brilliant rose.
**GRAZIOSA —** Intense dark lilac.
**SPLENDENS —** Brilliant dark purple.
**VARIABILIS—**White, marked purple, fading to rose.
Price of any of above six kinds—Per oz., 75c.; ¼ oz., 25c.; pkt., 10c. Any 3 pkts., 20c.; 6 pkts., 1 of each kind, for 35c. oz., 60c.; ¼ oz., 20c. All colors mixed: Per pkt., 5c.; ¼ oz., 20c.; oz., 60c.

KUNZE CHIC

Centaurea Giant Fragrant.

**NEW CALIFORNIA POPPY, "ROSY MORN."**
Eschsoltzia California Caniculata Rosea. This is a novelty of undoubted merit, and deserves the attention of all lovers of flowering annuals. A distinct new shade, producing flowers of a form hitherto unknown in the Eschsoltzia species. The rosy, white petals are delicately channeled or fluted with tiny folds radiating from the center and richly adorned with a soft primrose yellow hue, enhancing the beauty of this charming flower, which will gain admiration and praise wherever cultivated. Large pkt., 10c.; 3 for 25c.

**NEW TUFTED CALIFORNIA POPPY —** One of the prettiest of the Eschsoltzia family. The bushy plants grow only 6 inches in height and are covered with a great many brilliant golden - yellow flowers, which measure about 1 inch across. Pkt., 10c.

**LITTLE BROWNIE MARIGOLD—**One of the prettiest and handsomest of the Marigolds. The plants grow 9 inches high, are insect and drought proof and will bloom from the middle of summer until late in fall. Flowers rich, golden yellow marked with velvety brown. Pkt., 5c.

Marigold—Little Brownie.

**THE "MAYFLOWER" VERBENA—**This is of the same trailing habit as the Arbutus or Mayflower, its branches creeping over the ground and hugging it closely. Its blossoms appear in clusters at the ends of the creeping vines, and are of the same shape and about the same size. Pkt., 6c.

**CANDYTUFT LITTLE PRINCE—**It appears like the Giant Hyacinth-Flowered, illustrated here. The bushes grow only about 6 inches high, the spikes are very massive, pure white and planted in a row or a mass the effect is very fine. It also makes a fine pot plant. Pkt., 10c.; ¼ oz., 25c.

Candytuft—Little Prince.

## ALPINE SNOWFLOWER.

No other flower in the whole universe, not even the rarest orchid, has cost so many lives as this chaste little Alpine Beauty. A recent publication states that "scores of lives" are lost annually by venturesome tourists in their efforts to obtain it. It is well known that travelers circling the globe, will stop at the mountains of Switzerland and climb to almost inaccessible heights to be the proud possessors of the precious little treasure. It requires patience, courage, strength, endurance, and a perilous task it is. No wonder, therefore, that it is prized so highly, that the ladies ornament their hats with it as trophies. No wonder that gathering the plants in their native home by crafty guides, who know their value, is now prohibited for fear of their extermination.

Like the wonderful Rose of Jericho from Syria, and the Resurrection plant from Mexico, the "Snow Flower" is a natural curiosity, for one may say the "flower never dies." It remains as white as the snow from which it sprung, and soft and velvety even longer than human life.

There is some romance connected with it also, it being an ancient local custom for the Tyrolian lover to present his affianced as an engagement flower, one that he has gathered himself from amongst the snow clad rocks, the higher the altitude the more it is cherished. The flowers are certainly rare and beautiful, as white as snow, and as soft as velvet, growing sometimes thirty on one plant, with greyish white foliage and spreading rosette. Naturally as hardy as a rock, they grow in any way on sandy moist soil, gritty and well drained, or on raised rockwork, and even as a border plant, in chalky open soil. Lasting for years in beauty, it will certainly prove a wonderful attraction aside from its intrinsic value and the many ways in which they can be used. Pkt., 10c.

Pennisetum Rueppellianum.

PENNISETUM RUEPPELLIANUM—A gigantic Grass, resembling the Pampas grass, of South America, quite hardy, enduring the winters of Minnesota by a covering of leaves or litter to a depth of 4 to 6 inches. This is the finest and most graceful Ornamental Grass grown, producing a great number of the most lovely crimson colored spikes. Superior in beauty to the well known Pampas plumes. Pkt., 10c.

SALVIA SPLENDENS SILVERSPOT—The most distinct feature of this novelty is its strikingly handsome spotted foliage. The leaves are rich, soft dark green with light sulphur or cream-colored spots of various size, liberally sprinkled over them. The unique and elegant foliage is very abundant and has an extremely fresh and healthy appearance. The intense bright scarlet flowers are very large, and the plants of neat, compact habit, and very floriferous. A charming variety of great effect. Pkt., 15c. (See cut.)

Cinnamon Vine.

CINNAMON VINE.—This beautiful climber possesses the rare quality of emitting from its flowers the delightful odor of cinnamon. Perfectly hardy, growing so rapidly as to completely cover any trellis or arbor very early in the season. It is propagated from small bulblets, which will make from ten to twenty feet of vine, heart-shaped leaves, bright green, peculiar foliage and clusters of delicate white flowers sending forth a delicious cinnamon odor, render it one of the most desirable climbers in cultivation. Large tubers by mail, postpaid, for 10c each, three for 25c.; bulblets, four for 10c. or 25c. per dozen.

Salvia Silverspot.

Cut and Come Again Sunflower

"CUT AND COME AGAIN" SUNFLOWERS—Helianthus Cucumerifolius—New types. These improved profuse-flowering, branching single Sunflowers are becoming exceedingly popular, not only for showy display in the garden, but for cut flowers. The plants form many branched pyramidal bushes 3 to 4 feet high, bearing from base to summit a continuous succession of flowers from June until frost, veritable pyramids of gold. The perfectly formed single flowers, 3 to 4 inches across, are poised on long, graceful stems, which "vase" beautifully. They are easily grown, commencing to flower in a few weeks from seed. (See cut.)

WHITE STAR—Almost pure white with black eye..............Pkt., .10
SIRIUS—Lemon-yellow with dark center...................Pkt., .10
MARS—Intense golden yellow with dark eye ...............Pkt., .10
CACTUS-FLOWERED—Quilled and twisted petals—cream, lemon and golden flowers with dark centers —very aesthetic ..........Pkt., .10
PERKEO—A miniature plant only 12 inches high by 18 inches in diameter; flowers 3 inches across, golden with black eye......Pkt., .10
MIXED "Cut and Come Again" Sunflowers, all colors and new types ....................Pkt., .10

# PREMIUMS, NOVELTIES AND SPECIALTIES.

This handsome mantel clock is elegantly finished in bronze, making the best ornament for the parlor and sitting room. It is a very durable clock, never getting out of order, and a very correct timekeeper. We have had one of these clocks upon our shelf for several years already, and it has kept excellent time and never was out of order. We know that everybody will be well pleased with it.

We offer this handsome clock as a premium with a $20 order of our Clover-Grass Mixtures at catalogue prices, selected from pages 9, 10 and 11, and also with a $30 order for Farm Seeds and Seed Potatoes, selected from pages 15 to 31 of our catalogue.

Please notice that Timothy and Alsyke, and Timothy and Red Top Mixtures, also all Clover and Grass Seeds are excluded from the above offers, as these are sold on a very small margin; but Vegetable and Flower Seeds and Plants may be included.

By making up a club order, inducing your neighbors to order with you together, you will surely be able to secure one of these handsome and valuable premiums described on this and the previous page.

In order to enable those who cannot use such large quantities of Seeds to secure this handsome mantel clock, we make the following offer: For every dollar that you are short on $20 to secure this premium with Clover-Grass Mixtures, send us 7½ cents extra. For instance, if your order for Clover-Grass Mixture should be only $10, send us 75 cents extra.

If this clock is ordered separate it will be sent per express, but if ordered with Seeds it can be packed with them together and be shipped per freight.

Our cash price of this handsome mantel clock is only $1.50.

Liberty Bell.

Puritan Watch.

## PURITAN WATCH.

This cut represents the "Puritan" watch, the handsomest and most beautifully engraved gold plated watch ever offered for an extremely low price. The movement is of regular 16 size and only ⅝ of an inch in thickness. Lantern pinions (the smallest ever made), American lever escapement, polished spring, encased in barrel, stem wind; weight, complete with case, only 3 ounces; quick train movement; 240 beats per minute; runs 30 to 36 hours with one winding; hour, minute and second hands. Heavy bevel crystal, Roman dial, fancy engraved case, with special gold plate finish. These watches are tested, timed and regulated, and a guarantee for one year is in back of each case. The "Puritan" is up-to-date in high-class workmanship, as well as in good finish. It is a first-class timekeeper, and will last as long as the most expensive watch.

We offer the "Puritan" as premium with an order for $25 worth of our Clover-Grass Mixtures, selected at catalogue prices from pages 9, 10 and 11, or with an order for $30 worth of Farm, Garden and Flower Seeds and Fruit Plants ordered from pages 15 to 72 of our catalogue at the prices given therein. Grass and Clover Seeds described on pages 1 to 8 are excluded from this offer. We offer this elegant watch for the low cash price of $2.

Should your order for Clover-Grass Mixtures not amount to $30, please add 7 cents for each dollar lacking on $30, extra, and for Farm and Garden Seeds, please add 6 cents for each dollar short of $30, extra, to the amount you send us, to obtain the "Puritan" watch.

## CHAMPION WATCH.

The movement of this watch is exactly the same as that of the "Puritan," is also a 16 size, 3-ounce watch, stem winder, the only difference being in the engraving, as the Champion has a plain gold-plated case, open face and Roman dial, hour, minute and second hands, the same as the Puritan. Every watch has been carefully tested, timed and regulated, and a guarantee is in back of each case. It should, for this reason, not be compared with the so-called cheap watches, which, being out of order in a short time, have to be cast aside, while the firm who manufacture these watches for us guarantees every watch for one year.

This watch we offer, also, the same as the Little Seeder and the handsome Mantel Clock, as premium on $20 worth of Clover-Grass Mixtures ordered at catalogue prices from pages 9, 10 and 11, and with an order or $25 worth of Farm, Vegetable and Flower Seeds and Small Fruit Plants, selected from pages 15 to 72, at catalogue prices. Collections of Vegetable and Flower Seeds and Implements are excluded from this offer.

If your order should not be large enough to secure any of these premiums, then you may add 7½ cents for each dollar short on $20 extra, to the amount of your order to get this premium.

We sell this watch for the low price of $1.50.

Champion Watch.

For many generations housekeepers have been VEXED with dull knives and scissors. But this woe is now past, for with our "SCIENTIFIC" KNIFE AND SCISSORS GRINDER you can grind a dull knife or a dull pair of scissors in less than one minute and do it as well as the most experienced expert, and save your ten cents that you usually pay to have it done.

This fact has brought this little machine into great demand wherever it has been introduced, and as it is in demand in every home, dealers have found it a very rapid seller. No housekeeper, after knowing its real merit, will think of doing without it, for everybody recognizes the fact that the low price we are asking is not nearly commensurate with its real value. Price, $1.00, per freight or express, at purchaser's expense.

We also offer this Grinder as a premium with a $15 order of Seed Grain and Seed Potatoes at catalogue prices, selected from pages 18 to 31 of our catalogue.

Schofield's "Scientific" Knife and Scissors Grinder.

SEEDS FOR ALL — SEEDS DIRECT FROM THE GROWER — GREAT BARGAINS IN SEEDS

**Seldom Equaled. Never Excelled.**

The following list embraces the best of the old and thoroughly tried standard sorts of Vegetable Seeds. In it will be found everything required for a first-class garden, and Seeds that are sure to grow under ordinary favorable conditions.

We grow large quantities of Vegetable Seeds, and by our painstaking methods it is not possible to grow a purer or better stock. Such varieties as we cannot grow are grown for us by reliable growers in their special lines. We personally inspect these crops and know to a certainty that the work is carefully and conscientiously done. Our prices include postage on packets, ounces, quarter pounds and pounds; also, half pints and pints. On quarts and larger quantities of Peas, Beans and Corn, add at the rate of 15 cents per quart if to be sent by mail.

## Asparagus Seed.

**COLUMBIAN MAMMOTH WHITE**—A new, distinct variety, with pure white shoots, which remain white as long as fit for use without earthing up or artificial blanching. Pkt., 5c.; oz., 10c.; ¼ lb., 25c.; lb., 75c.

**CONOVERS' COLOSSAL**—A well tried, standard variety of large size, quick growth and excellent quality. Pkt., 4c.; oz., 5c.; ¼ lb., 20c.; lb., 55c.

**PALMETTO**—Very early, of large size, even and regular in growth and appearance, and of excellent quality. Pkt., 4c.; oz., 10c.; ¼ lb., 20c.; lb., 60c.

One-year-old roots of any of the above varieties by mail, postpaid, 12 for 30c., 25 for 50c. By express, at your expense, 25 for 35c., 100 for $1.00.

**EARLY GIANT ARGENTEUIL**—This deserves the attention of market gardeners and private planters, for it is a Mammoth sort and the earliest variety in existence. Gardeners who want large Asparagus and want it early can find no better sort than the Early Giant Argenteuil. Pkt., 5c.; oz., 15c.; ¼ lb., 40c. Roots one year, postpaid, 12 for 40c., 25 for 60c.

## Artichoke Seed.

**LARGE GREEN GLOBE**—Pkt., 4c.; oz., 25c.

## Borecole or Kale.

**DWARF GERMAN GREEN CURLED**—Very hardy, leaves are curly, bright green; very tender and of delicate flavor. Pkt., 4c.; oz., 10c.; ¼ lb., lb., $1.00.

**DWARF PURPLE KALE**—Like Dwarf German Green Curled, except the color, which is purple. Pkt., 4c.; oz., 10c.; ¼ lb., 30c.; lb., $1.10.

**TALL GREEN SCOTCH**—Fine curled leaves. Pkt., 4c.; oz., 10c.; ¼ lb., 30c.; lb., $1.00.

**Asparagus, Columbian Mammoth White.**

**Kale, Dwarf Green Curled.**

## Asparagus Culture.

Beds are usually formed by setting plants one or two years old, which can be procured of us, but if you wish to grow them yourself, pour hot water on the seed and allow it to stand until cool, pour it off and repeat with fresh hot water once or twice and then sow in drills one foot apart and two inches deep in light, rich soil. When the plants are well up, thin to about one inch apart, and give frequent and thorough cultivation during the summer. If this has been well done, the plants will be fit to be set the next spring. The permanent beds should be prepared by deep plowing or spading and thoroughly enriching the ground with stable manure or other fertilizers. If the subsoil is not naturally loose and friable, it should be made so by thoroughly stirring with a subsoil plow or the spade. Set the plants about four inches deep and one to two feet apart in rows four to six feet apart. After the plants are well started give frequent and thorough cultivation. Early the next spring spade in a heavy dressing of manure, and one quart of salt to each square rod and cultivate well as long as the size of the plants will permit or until they begin to die down. The next season the bed may be cut over two or three times.

## Brussels Sprouts.

Although not in general use in this country, this is a most delicious vegetable. The small heads which grow along the stem are the edible parts of this vegetable, and, when boiled like cabbage, or stewed with cream like cauliflower, are very tender and delicious. Where the winters are not very severe they may remain in the ground, to be cut as needed; the sprouts are much improved by a moderate frost.

**IMPROVED DWARF**—The best variety. Pkt., 4c.; oz., 15c.

**Broccoli.**

## Broccoli.

Very much like the Cauliflower, but hardier and preferred by many to that vegetable.

**LARGE WHITE CAPE**—The best large headed white variety. Pkt., 5c.; oz., 30c.; ¼ lb., $1.00.

**PURPLE CAPE**—Very fine for use in the North, and more extensively grown. Pkt., 5c.; oz., 30c.; ¼ lb., $1.00.

**Brussels Sprouts.**

# Bush Beans, Wax Varieties

Dwarf Butter Wax Bismarck.

German Black Wax or Butter Bean.

**THE BISMARCK**—This is one of the most attractive and famous varieties of Wax Beans known in Germany. It is very early; the pods are produced in great profusion and will average 6 inches in length, are almost transparent, exceedingly brittle and of very delicate flavor. Pkt., 4c.; ½ pint, 15c.; pint, 25c., prepaid; quart, 30c.; peck, $1.75; bu., $6.50, not prepaid.

**WARDWELL'S KIDNEY**—One of the earliest, hardiest and most productive of Wax Beans. It is almost entirely free from rust and spots. The pods are long and showy, very tender (stringless), and of delicate, waxy yellow color; quality excellent. A great favorite with market gardeners. Pkt., 4c.; ½ pint, 15c.; pint, 25c., prepaid; quart, 30c.; peck, $2.00, not prepaid.

**CRYSTAL WAX**—Pods waxy white, transparent, of fair size; stringless, and a good flavor; seeds white. Pkt., 4c.; ½ pint, 15c.; pint, 25c., prepaid; qt., 30c.; peck, $1.75, not prepaid.

**JONE'S STRINGLESS WAX**—A new and desirable yellow pod bush bean, with white seeds. The pods are round and plump, and attain a length of five to seven inches. They are thick and fleshy, and as handsome in the basket as on the bush. The pod is perfectly stringless, of prime quality in every way, and delicious to the taste. The plants make a vigorous growth and are uniformly productive. A most valuable variety. Pkt., 5c.; ½ pt., 15c.; pint, 25c.; qt., 45c., prepaid.

**GERMAN BLACK WAX OR BUTTER BEAN**—This is no doubt the earliest and one of the most productive of all, and is positively proof against rust. Not only is it rust-proof, but it possesses the most excellent and most desirable quality of being exceedingly crisp and tender, entirely stringless, and of delicious flavor. The pods are large and of beautiful waxy yellow color. Pkt., 4c.; ½ pint, 15c.; pint, 25c., prepaid; qt., 30c.; peck, $1.75; bu., $6.25, not prepaid.

**DAVIS KIDNEY WAX BEAN**—The large Beans are pure white, kidney shaped, excellent for cooking green or dry. The pods while young are stringless, tender and of excellent flavor, very long, straight and uniform in size and shape and of a clear waxy white color. Pkt., 4c.; ¾ pint, 15c.; pint, 25c., prepaid; quart, 30c.; peck, $1.50, not prepaid.

**VALENTINE WAX BEAN**—Our experience has proved this Bean to be remarkably early. The pods are thick and fleshy, with but very little string; vigorous and productive. Pkt., 5c.; ½ pint, 15c.; pt., 25c.; qt., 45c.; prepaid; pk., $1.75; bu., $6.50.

**RUST-PROOF GOLDEN WAX**—The best general crop Bean. Very early and of excellent quality; pods stringless, golden yellow, very fleshy; can be used either for snaps, green, shelled, or when ripe and dried. Pkt., 4c.; ½ pint, 15c.; pint, 25c., prepaid; quart, 25c.; peck, $1.50, not prepaid.

Rust-Proof Golden Wax Beans.

Early Valentine.

## Green Pod Varieties

**EXTRA EARLY RED VALENTINE**—A select strain of Early Red Valentine, ripening very uniformly and producing enormously. Pods tender and succulent; the most profitable sort for the gardener; ready to pick in 35 days. Pkt., 5c.; ½ pint, 12c.; pint, 20c., prepaid; qt., 25c.; peck, $1.50, not prepaid.

**EXTRA EARLY REFUGEE**—This is the earliest of the green podded Beans, and has all the good qualities of the well known Refugee, and the additional advantage of being ready for table at least ten days earlier. Immense yielder and sure cropper. Pkt., 4c.; ½ pint, 12c.; pint, 20c., prepaid; qt., 25c.; peck, $1.25, not prepaid.

## GREEN POD VARIETIES—Continued.

**BEST OF ALL BEANS**—A new variety which originated in Germany. Pods are about twice as long as of the Red Valentine, very fleshy, tender, stringless, and of excellent flavor. One of the best, or the "best of all" for market or family use. It is very productive. Pkt., 4c.; ½ pint, 15c.; pint, 25c., prepaid; qt., 30c.; peck, $1.75, not prepaid.

**EMPEROR WILLIAM BEAN**—One of the real good green podded Beans that pleases everybody. It is extra early, very productive, and certainly worth a place in every garden. For private or market use it is one of the grandest Beans that can be secured. Pkt., 4c.; ½ pint, 12c.; pint, 20c., prepaid; qt., 25c.; peck, $1.40, not prepaid.

**LONG YELLOW SIX WEEKS**—Extra early and a most excellent variety; the leading market sort; has full flat pods Pkt., 4c.; ½ pint, 12c.; pint, 20c., prepaid; qt., 25c.; peck, $1.40, not prepaid.

**DWARF HORTICULTURAL**—Pods medium length, round, curved, with splashes of bright red on a yellowish ground. The ripe beans are large, oval, plump, and nearly covered with splashes of bright red. This is undoubtedly the best variety as a green shelled bean, and when in this condition the beans are very large, easily shelled, and although of quite different form, are about equal to the Lima in quality. Pkt., 5c.; ½ pint, 15c.; pint, 25c., prepaid; qt., 30c.; peck, $1.75; not prepaid.

**HENDERSON'S BUSH LIMA**—A perfect bush, about 18 inches high, maturing its first beans 2 weeks before any Pole Lima, and continuing to bear its load of well-filled pods until stopped by frost. The beans are the size of the Sieva or small Pole Lima, and of delicious quality. Pkt., 4c.; ½ pint, 15c.; pint, 25c.; qt., 40c., prepaid by mail.

**BURPEE'S DWARF LIMA**—The bushes grow 18 to 20 inches in height, yet branching so vigorously that the plants develop into a magnificent circular bush from 2 to 3 feet in diameter, each bush bearing from 50 to 200 of handsome large pods, well filled with very large Beans, which are of the same size as the well known large Pole Limas. Pkt., 5c.; ½ pint, 15c.; pint, 30c., prepaid by mail.

## FIELD BEANS.

Tree Bean.

**CALIFORNIA WONDER OR IMPROVED TREE BEAN**—This is easily the heaviest yielding Bean known. The seed resembles the well known "Navy Bean," but cooks in less time and is of better flavor, and on account of its whiteness and small size commands the highest price in all markets. They should be planted in rows 2½ feet apart and 20 inches apart in the rows, so they will not crowd each other. Ours is pure stock. Pkt., 4c.; ½ pint, 10c.; pint, 18c., prepaid; quart, 18c.; peck, $1.00; bu., $3.50.

**BROAD WINDSOR BEANS**—Pkt., 4c.; ½ pint, 10c.; pint, 20c.; qt., 35c., prepaid by mail.

Market Gardeners as Farmers in need of larger quantities than here quot'd, will please write for prices.

**BURLINGAME MEDIUM**—The Beans are pearly white, do not rust; 40 bushels to the acre is no uncommon yield. The leading Field Bean. Pkt., 4c.; ½ pint, 10c.; pint, 18c., prepaid; quart, 18c.; peck, 90c.; bu., $3.25, not prepaid.

**IMPROVED NAVY OR BOSTON PEA BEAN**—This Bean is very largely grown as a field crop. Ripens early, and yields immensely. The Beans are small, white and of superior quality for baking. Pkt., 4c.; ½ pint, 8c.; pint, 16c., prepaid; quart, 15c.; peck, 80c.; bu., $3.25, not prepaid.

**WHITE MARROWFAT**—Standard variety for field culture. Very early, productive, of excellent quality, either when green or dry. Pkt., 4c.; ½ pint, 10c.; pint, 18c., prepaid; quart, 20c.; peck, $1.00; bu., $3.50, not prepaid.

Golden Cluster.

## POLE BEANS.

**KENTUCKY WONDER**—The best variety for use in a green state. The pods are entirely stringless, silvery green in color, resembling in this particular the Refugee, and although very large, are tender and melting when cooked. It is enormously productive. Pkt., 4c.; ½ pint, 15c.; pint, 25c.; qt., 45c., prepaid by mail; pint, 15c.; qt., 30c., not prepaid.

**TALL GERMAN BLACK WAX**—A very good snap sort, maturing in seventy days from germination; also, excellent for shell Beans. Seeds are glossy black. Pkt., 5c.; ½ pint, 15c.; pint, 25c., prepaid; qt., 25c., not prepaid.

**HORTICULTURAL OR SPECKLED CRANBERRY**—An old favorite, excellent as a snap or shell Bean. Beans are large and of fine flavor. Pkt., 3c.; ½ pint, 10c.

**DUTCH CASE KNIFE**—Vines moderately vigorous, climbing well, but not twining so tightly as some, and so may be used for a corn hill bean. Pods very long, flat, irregular, green, but becoming cream white; beans broad, kidney shaped, flat, clear white, and of excellent quality, green or dry. Pkt., 4c.; ½ pint, 15c.; pint, 25c., prepaid; qt., 30c.; peck, $2.00, not prepaid.

**KING OF THE GARDEN LIMA**—Pods are very long, from 7 to 8 inches, producing 4 to 7 Beans to the pod, all perfectly formed and of superior quality. Pkt., 3c.; ½ pint, 15c.; pint, 25c., prepaid; qt., 30c.; peck, $2.00, not prepaid.

**GOLDEN CLUSTER BEAN**—A strong, vigorous grower, requiring a pole 6 to 8 feet high. It bears its bright golden yellow pods, in clusters of from 3 to 6, in the greatest abundance from July until cut down by the frost. Is stringless, and of very delicate flavor. The pods are 6 to 8 inches long. Pkt., 4c.; ½ pint, 10c.; pint, 20c.; qt., 35c., prepaid by mail; pint, 12c.; qt., 20c., not prepaid.

**CUT SHORT, or CORN HILL**—An old variety, very popular for planting among corn, and it will give a good crop without the use of poles; vines medium, pods short, cylindrical and tender; beans nearly oblong, cut off diagonally at the ends, white, covered at one end with reddish brown dots. Per pkt., 5c.; pt., 25c.; qt., 45c., prepaid.

**YARD LONG or CUBAN ASPARAGUS**—This is a real curiosity. We have measured pods over three feet long, though two feet is a more common length. Quality very good, and pods freely borne. Pkt., 10c.

Kentucky Wonder.

# TABLE BEETS.

Early Egyptian.

**ECLIPSE**—The roots are nearly globe-shaped and smooth, are of intense blood-red flesh and skin, fine grained and sweet. Its small top and extreme earliness recommend it to market gardeners. Pkt., 4c.; oz., 8c.; ¼ lb., 15c.; lb., 50c.

**DEWING'S IMPROVED BLOOD TURNIP**—Earlier and better than the old Early Blood Turnip and desirable for main crop; globe shal-e; deep blood-red color and of fine flavor. Pkt., 3c.; oz., 8c.; ¼ lb., 15c.; lb., 50c.

**MARKET GARDENERS' BEET**—This is the ideal and most profitable Beet for market gardeners as well as for the private garden, and the best general purpose Beet in cultivation. It is very symmetrical in form, with but few fibrous roots and small tap root. At the age of Egyptian it is larger and continues to grow until late in the fall, attaining a large size and making a good selling and eating Beet for winter. One sowing only is necessary to produce early Beets for market and main crop for winter use. When cooked they are a beautiful dark red throughout, fine grained and unsurpassed in quality. The color outside is a deep blood red, inside layers of blood red and light red alternately. Pkt., 5c.; oz., 10c.; ¼ lb., 18c.; lb., 60c.

**IMPROVED EARLY EGYPTIAN**—The standard early market sort; bulbs medium size, of very deep red color and fine quality, tender and sweet, of very quick growth, and best for early market. Pkt., 5c.; oz., 8c.; ¼ lb., 15c.; lb., 50c.

**EARLY BASSANO**—Very early; flesh light color, sweet and tender. Pkt., 3c.; oz., 7c.; ¼ lb., 16c.; lb., 48c.

**SWISS CHARD, SILVER OR SEA KALE**—Cultivated for its leaves only, which are used like Spinach. Pkt., 3c.; oz., 7c.; ¼ lb., 14c.; lb., 50c.

Market Gardeners'.

**EDMAND'S IMPROVED BLOOD TURNIP**—A new and very superior variety. The roots re of very good form, round, with only one single small tap root; top is very small; the flesh is of a deep red color and very sweet and tender. It is one of the best for the market gardener and table use. Pkt., 3c.; oz., 8c.; ¼ lb., 15c.; lb., 45c.

Columbia.

**NEW HALF LONG BLOOD**—This is an entirely new variety. In form it is thick at the top and tapers to a point, and is only half as long as the Long Blood. It is always smooth and handsome; and the rich, dark red flesh is very sweet, crisp and tender, and never becomes woody. Pkt., 4c.; oz., 8c.; ¼ lb., 15c.; lb., 50c.

**LONG BLOOD**—A well known winter sort; good shape, sweet and tender. Pkt., 4c.; oz., 8c.; ¼ lb., 15c.; lb., 50c.

**CROSBY'S IMPROVED EGYPTIAN**—The best and most popular Extra Early Beet. Nothing better for market or home table. Pkt., 3c.; oz., 6c.; ¼ lb., 12c.; lb., 42c.

**EXTRA EARLY BLOOD TURNIP**—A standard early sort with small top. Pkt., 3c.; oz., 6c.; ¼ lb., 15c.; 1 lb., 45c.

**NEW COLUMBIA** — (Carter's Excelsior)—Round, smooth, deep red flesh. Pkt., 4c.; oz., 7c.; ¼ lb., 15c.; 1 lb., 45c.

Edmand's Improved Blood Turnip.

## Cress or Pepper Grass.

**WATER CRESS** — A hardy perennial, grown in wet places or on borders of ponds, streams and ditches. As a salad it is highly appetizing and of delicious flavor. Pkt., 4c.; oz., 30c.

**CURLED GARDEN** — A small salad much used with lettuce, to which its warm, pungent taste makes a most agreeable addition. Pkt., 4c.; oz., 7c.; ¼ lb., 15c.; lb., 45c.

## Collards.

**TRUE GREGORIAN OR CREOLE**—Excellent for green; quite extensively grown in the South. Sow for succession from June to August, and treat as Cabbage. Pkt., 5c.; oz., 10c.; ¼ lb., 30c.; lb., $1.00.

**CHICORY** (Large Rooted)—Much used in Europe as a substitute for coffee. In the fall the roots should be taken up and dried, and when required for use should be roasted and ground like coffee. Pkt., 3c.; oz., 6c.; ¼ lb., 15c.; lb., 50c.

## Coffee Berry or Soja Bean.

**COFFEE BERRY OR SOJA BEAN**—This bean is largely advertised under the name of "German Coffee Berry" at high prices. The berries ripen in about 4 months from time of planting and produce a crop of 20 to 30 bushels to the acre, and are as easily grown as other Beans. When roasted and ground it resembles coffee and tastes quite similar. Some mix half and half with coffee when using.

It can be sown broadcast at the rate of one-half bushel to the acre or it may be planted in drills 3 feet apart and one foot between plants. Price by mail postpaid; Pkt., 5c.; ¼ lb., 15c.; lb., 40c. By freight or express: Peck, $1.00; bu., $3.50.

Bear in mind our prices by the pound are postpaid. If by express or freight, deduct 8c. per lb.

Coffee Berry.

Corn Salad.
Pkt., 3c.; oz., 7c.; ¼ lb., 18c.; lb., 60c.

*Marblehead Mammoth Cabbage.* ## CABBAGE. *Early Spring Cabbage*

Again comes the news that Cabbage Seed is a short crop generally; but we have been fortunate in securing a good supply of first-class Seed, and our prices will remain the same as last year, with one or two exceptions.

Hardly another crop requires a more careful selection of Seed than Cabbage. Seed grown in France and other parts of Europe can be bought very cheap, but is usually worthless when sown in this country; still many dealers handle nothing else but this cheap European Cabbage Seed. It is not sufficient that the seed germinates well, but it must be true to name, of uniform type, grown from perfect, solid heads and in a climate especially adapted for producing the best and most solid heads. We have such seed, and know that our Northern Grown Seed can be relied upon to produce sure and solid, fine heads. **Our Packets of Cabbage contain on an average about 1,000 seeds.**

**NEW WASHINGTON WAKEFIELD CABBAGE**—First in head! First in the market! First in the hearts of gardeners. This expresses the qualities of this grand variety. All gardeners are so familiar with the Wakefield Cabbages that description is unnecessary. The engraving shows the character of the WASHINGTON WAKEFIELD, and it is perhaps sufficient to say that this leads all other strains of this popular variety in earliness, size of head and purity of stock. It grows remarkably uniform, the heads being of very even size and shape. Unequaled for either the market or family garden. Pkt., 8c.; 3 pkts., 20c.; oz., 30c.; ¼ lb., 85c.; lb., $3.00.

**MINNESOTA'S EARLIEST**—Will produce good sized marketable heads 70 days from sowing the seed. It is conical shaped, and has but very few loose leaves. Pkt., 5c.; oz., 20c.; ¼ lb., 60c.; lb., $1.85.

Early Summer.

Washington Wakefield.

**EARLY JERSEY WAKEFIELD**—The standard sort and market gardener's favorite. The heads are very hard, compact, solid, and of conical shape. No other stock is superior to this, which we offer, except the Washington Wakefield. Pkt., 5c.; oz., 20c.; ¼ lb., 60c.; lb., $2.00.

**EARLY SUMMER** (Henderson's)—This superior Cabbage is about double the size of Jersey Wakefield, and ten days later. Having short outer leaves it can be planted closer than most sorts. The heads are not liable to burst. Pkt., 4c.; oz., 20c.; ¼ lb., 55c.; lb., $1.85.

**ALL-HEAD EARLY CABBAGE**—A splendid new Cabbage. Grows to a larger size than any other new early variety, and stands drought remarkably. Head very solid, flat and deep, with few loose leaves; very uniform in size and color. It is the earliest of all large, and an all-the-year around Cabbage. Any one planting but one variety of Cabbage could get none that would answer all purposes as well as this variety. Pkt., 5c.; 3 pkts., 12c.; oz., 20c.; ¼ lb., 60c.; lb., $1.60.

**EARLY WINNINGSTADT**—Heads pointed, very hard and solid; does well on light soil; is of fine flavor, crisp and tender. Pkt., 4c.; oz., 15c.; ¼ lb., 50c.; lb., $1.85.

**FILDERKRAUT**—A great favorite of the Germans. Pkt., 4c.; oz., 15c.; ¼ lb., 50c.; lb., $1.85.

**HENDERSON'S SUCCESSION**—Is about a week later than the Early Summer, but double the size, and remarkably uniform in size and shape. It is certainly a good Cabbage, and should be included in every order. Pkt., 4c.; oz., 18c.; ¼ lb., 65c.; lb., $2.00.

All Head Early.

## Red Cabbages.

**EXTRA EARLY DARK RED ERFURT**—The earliest and finest red Cabbage. Pkt., 4c.; oz., 18c.; ¼ lb., 70c.

**LARGE RED DRUMHEAD**—Very solid and large heads; round, of a deep red color. Pkt., 4c.; oz., 18c.; ¼ lb., 70c.

**MAMMOTH ROCK RED**—Heads as large as the Flat Dutch, deep red to the center; highly recommended. Hard as a rock. Pkt., 5c.; ½ oz., 15c.; oz., 25c.; ¼ lb., 75c.; lb., $2.50.

## Savoy Cabbages.

**IMPROVED AMERICAN**—An excellent variety, of fine flavor, heads very compact, showy, with fine savoyed or crumpled leaves. The best late Savoy. Pkt., 4c.; oz., 15c.; ¼ lb., 55c.

**DWARF ULM SAVOY**—A very good early variety. Pkt., 3c.; oz., 15c.; ¼ lb., 55c.

Dwarf Ulm Savoy.

**ERFURT ROUND SUGAR**—This entirely new and distinct variety was recently introduced by a seed grower in Germany. It is the finest pickling sort now in cultivation. It is a very close and heavy, tender, smooth, round-headed variety, a good keeper, and when held over winter comes out having a fine golden color, thus presenting a more appetizing and finer appearance than others, which turn a grayish white. Pkt., 8c.; 3 pkts., 20c.; oz., 30c.

**HARVEST HOME**—The best late cabbage, and noted for its reliability of heading, uniformity of size, and solid heads. No other cabbage of equal quality will yield as large a weight from a given area as this variety. Pkt., 5c.; oz., 20c.; ¼ lb., 70c.; lb., $2.25.

**FOTTLER'S BLUE BRUNSWICK**—It forms large and solid heads. The leaves have a bluish tint, hence the name. It is a good keeper. Pkt., 4c.; oz., 15c.; ¼ lb., 55c.; lb., $1.85.

**GERMAN EXPORT or IMPROVED LATE DRUMHEAD**—One of the finest main crop and winter Cabbages, a splendid keeper, selling for more than other varieties in the spring. Pkt., 5c.; oz., 20c.; ¼ lb., 70c.; lb., $2.25.

**NEW LUPTON**—A very good late Cabbage; is always sure to head and keeps well. Pkt., 5c.; oz., 20c.; ¼ lb., 60c.; lb., $2.00.

**SELECT LARGE LATE FLAT DUTCH**—Through careful selection this deservedly popular Cabbage can be depended on to produce large heads of uniform size and of excellent quality. A good one for main crop and an excellent keeper. Pkt., 4c.; oz., 15c.; ¼ lb., 55c.; lb., $1.85.

Luxemburger.

**LUXEMBURGER or HARD HEAD**—It makes a very hard head of good size and extraordinary weight, and is remarkable for its keeping qualities when buried over winter, and will then command the highest price after all the other sorts are gone. One of the most profitable to grow, especially for the market gardener. This variety was first grown by a German gardener near Chicago, and proved so valuable that the seed has frequently been sold at $1 per ounce, and more when it was scarce, as it always has been in demand by the gardeners who knew of it. Pkt., 4c.; oz., 20c.; ¼ lb., 70c.; lb., $2.50.

**SHORT STEM DRUMHEAD**—Heads very large, extra hard, solid, round, flattened on the top, uniform in size and shape. It has a very short stem, and grows very compactly, the leaves all turning in to form the head, with very few leaves, thus allowing it to be set very close together. Pkt., 4c.; oz., 15c.; ¼ lb., 45c.; lb., $1.65.

Holland Ball Head Cabbage.

100 Weight.

**LUXEMBURGER or HARD HEAD**—It makes a very hard head of good size and extraordinary weight, and is remarkable for its keeping qualities when buried over winter, and will then command the highest price after all the other sorts are gone. One of the most profitable to grow, the seed has frequently been sold at $1 per ounce, and more when it was scarce, as it always has been in demand by the gardeners who knew of it. Pkt., 4c.; oz., 20c.; ¼ lb., 70c.; lb., $2.50.

**SHORT STEM DRUMHEAD**—Heads very large, extra hard, solid, round, flattened on the top, uniform in size and shape. It has a very short stem, and grows very compactly, the leaves all turning in to form the head, with very few leaves, thus allowing it to be set very close together. Pkt., 4c.; oz., 15c.; ¼ lb., 45c.; lb., $1.65.

**THE HOLLAND CABBAGE or DANISH BALL HEAD**—The most remarkable Cabbage yet produced, and although introduced only a few years ago, is a great favorite with all who have grown it. The heads, which are very solid and deep, are of medium size, averaging about 8 lbs. in weight; in color they are entirely distinct, being a fine white. Their quality is superior and they keep better than any other sort, the heads being as solid and perfect when taken up in the spring as when put away in the fall. Our seed is American grown and sure to produce the finest and best heads. Pkt., 5c.; oz., 25c.; ¼ lb., 75c.; lb., $2.50.

Premium Flat Dutch.

**NEW 100 WEIGHT**—This is the largest Cabbage known; remarkable for its immense size, firm heart and superior heading properties. Pkt., 5c.; oz., 20c.; ¼ lb., 70c.; lb., $2.50.

**BRIDGEPORT DRUMHEAD**—It is shipped more largely than any other from the Chicago market, and possesses all the points desired by large growers. It makes a large, firm, round head, which seldom bursts. Pkt., 5c.; oz., 20c.; ¼ lb., 70c.; lb., $2.50.

**PREMIUM FLAT DUTCH**—The well known standard late sort and among the best for winter use. It is of very handsome appearance and always sure to head. The well developed heads measure about 12 to 14 inches in diameter and weigh from 12 to 16 pounds each; they are true to type, hard, solid and fine grained, and among the best of keepers. Our seed of this old and reliable sort is as good as any offered. Pkt., 5c.; oz., 20c.; ¼ lb., 60c.; lb., $2.00.

**AUTUMN KING**—It produces enormous, solid heads of that dark shade of green which is most desirable in a Cabbage. It is always sure to head hard, and as solid as a rock. The large, broad heads are very thick through, rounded at the top, fine grained and tender. It has such small outer leaves that it can be planted much closer than the ordinary late sorts. Pkt., 5c.; oz., 20c.; ¼ lb., 70c.; lb., $2.25.

Autumn King.

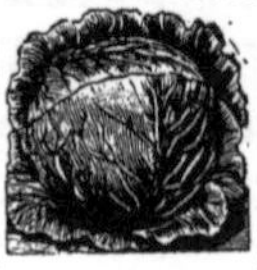

Surehead.

**SUREHEAD**—A good main crop variety. Always very sure to make fine heads, even in most unfavorable seasons. The heads are remarkably uniform, very hard, firm and fine in texture, and weigh from 10 to 15 lbs. each. Pkt., 5c.; oz., 20c.; ¼ lb., 70c.; lb., $2.25.

# Cauliflower.

**Dwarf Erfurt.**

**EARLY PADILLA**—A variety of Cauliflower which is a great favorite with some market gardeners and one which we can recommend. Pkt., 10c.; oz., $1.50; ¼ lb., $5.00.

**EXTRA EARLY PARIS**—Good for forcing; a standard early variety. Pkt., 8c.; ½ oz., 40c.; 1 oz., 70c.; ¼ lb., $2.25.

**AUTUMN GIANT**—A large, late variety, well protected by foliage. Pkt., 5c.; oz., 50c.; ¼ lb., $1.75.

**WALCHEREN**—Very late and hardy. Pkt., 8c.; oz., 40c.; ¼ lb., $1.40.

**Snowball Cauliflower.**

**EXTRA EARLY DWARF ERFURT CAULIFLOWER**—The best that can be had at any price, and growers will find this a very superior strain. Our seed comes from the city of Erfurt, Germany, where for more than half a century the finest seed known has been produced, and there is none better. It is of dwarf, compact growth, with short stalk. The heads are beautiful; white, very large and firm, measuring from 8 to 10 inches across, of fine grain, and form quickly. Pkt., 20c.; ¼ oz., 60c.; ½ oz., $1.00; 1 oz., $1.75.

**HENDERSON'S EARLY SNOWBALL**—A well-known American variety; is very early and reliable in heading. Pkt., 20c.; ¼ oz., 60c.; oz., $1.75.

**LARGE LATE ALGIERS**—This is one of the best late varieties. It is largely grown for fall use, never failing to produce large, fine heads. Very popular with market gardeners and canners. 8c. pkt., 50c. oz., $2.00 ¼ lb.

# Best Carrots for Stock.

**Victoria Carrot.**

**Mastodon Carrot.**

Of all root crops there is none so well adapted for horses, and particularly for colts, as Carrots. In Europe they are largely grown for this purpose, and the farmers there know the value and beneficial results to be had from feeding the Carrots, and large quantities are also used for the cavalry horses in the army. Every farmer who feeds Carrots regularly to his horses during the early winter, and, if possible, through the winter and in the spring, will find them better than all condition powders. Distemper and similar diseases among his horses will be unknown to him. Try a small patch of Carrots, fi 'ers, and see if they don't pay.

The seed should be sown as 'ly in spring as the ground can be worked, in drills fi ough apart so they can be cultivated with a horse cu 'or. Three to five pounds of seed are required to sow on re.

**MASTODON CARROT**—This will give the greatest yield per acre of any carrot grown. The roots are short and very heavy at the shoulder; consequently they are easily harvested. The flesh is white, crisp, solid and very sweet in flavor. A yield from 15 to 20 tons per acre and more is very frequently obtained. They do not easily break in pulling or storing. Price postpaid by mail: Pkt., 5c.; oz., 8c.; ¼ lb., 25c.; lb., 85c. By express or freight: Lb., 30c.; 5 lbs., $3.75.

**VICTORIA CARROT**—The largest and unquestionably the heaviest cropping Yellow Carrot in cultivation. The roots are remarkably fine, very symmetrical, and of excellent quality, possessing high feeding properties. It is especially adapted for rich land, although a heavy cropper on all soils. It is easily harvested, as the roots grow much more above the ground, and will suit all those who grow it. Price postpaid by mail: Pkt., 5c.; oz., 8c.; ¼ lb., 25c.; lb., 85c. By express or freight: Lb., 30c.; 5 lbs., $3.75.

**LONG WHITE BELGIAN CARROT**—A very productive white Carrot which has become the standard variety for stock feeding. They grow one-third above ground, and to a large size. The lower part of the root is white; that growing above ground and exposed to the air is green. The flesh is yellowish white, sweet, and excellent for stock feeding. Price postpaid by mail: Pkt., 3c.; ¼ lb., 14c.; lb., 45c. By express or freight: Lb., 35c.; 5 lbs., $1.65.

**LARGE YELLOW BELGIAN**—A large growing favorite variety, grown very largely for feeding purposes. Price postpaid by mail: Pkt., 3c.; ¼ lb., 15c.; lb., 45c. By express or freight: Lb., 35c.; 5 lbs., $1.65.

**MAMMOTH WHITE VOSGES**—A field variety; one of the best for feeding cattle. The roots are very broad at the neck, narrowing abruptly to the point; they are about 8 inches long, with a diameter of from 4 to 5 inches. It is easily pulled and is especially suitable for shallow soils. Pkt., 3c.; ¼ lb., 12c.; lb., 40c. By express or freight: Lb., 30c.; 5 lbs., $1.40.

## Table Carrot

One ounce of seed is sufficient for one hundred feet of drill, three to four pounds are required for an acre. One packet contains about 45000 seeds.

**FRENCH FORCING** — The earliest variety, and very valuable for forcing. It makes a small, almost globe-shaped root, of orange red color, and is of excellent quality. Pkt., 4c.; oz., 7c.; ¼ lb., 18c.; lb., 60c.

**OXHEART** — Or GUERANDE—A thick Carrot, 5 or 6 inches long and often 3 or 4 inches in diameter. and short, stump rooted. It is of very fine quality for table use. very tender and of good flavor. Where other sorts require digging. Ox Heart can be easily pulled. Pkt., 4c.; oz., 8c.; ¼ lb., 20c.; lb., 65c.

**SCARLET HORN** — One of the most popular varieties grown; stump rooted, about 5 inches long. Pkt., 4c.; oz., 8c.; ¼ lb., 20c.; lb., 65c.

**IMPROVED LONG ORANGE** — Similar to the Altringham, but the roots are of a dark orange color and grow to large size. It is suitable for the table and the main field crop. Pkt., 3c.; oz., 8c.; ¼ lb., 18c.; lb., 60c.

**CHANTENAY** — A first-class table variety; stump rooted, smooth, and about 5 to 6 inches long and broad-shouldered. The flesh is of a beautiful rich orange color and of the finest quality; is medium early, with small tops. Pkt., 3c.; oz., 8c.; ¼ lb., 18c.; lb., 60c.

**DANVERS HALF LONG** — This is considered the best variety for general crop, and a first-class Carrot for all kinds of soil. It is of a rich dark orange color, grows to good and large size, is smooth and very handsome. It generally grows with a stump root, is quite easily harvested and a good keeper. It is excellent for table use, and owing to its productiveness is also largely grown for feeding purposes. Pkt., 4c.; oz., 8c.; ¼ lb., 20c.; lb., 65c.

**F. S. CO.'S SUPERIOR MARKET**—Resembles Danvers Half Long, but of finer texture; flesh deep orange nearly to the center, leaving but a very small core; finest Carrot for the market or table use, and one of the best stock Carrots, being a heavy yielder and of great feeding value. Pkt., 5c.; oz., 15c.; ¼ lb., 30c.; lb., 80c.

**LONG RED ALTRINGHAM**—A well known standard sort. Roots are of large size, bright color, smooth, fine grained and of superior quality. The yield is very large, especially on light, deep soil. Pkt., 3c.; oz., 8c.; ¼ lb., 18c.; lb., 60c.

## CELERY.

**DWARF GOLDEN HEART**—A well-known and popular variety. It is one of the best keepers. Pkt., 3c.; oz., 15c.; ¼ lb., 40c.; lb., $1.25.

**NEW GOLDEN SELF-BLANCHING**—A very popular variety, and one of the most profitable to grow. The growth is compact and vigorous; the ribs are straight, solid, crisp and tender, and of a most delicious flavor. It has the advantage of being self-blanching; without banking up or any covering whatever, even the outer ribs become of a handsome, fresh, yellowish-white color as it approaches maturity. The heart is large, solid, and of a beautiful, rich golden-yellow color. Pkt., 5c.; oz., 20c.; ¼ lb., 60c.; lb., $2.30.

**WHITE PLUME**—A handsome crisp sort, of very easy cultivation. It is of very best quality, crisp, solid, and of a rich nutty flavor. It is the earliest celery in cultivation. Pkt., 4c.; oz., 15c.; ¼ lb., 45c.; lb., $1.50.

**PINK PLUME**—One of the best of the Red Celeries. Of fine table quality and an excellent keeper. Pkt., 3c.; oz., 15c.; ¼ lb., 50c.

Celeriac Erfurt.

**NEW GIANT PASCAL**—The latest and best variety of celery. The stalks are very large, thick, solid, crisp, and of a rich, nutty flavor, free from any trace of bitterness. It blanches very easily and quickly, and retains its freshness a long time after being marketed. Pkt., 4c.; oz., 15c.; ¼ lb., 40c.; lb., $1.40.

**BOSTON MARKET**—A popular dwarf variety. Pkt., 3c.; oz., 12c.; ¼ lb., 35c.; lb., $1.25.

## CELERIAC.

**LARGE ERFURT**—Roots large, smooth, turnip shaped, and of excellent flavor. Pkt., 4c.; oz., 12c.; ¼ lb., 40c.; lb., $1.25.

**NEW APPLE SHAPED**—Roots large, round, and smooth. Pkt., 4c.; oz., 12c.; ¼ lb., 40c.; lb., $1.25.

**KALAMAZOO CELERY**—It is of a beautiful cream color throughout; of very large size; is of quick growth and stiff, close habit; remarkably solid, thick and closely set. Considered the most solid, crisp-eating, and delicious flavored variety. Pkt., 5c.; oz., 18c.; ¼ lb., 60c.; lb., $2.25.

**OLD CELERY SEED**—Used in flavoring soups, pickles, etc. Oz., 5c.; ¼ lb., 10c.

Owing to the extremely short crop, we are reluctantly obliged to increase our prices on cucumber seed.

## CUCUMBERS.

Our Packets of Cucumbers contain on the average about 300 seeds.

**JAPANESE CLIMBING CUCUMBER**—The vines are of healthy vigorous growth, with rich dark green foliage, and throw out strong, grasping tendrils, which enable it to climb trellis, wire netting, brush or any other suitable support. It clings so tightly that it is not prostrated by heavy storms of wind or rain. The Cucumbers are thick, exceedingly tender, and of delicate flavor; flesh pure white. They are of good quality, and when young make attractive pickles. With this variety of cucumbers the produce of a given area of ground can be increased three-fold, thus making it particularly valuable in small gardens or to grow on high-priced land. Pkt., 5c.; oz., 18c.; ¼ lb., 60c.; lb., $2.00.

**IMPROVED WHITE SPINE**—The old standard variety; none better or more generally and favorably known. Color, deep green; shape, uniform, somewhat tapering at both ends. Quality is excellent, crisp and tender. Pkt., 4c.; oz., 15c.; ¼ lb., 45c.; lb., $1.50.

**EARLY FRAME**—Fruit straight and handsome, with crisp, tender flesh, and makes excellent pickles. Pkt., 4c.; oz., 15c.; ¼ lb., 50c.; lb., $1.75.

**CHICAGO PICKLING**—Used almost exclusively by the large factories in Chicago, and is undoubtedly the best Cucumber for pickles. Color green; yielding between 200 and 400 bushels per acre. Pkt., 4c.; oz., 15c.; ¼ lb., 50c.; lb., $1.75.

Cool and Crisp.

**COOL AND CRISP**—Extra early, very prolific, and bears the whole season. At the pickling stage the cucumbers are straight, long, even and slim, of very dark or almost black color. While primarily a pickling variety, it is also most useful for slicing, the cucumbers when fully matured being of good size and very tender and crisp. Pkt., 4c.; oz., 15c.; ¼ lb., 50c.; lb., $1.75.

**GIANT WHITE**—This grows from 12 to 16 inches long, and the fruit is always of a pure waxy white color, very uniform, straight, and perfectly smooth. The flesh is very solid, pure white, with few seeds, crisp and of most perfect flavor. Pkt., 4c.; oz., 12c.; ¼ lb., 40c.; lb., $1.40.

**GIANT PERA**—A very large and most prolific variety; from 18 to 22 inches long, and uniformly grows very smooth and straight.

**NICHOL'S MEDIUM GREEN**—Very prolific, medium size, always straight, smooth and handsome. Color, dark green; flesh crisp and tender; good for early forcing, and for pickling or slicing is unsurpassed. Pkt., 4c.; oz., 15c.; ¼ lb., 50c.; lb., $1.75.

**EARLY GREEN PROLIFIC or BOSTON PICKLING**—Largely grown by market gardeners for both pickling and as a table variety. It is early, very prolific, and a great favorite in Eastern markets as a choice pickling sort. Pkt., 4c.; oz., 15c.; ¼ lb., 50c.; lb., $1.75.

**IMPROVED LONG GREEN**—Forms fruit fit for the table nearly as early as the shorter sorts; about 12 inches long, firm and crisp, with very few seeds. The young fruit is well shaped for pickles, both sour and sweet. Pkt., 4c.; oz., 15c.; ¼ lb., 50c.; lb., $1.75.

Boston Pickling.

**F. S. CO.'S QUEEN OF PICKLERS**—A new cucumber, and without doubt a triumph and the best of pickles. We have been working up this variety for years, now think it perfected as to medium even size and solid perfect picklers. Leading pickling factories that gave same a trial last year are clamoring for seed. We have but a small quantity of seed this year and want our customers to have first chance. Also valuable for slicing, fine flavor, never being overgrown and seedy. Pkt., 5c.; oz., 18c.; ¼ lb., 60c.; lb., $2.00, postpaid.

**NEW SIBERIAN**—A remarkable early variety which produces fruit 5 inches long, in the open ground, from seed, in 55 days. A surprise for market gardeners and truckers who have grown the early Russian so far for earliest. The size is just right. It is a splendid free bearer, fruit straight and smooth, flesh tender and crisp. Pkt., 4c.; oz., 15c.; ¼ lb., 50c.; lb., $1.75.

**WHITE PEARL**—The Cucumbers grow so thickly together that they actually lie piled one upon the other. The skin is very smooth and entirely free from spines. In color they are a beautiful pearly white; even the young fruit is of a very light color, nearly as pure white as when ready for use. Pkt., 4c.; oz., 12c.; ¼ lb., 40c.; lb., $1.40.

**SERPENT or SNAKE**—A remarkable and very interesting curiosity. The cucumbers grow curled up like a snake with the head protruding, and sometimes are 6 feet in length, and, although they attain great size, the quality is fair. Pkt., 5c.; oz., 20c.

SNAKE CUCUMBER.

# FANCY CLIMBING GOURDS

## ENDIVE.

**WINTER OR GREEN CURLED**—The standard sort for summer and winter use. Very hardy and ornamental, with curled, dark green leaves, which blanch white and crisp and are very tender. Pkt., 4c.; oz., 15c.; ¼ lb., 50c.

**MOSS CURLED**—Beautiful curled, tender and of fine quality. Pkt., 4c.; oz., 15c.; ¼ lb., 50c.

**BROAD LEAVED**—Leaves, large, broad, slightly curled; if tied at the top when full grown they will blanch and make an excellent salad. Pkt., 4c.; oz., 15c.; ¼ lb., 50c.

## EGG PLANT.

**IMPROVED NEW YORK PURPLE**—The leading market variety, and one of the best varieties in cultivation, early, a sure cropper and of fine quality. Pkt., 6c.; oz., 32c.; ¼ lb., $1.15.

**BLACK PEKIN** — Shape nearly round, of largest size, skin jet black, glossy and smooth; fine grained and delicate in flavor. Pkt., 6c.; oz., 32c.; ¼ lb., $1.15.

Egg Plant.

## KOHLRABI.

**EARLY WHITE VIENNA**—Excellent for forcing and open ground; flesh white and very tender; leaves very short. Pkt., 6c.; oz., 15c.; ¼ lb., 50c.; lb., $1.75.

**EARLY PURPLE**—Very similar to the last, except in color, which is a bright purple. A desirable sort. Pkt., 6c.; oz., 15c.; ¼ lb., 50c.; lb., $1.75.

Kohlrabi.

Moss Curled Endive.

## GOURDS.

**SUGAR TROUGH**—They grow to hold from 4 to 10 quarts each; have thick, hard shells, are very light, but durable. They are useful for many purposes. Pkt., 3c.; oz., 10c.; ¼ lb., 30c.

**DIPPER GOURD**—Very useful for many purposes; holding about a quart; with a long handle. Pkt., 4c.; oz., 8c.; ¼ lb., 25c.

**NEST EGG**—Very ornamental and useful for nest eggs. Pkt., 3c.; oz., 8c.; ¼ lb., 25c.

**HERCULES CLUB**—Pkt., 4c.; oz., 8c.; ¼ lb., 20c.

**APPLE-SHAPED**—Pkt., 3c.; oz., 8c.; ¼ lb., 20c.

**PEAR-SHAPED**—Pkt., 3c.; oz., 8c.; ¼ lb., 20c.

## GARLIC.

The Garlic is much esteemed for flavoring soups, stews, etc. Bulbs, lb., 48c.; ¼ lb., 18c.

## MUSTARD.

**WHITE**—Grown for salads. Pkt., 3c.; oz., 6c.; ¼ lb., 12c.; lb., 45c.

**BROWN OR BLACK**—Pkt., 3c.; oz., 5c.; ¼ lb., 10c.; lb., 30c.

**NEW CHINESE**—Leaves twice the size of the white; flavor sweet and pungent. Pkt., 4c.; oz., 7c.; ¼ lb., 15c.; lb., 50c.

**SOUTHERN GIANT CURLED**—This variety is very highly esteemed in the South. Plants about 2 feet high and form immense bunches. Pkt., 3c.; oz., 10c.; ¼ lb., 20c.; lb., 50c.

## NASTURTIUM—INDIAN CRESS.

**TALL**—The seeds while young are used for pickles; also very ornamental as a flowering plant. Pkt., 3c.; oz., 8c.; ¼ lb., 30c.

**DWARF**—Beautiful colored flowers. Pkt., 3c.; oz., 8c.; ¼ lb., 30c.

## LENTILS.

Largely used in Oriental countries, and is one of their principal articles of diet. It was from these that the dish of pottage was made for which Esau sold his birthright to Jacob in Bible times, and many will be interested in them for that reason. Sow and cultivate same as garden Peas, and thresh out in the fall. Large pkt., 5c.; lb., 28c., prepaid by mail; lb., 20c.; 10 lbs., $1.80, not prepaid.

## GARDEN LEMON.

Resembles the Vine Peach in manner of growth. The fruit is round, somewhat smaller than Vine Peach, has thinner flesh and has decidedly more acid. Pkt., 5c.; oz., 15c.

## VINE PEACH.

The fruit is about the size of a large Peach, oval-shaped, and of bright orange-yellow color, somewhat russeted. For sweet pickles, pies, preserving, they are superb. Require the same cultivation as Musk Melons, are easily grown and wonderfully prolific. Pkt., 5c.; oz., 15c.

## LEEK.

**MUSSELBURG**—This variety grows to extra large size, and is very hardy. The leaves are large and broad; the edible stem grows to large size, and is of mild flavor. Pkt., 4c.; oz., 18c.; ¼ lb., 58c.; lb., $1.90.

**LONDON FLAG**—Large, with broad leaves. An excellent large growing variety. Pkt., 4c.; oz., 15c.; ¼ lb., 50c.; lb., $1.75.

Leek Musselburg.

*Peck O' Day Sweet Corn*

# SWEET CORN.

**FIRST OF ALL**

**FIRST OF ALL**—Numerous tests and experiments proved this variety to be a full week earlier than the Early Cory, which is an important consideration in getting early Corn on the market; besides, the ears are larger than other extra early varieties. Sweet and of a delicious flavor. Pkt., 4c.; ½ pt., 8c.; pt., 15c., prepaid; qt., 18c.; pk., $1.00; bu., $8.50, not prepaid.

**NEW EARLY WHITE CORY**—A greatly improved variety from the old and well known Cory; has white cobs and white kernels, and is fully as early. Pkt., 4c.; ½ pt., 8c.; pt., 16c.; prepaid; qt., 15c.; bu., $3.00, not prepaid.

**CORY RED COB**—A very early variety with good sized ears and large grains. Pkt., 5c.; ½ pt., 8c.; pt., 15c., prepaid; qt., 20c.; pk., 80c.; bu., $3.00, not prepaid.

**COUNTRY GENTLEMAN**—The sweetest and most tender of all the Sweet Corns, and the finest for the private table. The ears average 8 to 10 inches in length, the cob is unusually small, and the pearly white kernels very long. It produces 3 and 4 ears to a stalk, all the average size, and well filled from end to end with plump and fully developed kernels. Pkt., 4c.; ½ pt., 9c.; pt., 16c.; qt., 30c., prepaid; pt., 10c.; qt., 20c.; pk., 80c.; bu., $3.00, not prepaid.

**EARLY MINNESOTA**—The standard early sweet corn; ears 8-rowed; good size; kernels broad, sweet and tender. Pkt., 3c.; ½ pt., 8c.; pt., 16c., prepaid; qt., 15c.; pk., 80c.; bu., $3.00, not prepaid.

**PORTLAND**—Not quite so early as the Cory, but in sweetness and flavor it excels any early Sweet Corn grown. It is one of the best all around varieties. Market gardeners capture the trade with it, and it is a great favorite with canning factories. Pkt., 4c.; ½ pt., 10c.; pt., 18c., prepaid; qt., 20c.; pk., 80c.; bu., $3.00, not prepaid.

**PERRY'S HYBRID**—A large, early variety, ripens about the same time as Early Minnesota. Ears of a larger size, usually contain about 12 to 14 rows of kernels well filled to the end; the kernels are large, sweet, tender and pure white; cob red. Pkt., 5c.; ½ pt., 10c.; pt., 15c.; prepaid; qt., 20c.; pk., 80c.; bu., $3.00, not prepaid.

**MAMMOTH WHITE CORY**—(See cut.) The largest and best extra early sweet Corn. The stalks are no larger than those of the Cory, and mature their ears fully as early, but the ears are 12 instead of 8 rowed, very much larger and quite free from the open space between the rows which is such an objectionable feature of the old Cory. The quality is good, and the size and beauty of the ears give this variety ready sale. Pkt., 5c.; ½ pt., 10c.; pt., 18c.; qt., 35c., prepaid; pk., $1.00; bu., $3.50, not prepaid.

**ACME**—Very productive; it will produce more bushels of ears to the acre than any other variety. Pkt., 5c.; ½ pt., 10c.; pt., 18c., prepaid; qt., 20c.; pk., $1.00; bu., $3.50, not prepaid.

**CROSBY**—A great favorite. Pkt., 3c.; ½ pint, 8c.; pint, 16c., prepaid; qt., 15c.; pk., 80c.; bu., $3.00, not prepaid.

**OLD COLONY**—A remarkably productive medium early variety. Pkt., 3c.; ½ pint, 8c.; pint, 16c., prepaid; qt., 20c.; peck, 80c.; bu., $3.00, not prepaid.

**BLACK MEXICAN**—Is the sweetest and most sugary of all kinds; highly prized for table use. Pkt., 3c.; ½ pint, 16c., prepaid by mail.—Pint, 8c.; quart, 15c.; peck, 80c.; bu., $3.00, not prepaid.

Stowell's Evergreen.

**STOWELL'S EVERGREEN**—This is more largely planted than any other variety, being the general favorite with canners and market gardeners. Pkt., 3c.; ½ pint, 8c.; pint, 16c., prepaid by mail; pint, 8c.; quart, 15c.; peck, 80c.; bu., $3.00, not prepaid.

# POP CORN.

**NEW RED RICE**—For beauty, earliness, productiveness, crispness and tenderness it cannot be equaled. Pkt., 5c.; ½ pt., 15c., prepaid.

**WHITE RICE**—One of the finest and most prolific Pop Corns grown; largely planted; very good. Pkt., 5c.; ½ pt., 15c., prepaid.

**MAPLEDALE**—It pops a clear white, and of the finest quality. The originator of this variety has counted as many as nineteen ears to a stalk, and it certainly is at the head of the list of pop corns. Pkt., 5c.; ½ pt., 20c.; pt., 30c.; qt., 55c., prepaid.

**QUEEN'S GOLDEN**—A splendid sort. Above all is its exceeding tenderness when popped, together with its delicious and delicate taste; splendid for all purposes. By mail, pkt., 5c.; ½ pt., 20c., prepaid.

Give the boys on the farm an acre to plant Pop Corn for the market. It pays.

# LETTUCE.

Our packets of Lettuce contain on the average about 3,000 Seeds.
We wish to call your attention to the very low prices for our large and well filled packages, and our prices on larger quantities are correspondingly low. Nowhere can you buy better Seed, and at no other place can you buy good Seeds for as little money as we ask.

**Grand Rapids Forcing.**

**GRAND RAPIDS FORCING LETTUCE**—The best sort to grow for early market and for shipping. It is of handsome appearance, crisp and tender; a strong grower, not apt to rot, and will keep from wilting longer, when exposed for sale, than other varieties. It requires but little care and stands neglect of watering or ventilation, and grows more weight in the same space than any other kind. In addition to its desirable forcing qualities it is excellent for early spring sowing in the open ground. Pkt., 5c.; oz., 8c.; ¼ lb., 20c.; lb., 65c.

**EARLY CURLED SILESIA**—The earliest variety, does not form any heads, but the leaves are exceptionally tender, crisp and well flavored, and ready for the table long before any other variety. Pkt., 4c.; oz., 8c.; ¼ lb., 20c.; lb., 70c.

**NEW ICEBERG LETTUCE**—One of the very best head or Cabbage varieties. The heads are so compact and solid that they seldom go to seed. The inside is thoroughly blanched, and of the finest flavor. During the hottest and driest weather it remains crisp and tender. Pkt., 5c.; oz., 10c.; ¼ lb., 25c.; lb., 75c.

**CHICAGO FORCING**—The best variety for forcing, or green house culture. It is of rapid growth, with excellent flavor, crisp and tender. Pkt., 4c.; oz., 8c.; ¼ lb., 20c.; lb., 70c.

**Rudolf's Favorite.**

**RUDOLF'S FAVORITE or NEW BUTTERCUP**—This new and valuable variety originated in Germany. It is a head or Cabbage Lettuce; very early; forming large, solid heads, with delicate golden yellow foliage. It is very crisp, tender, and excellent in flavor, long standing, remaining fit for eating longer than any other variety. Also valuable for forcing or early spring crop. Pkt., 5c.; oz., 10c.; ¼ lb., 30c.; lb., $1.00.

**The Deacon.**

**EARLY CURLED SIMPSON**—Forms a close, compact mass of curly leaves of a yellowish green. It is earlier than the head varieties, and is the kind that is planted mostly. In cold frames, but is also largely grown as an open-air variety. Pkt., 4c.; oz., 8c.; ¼ lb., 20c.; lb., 65c.

**THE DEACON LETTUCE**—A fine Butter Head Lettuce. It stands hot weather without becoming bitter or running to seed, and forms fine large heads, light green outside and within a beautiful cream-yellow; of delicious, rich, buttery flavor. A great favorite to plant for home use as well as to sell on the market. Pkt., 4c.; oz., 8c.; ¼ lb., 20c.; lb., 65c.

**WHITE SUMMER CABBAGE**—An excellent variety for summer use, with close heads of good size. Pkt., 4c.; oz., 8c.; ¼ lb., 20c.; lb., 60c.

**LETTUCE, WONDERFUL**—Introduced two years ago and continually growing in favor. The large, white heads resemble cabbage in their solidity, and frequently weigh 2 and 3 pounds each. The quality is superb, being crisp, rich and tender. Pkt., 5c.; oz., 20c.; ¼ lb., 60c.

**IMPROVED HANSON**—Forms very large, deliciously sweet, crisp and tender heads, which are firm, resembling a Cabbage, green outside and white within. Very good for outside culture, and one of the best sorts to resist heat. Pkt., 4c.; oz., 8c.; ¼ lb., 20c.; lb., 65c.

**BLONDE BLOCKHEAD, SUNSET or BLONDE BEAUTY**—A new head Lettuce of excellent quality and beautiful appearance. It forms large, solid heads of rich golden yellow; is an excellent keeper after being cut, making it desirable for shipping. Is tender, crisp, sweet and juicy when many sorts have become bitter. It resists heat to a remarkable degree and stands a long time before going to seed. We can recommend it for both the home garden and to market gardeners. Pkt., 4c.; oz., 8c.; ¼ lb., 20c.; lb., 65c.

**Black Seeded Simpson.**

**BLACK SEEDED SIMPSON**—This is one of the most popular varieties. It forms a large, loose head of yellowish green color; the leaves are large, thin, very tender, and of good quality. One of the best sorts for the frame or hothouse, as well as for outdoor planting. Pkt., 4c.; oz., 8c.; ¼ lb., 20c.; lb., 65c.

**BROWN DUTCH** — A well-known favorite variety. Pkt., 4c.; oz., 8c.; ¼ lb., 20c.; lb., 70c.

**Improved Hanson.**

**CALIFORNIA CREAM BUTTER LETTUCE**—A medium early and one of the best summer varieties of Head Lettuce. It forms round, solid heads. The leaves are of a very rich cream yellow color, and particularly rich and buttery to the taste. This is a variety which should have a place in every farmer's garden, and is also a first-class variety to grow for the market. Pkt., 5c.; oz., 10c.; ¼ lb., 25c.; lb., 75c.

## Cos Lettuce.

**PARIS WHITE COS**—An old standard variety, one of the best, tender and crisp. Pkt., 4c.; oz., 10c.; ¼ lb., 25c.; lb., 85c.

**EARLY WHITE, SELF-FOLDING COS**—Leaves are yellowish white, long, narrow, folding into a solid head. Very crisp and tender. Pkt., 4c.; oz., 10c.; ¼ lb., 25c.; lb., 85c.

Minnesota Perfection Musk Melon.



Musk Melon

## Musk Melons.

Our Packets of Musk Melon contain on the average about 250 Seeds.

**EMERALD GEM**—New, extra early, and prolific. The skin, while ribbed, is generally smooth, and of a very deep emerald green color. The flesh is of a beautiful salmon color, and ripens thoroughly to the extremely thin rind, and the flavor is sweet and luscious. **Pkt., 4c.; oz., 15c.; ¼ lb., 30c.; lb., $1.00.**

**DELMONICO**—A new oval-shaped Musk Melon of large size, finely netted, and has beautiful orange pink flesh, and is pronounced to be a Melon PAR EXCELLENCE. We offer the Delmonico with full assurance that it will be found a most delicious variety. **Pkt., 4c.; oz., 10c.; ¼ lb., 25c.; lb., 80c.**

**OSAGE**—Skin dark green, slightly netted on the lobes on the upper side, flesh of a rich salmon color. The shape is pointed oval, medium sized, and the whole crop is very even and extra heavy, owing to thickness of meat. **Pkt., 4c.; oz., 15c.; ¼ lb., 30c.; lb., $1.00.**

Extra Early Hackensack.

**THE ROCKY FORD MUSK MELON**—This melon has taken its name from the little town of Rocky Ford, Colorado, where the growing and shipping of these Melons has become the leading industry of the town. The reason for the widespread popularity of these melons is two-fold. First its superb table qualities, being firm, sweet, and remarkably solid. Second, its wonderful shipping qualities, which enable it to be carried great distances, and yet arrive in first-class condition for market. It is very early, and wonderfully productive. The fruit is of medium size, oval shaped, heavily netted and very solid. The flesh is green, thick and juicy. There is a great demand for this popular melon. We obtained our seed at high cost and it comes direct from Rocky Ford, and can be relied upon as the genuine stock. **Pkt., 5c.; oz., 10c.; ¼ lb., 30c.; lb., $1.00.**

Rockyford Musk Melon.

**EXTRA EARLY HACKENSACK**—Several years' trial has proven it to be the earliest, best, hardiest and most prolific of all the netted Melons. They weigh from 4 to 6 pounds each, and are of delicious flavor. **Pkt., 4c.; oz., 10c.; ¼ lb., 25c.; lb., 80c.**

**PAUL ROSE**—This is the result of a cross of the Osage and Netted Gem, and combines the sweetness and high flavor of the former with the fine netting of the Gem. They are of very uniform shape and average about 1½ lbs. each in weight. It surpasses all Melons as a shipper and long keeper, and is of peculiarly sweet, rich, delicious flavor. The flesh is very thick and the seed cavity very small. It is the best Musk Melon introduced for several years. **Pkt., 5c.; oz., 12c.; ¼ lb., 40c.**

**YELLOW MEATED JAPAN**—This can be considered the best yellow meated Melon on the market on account of its sweetness, thickness of flesh and delicate flavor. The melons are of large size, quite early and yield very heavy. **Pkt., 5c.; oz., 12c.; ¼ lb., 40c.**

**NETTED GEM**—GOLDEN GEM, or GOLDEN JENNY—Very early and prolific, quite uniform in size and shape, weighing from one and one-quarter to two pounds; skin green, thickly netted; flesh very thick, of a light green color, of very superior quality, rich and sugary. **Pkt., 4c.; oz., 12c.; ¼ lb., 30c.; lb., $1.00.**

Black Diamond Water melon,

## Watermelon.

Kleckley Sweets Water Melon

**KLONDIKE**—This Melon is offered with the full assurance of not only being remarkably early, but as sweet, delicate, and melting in flavor as any variety grown. The flesh is of deep scarlet, rind thin. It is to all other varieties of Water Melons what the Early Minnesota is to Tomatoes—the earliest, and of quality second to none. It will ripen where it has not been thought possible to mature a good Water Melon. **Pkt., 5c.; oz., 18c.; ¼ lb., 35c.; lb., 92c.**

**SWEET HEART**—A grand sweet hearted kind for home and market use. It is very productive, ripening early. The fruit is large, oval, very heavy. The flesh is bright red, firm, solid, but very tender, melting and sweet. **Pkt., 4c.; oz., 10c.; ¼ lb., 20c.; lb., 70c.**

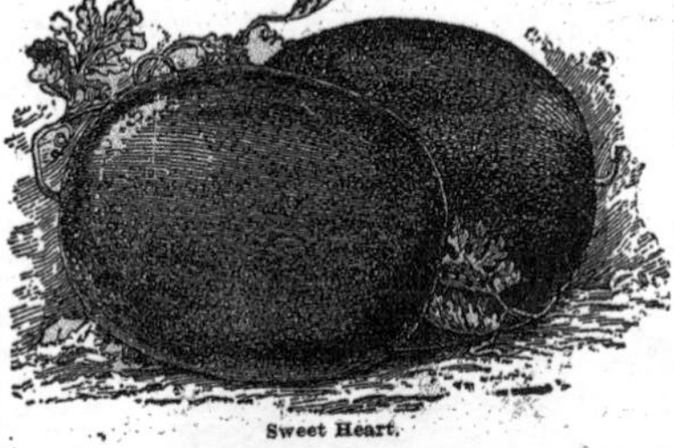

Sweet Heart.

**KOLB'S GEM**—Melon dealers say that as a shipping Melon it has hardly an equal. It is an early variety that is largely grown, particularly in the South, for shipment to the Northern markets. The fruit is nearly round, dark green, and marbled with lighter shades. **Pkt., 3c.; oz., 8c.; ¼ lb., 18c.; lb., 55c.**

**STOKES' EXTRA EARLY**

"The earliest of all." Nearly round, dark green skin, slightly mottled with white. Flesh very solid, deep scarlet, and not excelled in its delicious sugary flavor. Seeds very small, wonderfully productive, for family use unsurpassed. **Pkt., 5c.; oz., 10c.; ¼ lb., 25c.; lb., 85c.**

**KENTUCKY WONDER**—One of the very best Melons for home use or market. In form it is quite long, of good size, weighing forty to sixty pounds; skin dark green, striped and marbled with light green; flesh very firm, solid and never mealy, very fine sugary flavor. **Pkt., 3c.; oz., 7c.; ¼ lb., 18c.; lb., 60c.**

**CUBAN QUEEN**—This is a large variety, often weighing eighty pounds and upwards. The rind is marked with regular stripes of light and dark green. It is very showy and of good quality. **Pkt., 3c.; oz., 7c.; ¼ lb., 16c.; lb., 50c.**

**PEERLESS** or **ICE CREAM**—An excellent one for home use, medium size, oblong, light green skin; with very sweet, melting, deliciously flavored crimson flesh; seeds white. **Pkt., 3c.; oz., 7c.; ¼ lb., 16c.; lb., 52c.**

**THE DIXIE**—This new Watermelon has excellent merits, and we can recommend it as the **best shipping Melon** grown; being even **larger, earlier, and far more productive** than Kolb's Gem, which has heretofore been considered the best Melon for shipping. It is of a very fine appearance, while its eating qualities are unexcelled. **Pkt., 3c.; oz., 7c.; ¼ lb., 16c.; lb., 55c.**

**RUBY GOLD**—A new Melon of great beauty and excellence, of large size; forty pounds or more in weight. A prominent characteristic is its unapproachable beauty of flesh. A Melon cut crosswise presents a striking and unique appearance. A red star with many rays, some of them reaching nearly to the rind, ending in a curve, set in a beautiful golden ground, surrounded with a thin, white rind. Added to its great beauty, it is the juiciest of all Melons, and of delicate flavor. **Pkt., 4c.; oz., 8c.; ¼ lb., 18c.; lb., 60c.** Write for prices on five and ten pound orders.

**MOUNTAIN SWEET** — Oblong, dark green; rind thin, flesh red, solid and sweet. **Pkt., 3c.; oz., 6c.; ¼ lb., 16c.; lb., 52c.**

**COLORADO PRESERVING**—It makes beautiful, clear, transparent preserves. **Pkt., 4c.; oz., 7c. ¼ lb., 18c.; lb., 60c.**

**CITRON**—For preserving. A round, handsome fruit, of small size. **Pkt., 3c.; oz., 7c.; ¼ lb., 18c.; lb., 60c.**

## Choice New Drop Onion Seed.

We have a fine stock of well-matured seed (of our own growing) from selected bulbs. This stock cannot be excelled in purity, fine form and germinating qualities. Our pedigree onion seed is not in competition with stock of doubtful quality. Our aim is to produce the very best, regardless of expense, and offer the same at only a small margin above cost of production. However, if any of our reliable competitors offer you seed that you know to be right at a less figure, write us, and we will endeavor to satisfy you.

A WORD OF CAUTION—Do not be influenced by very low prices. The market is full of Old seed and many unscrupulous dealers are tempted to unload, on an unsuspecting public, seed that is old and worthless, at a very low price. Buy our Northern-grown seed, and be happy.

Our packets of Onion Seed contain on the average about 1,500 Seeds. One ounce will sow 100 feet of Drill; 4 to 5 lbs. are required per acre.

THE GLOBE WETHERSFIELD ONION—This is a RED GLOBE ONION of the finest and most select type, and differs from other kinds of Red Globe Onion, not only in purity of stock and perfection of shape, but in earliness, productiveness and beauty of color. They are most attractive in appearance, most economical in use and usually they command the highest price. They are more profitable to grow than flat varieties, as they occupy no more room in the row, but weigh more and measure better. This Onion is grown here around Faribault in large quantities, both the bulbs and the seed, and was introduced in 1898 under the name of Globe Wethersfield Onion. Our seed is the true stock. Pkt., 4c; oz., 10c; ¼ lb., 35c; lb., $1.20.

WHITE GLOBE—A large, globe-shaped Onion, firm, fine grained, of mild flavor and good keeping qualities. This is one of the handsomest Onions grown, of beautiful shape, clear white skin, and always commands the highest market price. Our seed is grown from the nicest and largest Onions, and will be found ripening early and evenly. We have found these White Globe Onions the best keepers of any. When kept in the cellar along with other varieties none were as nice and sound in the spring as the White Globe. Price, postpaid by mail—Pkt., 5c; oz., 15c.; ¼ lb., 55c.; lb., $2.00. By express or freight—Lb., $".60; 5 lbs., $9.00.

EARLY RED GLOBE—Very early and a great favorite in the best Onion seed districts. The Onions are of fine shape; beautiful rich red color; mature quickly from seed, ripen early and at a time when Onions bring a good price, and are therefore very profitable to grow. Price, postpaid by mail—Pkt., 5c; oz., 12c.; ¼ lb., 40c; lb., $1.25.

LARGE RED WETHERSFIELD—A favorite standard variety and the most profitable Red Onion for the market gardener and farmer. The bulbs are of large size, weighing from 1 to 2 pounds apiece; form round, somewhat flattened; skin deep purplish red, flesh purplish white, moderately fine grained and stronger in flavor than the yellow or white Onions. It is the best keeper. Price, postpaid, by mail—Pkt., 4c; oz., 10c; ¼ lb., 35c; lb., $1.30. By express or freight, not prepaid—Lb., $1.10; 5 lbs., $5.00.

Yellow Globe Danvers.

AUSTRALIAN BROWN—A new variety, ripening very early, and being wonderfully hard and solid; will keep in good condition longer than any other Onion. The color of the skin is a clear amber-brown and the quality is sure to please all. Pkt., 5c; oz., 12c; ¼ lb., 35c; lb., $1.00.

WHITE PORTUGAL—Very popular on account of its earliness and mild flavor. Is largely used for growing sets and pickles, but produces fine Onions from the seed. Pkt., 4c; oz., 20c; ¼ lb., 65c; lb., $2.15.

YELLOW GLOBE DANVERS—The Yellow Danvers Onion is known everywhere as a heavy yielder, and as being of superior quality. They are good keepers, are superior for shipping, and sell rapidly in any market. The Onions from which our seed is grown are carefully selected, and none but bulbs of good size are planted, and these will produce good and large heads, filled with plump and heavy seed, grown in our superior climate. We are sure that our stock will please everyone, and as we can make our prices very low, our Northern Grown Seed should be more largely planted. Price, postpaid, by mail: Pkt., 3c; oz., 8c; ¼ lb., 25c; lb., 90c. By express or freight, not prepaid: Lb., 80c; 5 lbs., $3.75.

EXTRA EARLY RED FLAT—Sometimes called Extra Early Red Wethersfield. A medium sized flat variety, good yielder. Ready for use about two weeks earlier than Large Red Wethersfield. Very desirable for early marketing. Best where seasons are very short. Good keeper. Pkt., 4c; oz., 10c; ¼ lb., 35c; lb., $1.30.

MAMMOTH SILVER KING—In appearance this is the most striking Onion grown. The bulbs are of attractive form, flattened but thick through. The average diameter is from five to seven and one-half inches, making the circumference from fifteen to twenty-five inches; single bulbs weighing from two and one-half to five pounds each. The skin is a beautiful silvery white; the flesh is snowy white and of a particularly mild and pleasant flavor. So sweet and tender is the flesh, that it can be eaten raw like an apple. It matures early and is of uniformly large size and fine shape. These qualities make it the best for exhibition at fairs, while for the home table it is unsurpassed. Price, postpaid, by mail: Pkt., 5c; oz., 20c; ¼ lb., 60c; lb., $2.00.

THE PRIZE-TAKER ONION—This has become a great favorite on account of its large size and great solidity. It has proved to be an excellent keeper, being of finest flavor and enormous size. It is handsome and very uniform in shape, a nearly perfect globe, with thin skin of a clean, bright straw color. The necks are very small, and the Onions always ripen up hard, and present the handsomest possible appearance in the market, while the pure white flesh is fine grained, mild and delicate in flavor. They grow to immense size, measuring from 12 to 16 inches in circumference, and Onions weighing from 4 to 6 lbs. each have been grown from the seed the first year. Price, postpaid, by mail: Pkt., 5c.; oz., 20c.; ¼ lb., 50c.; 1 lb., $1.75.

WHITE QUEEN—Small, early, white; used for pickling. Lb., $2.00; ¼ lb., 60c; oz., 20c; pkt., 5c.

EXTRA EARLY PEARL—Pearly white, very early, of a nic , medium size. Pkt., 5c.; oz., 20c.; ¼ lb., 65c.; 1 lb., $2.15.

YELLOW STRASBURG—Later, more flat and larger than the Yellow Danvers. Pkt., 4c; oz., 12c; ¼ lb., 40c.; lb., $1.20.

GIANT BROWN ROCCA—A fine globe-shaped Onion of very mild and delicate flavor, growing to immense size, weighing often 3 pounds each. Skin is light brown; a good keeper. Pkt., 4c; oz., 15c; ¼ lb., 50c; lb., $1.50.

EXTRA EARLY BARLETTA—This is the very earliest Onion grown, being fully two weeks' earlier than the Early White Queen. They are of a pure paper-white color, very mild and delicate in flavor, from 1 to 1½ inches in diameter and three-fourths of an inch in thickness, with finely formed bulbs. At maturity the tops die down directly to the bulb, leaving the neatest and most handsome little Onion imaginable. Pkt., 5c.; oz., 20c.; ¼ lb., 60c.; lb., $2.00.

WHITE MULTIPLIERS—Color pure silvery white, very productive, frequently producing as many as 20 bulbs in a single cluster from 1 bulb planted; of excellent quality and size for bunching green, or can be ripened for use as pickling onions. Pint. 15c.; qt., 30c; prepaid by express, pint, 12c.; qt., 22c.; pk., $1.25, not prepaid.

## ONION SETS.

Although Onions are grown cheapest from the black seed, a great many of our customers want green Onions only for early spring use, and these are best obtained by planting the sets. A quart or two is sufficient for a family.

YELLOW MULTIPLIER—We prefer these to any other Onions on account of their earliness; they are fully ripe and can be harvested the latter part of June. The large bulbs are then best sorted out for using and they will keep remarkably well. They are very productive, 5 to 15 bulbs growing from one small bulb set out. Pint, 15c; qt., 30c; 2 qts., 55c; 4 qts., $1.00, prepaid by mail. Not prepaid—Qt., 20c; 2 qts., 35c; 4 qts., 60c.

WHITE MULTIPLIER ONION SETS.

YELLOW BOTTOM SETS—Pint, 15c; qt., 30c; prepaid by mail. Not prepaid—pint, 12c; qt., 22c; peck, 90c.

RED BOTTOM SETS—Pint, 15c; qt., 30c, prepaid by mail. Not prepaid—Pint, 12c; qt., 22c; peck, 90c.

WHITE BOTTOM SETS—Pint, 15c; qt., 30c; prepaid by mail. Not prepaid—Pint, 12c; qt., 22c; peck, $1.00.

RED TOP SETS—Pint, 20c; qt., 30c; peck, $1.00. Not prepaid—Pint, 15c; qt., 25c; peck, $1.00.

EGYPTIAN OR PERENNIAL SETS—Once set out and established these come up year after year. Will stand any climate and furnish the earliest green Onions. Pt., 15c; qt., 30c, prepaid by mail. Not prepaid—Pt., 12c; qt., 22c; peck, 80c.

## OKRA OR GUMBO.

DWARF GREEN—The pods when young are used in soups. Pkt., 3c; oz., 7c; ¼ lb., 22c.

LONG GREEN—A tall, late variety. Pkt., 3c; oz., 7c; ¼ lb., 20c.

VELVET POD—The pods are round and smooth and much longer than other varieties; very prolific. Pkt., 3c; oz., 8c.; ¼ lb., 25c. 8c; ¼ lb., 25c.

OKRA OR GUMBO.

# Parsley.

Our Packets of Parsley Contain 1,500 to 2,000 Seeds.

**CHAMPION MOSS CURLED**—No variety is more attractive; when well grown it resembles a tuft of finely curled moss; is hardy and slow in running to seed. Pkt., 4c.; oz., 8c.; ¼ lb., 20c.; lb., 65c.

**DOUBLE CURLED**—Dwarf, finely curled. Pkt., 3c.; oz., 7c.; ¼ lb., 18c.; lb., 58c.

**FERN LEAVED**—A new and most beautiful variety for table decoration, as well as very ornamental for the garden. Pkt., 3c.; oz., 8c.; ¼ lb., 20c.; lb., 65c.

**PLAIN or SINGLE**—Useful for flavoring soups and stews and garnishing; for flavoring, the green leaves are used; or they may be dried crisp, rubbed to a powder and kept in bottles until needed. Pkt., 3c.; oz., 7c.; ¼ lb., 16c.; lb., 55c.

**HAMBURG or TURNIP ROOTED**—The roots are used in soups, giving them a fine, delicious flavor. Pkt., 3c.; oz., 8c.; ¼ lb., 20c.; lb., 60c.

# Parsnips.

Our Packets of Parsnip Contain from 1,000 to 1,500 Seeds.

**IMPROVED GUERNSEY**—Has a very smooth skin; is a great cropper; the flesh is fine grained, tender and sugary; considered the best Parsnip for general cultivation. Pkt., 3c.; oz., 7c.; ¼ lb., 15c.; lb., 45c.

**HOLLOW CROWN or LONG SMOOTH**—Smooth and large, tender, sugary; one of the best. Pkt., 3c.; oz., 8c.; ¼ lb., 15c.; lb., 45c.

**STUDENT**—A good half long variety, smooth, sweet and of delicious flavor. Pkt., 3c.; oz., 7c.; ¼ lb., 15c.; lb., 45c.

IMPROVED HOLLOW CROWN PARSNIP

# Pepper.

Our Packets of Pepper Contain about 400 Seeds.

**LARGE BELL or BULL NOSE**—Early, sweet and pleasant to the taste, and less pungent than the other sorts. Pkt., 4c.; oz., 15c.; ¼ lb., 50c.

**LONG RED CAYENNE**—A small, long pointed, slim pod, strong and pungent; furnishes the Cayenne pepper of commerce. Pkt., 4c.; oz., 20c.; ¼ lb., 65c.

**RUBY KING**—A very mild flavored variety which grows to a large size, often 5 or 6 inches long and 3 or 4 inches thick; of a bright ruby-red color when ripe, and remarkably mild and pleasant to the taste. Pkt., 5c.; oz., 20c.; ¼ lb., 65c.

Ruby King.

**KING OF THE MAMMOTHS**—The king of all and Big Show Pumpkin. It exceeds all in size and weighs about 200 pounds. Some specimens have been grown to weigh 300 pounds. It has a salmon colored skin, flesh bright yellow, fine grained and of excellent quality, a splendid keeper. Its greatest value, besides for feeding stock, is to have the biggest pumpkin for your fair, and if you wish to astonish your neighbors and win first premium at county or state fair, do not fail to include a package of the King of Mammoth Pumpkins in your order. Pkt., 8c.; oz., 15c.; ¼ lb., 50c.; lb., $1.75.

King of the Mammoths.

# Pumpkin.

**NEGRO, BLACK SUGAR, or NANTUCKET PIE PUMPKIN**—Oblong or bell-shaped, ribbed; outer color of skin very dark green, almost black. Pkt., 4c.; oz., 10c.; ¼ lb., 25c.; lb., 80c.

**JAPANESE PIE**—The flesh is very thick, solid, unusually fine grained, dry and sweet. It ripens early and keeps well. The seeds are curiously marked. Pkt., 4c.; oz., 10c.; ¼ lb., 25c.; lb., 80c.

**TENNESSEE SWEET POTATO**—Of medium size, pear-shaped, slightly ribbed; color of skin and flesh creamy white; flesh thick, very fine grained, dry, and of most excellent flavor. Pkt., 4c.; oz., 8c.; ¼ lb., 20c.; lb., 70c.

**CONNECTICUT FIELD PUMPKIN**—One of the best for field culture. Pkt., 4c.; oz., 8c.; ¼ lb., 15c.; lb., 45c.; 10 lbs. by freight or express, $3.50.

**QUAKER PIE**—A very distinct variety, oval in shape, of a creamy color inside and out; the flesh is fine grained and rich flavored and makes superior pies. It is an excellent keeper. Pkt., 4c.; oz., 10c.; ¼ lb., 25c.; lb., 80c.

**THANKSGIVING PUMPKIN**—A new, entirely distinct variety. The average size is about the same as that of the large Cheese Pumpkin, but the flesh is fully twice as thick. We have had specimens to weigh 55 pounds and only have 1¾ ounces of seed in them; the flesh being in some places 6 inches thick. On account of this extra thickness of flesh the yield in pounds is double that of other kinds, as the fruit is produced in as great abundance, if not more. The flesh is orange in color, of fine grain, sweet, and has the delicious pumpkin flavor essential to the making of a first-class pumpkin pie. Pkt., 5c.; oz., 15c.; ¼ lb., 40c.

Thanksgiving Pumpkin.

# PEAS.

Our prices for quarts, peck and bushel are not prepaid, as they are often ordered with large orders for farm seeds, and are then packed together and sent by cheap freight. When quarts are ordered to be sent by mail, please add fifteen cents for postage to the price of a quart.

Note our very low prices for our large packets and half pints which we send prepaid by mail. Our half pints cost less (and contain three times as much seed) than others will ask you for their packages.

One quart will plant about 100 feet of drill. One and one-half bushels to the acre.

## EXTRA EARLY VARIETIES.

First and Best.

**FIRST AND BEST**—This is the standard Extra Early Pea, and a great favorite with market gardeners. It grows very vigorous and ripens very early and ahead of any other, and is best of all in quality. It grows about 20 to 24 inches in height, is very productive, pods are long and well filled; Peas are of good size and of fine quality. Pkt., 4c.; ½ pint, 12c.; pint, 20c.; prepaid; qt., 25c.; peck, $1.65, not prepaid.

**ALASKA**—This extra early blue Pea is a great favorite for market as well as for home use. Vines are very stout, about 20 inches in height, loaded with large, dark green pods, well filled with smooth, blue Peas, much sweeter than any of the white sorts. Pkt., 4c.; ½ pint, 10c.; pint, 18c., prepaid; qt., 20c.; peck, $1.50, not prepaid.

**TOM THUMB**—Dwarf and early; 1 foot high; needs no brush; of excellent quality, and an abundant yielder. Pkt., 4c.; ½ pint, 12c.; pint, 20c., prepaid; qt., 20c.; peck, $1.50, not prepaid.

**AMERICAN WONDER**—One of the best and most largely grown varieties, and a great favorite everywhere. It grows only 8 to 10 inches high. Peas are large, green, wrinkled and fine flavored. It is very early and ripens in from 40 to 45 days; it needs no brushing and is very productive. Pkt., 5c.; ½ pint, 15c.; pint, 25c., prepaid; qt., 30c.; peck, $1.75, not prepaid.

**HORSFORD'S MARKET GARDEN**—A grand wrinkled variety, coming in between Little Gem and Advancer. Two feet high, very regular in growth. It is a prolific bearer, and has yielded more shelled peas per acre than any other American variety. The pods are numerous, and are literally packed with peas of a delicious sweet flavor. (See cut.) Pkt., 5c.; ½ pt., 12c.; pt., 20c.; qt., 40c.; postpaid; pk., $1.75; bu., $6.50, not prepaid.

**GRADUS** — This new First Early Wrinkled Pea, which is almost identical with the new sort called "Prosperity," is an extra heavy yielder. The peas are large and delicious and only 3 days later than the small round extra early kinds. We call it the Earliest Large Podded Pea in existence. Pkt., 6c.; ½ pint, 15c.; pint, 30c.; qt., 55c., postpaid. By express: Pint, 22c.; qt., 40c.; ½ peck, $1.50; peck, $2.90.

Gradus.

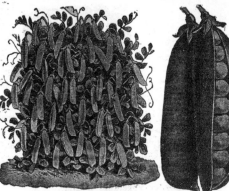

Little Gem Peas.

**LITTLE GEM**—This is a great favorite for its earliness, fine quality and productiveness; it grows about 12 to 14 inches high, needs no brush. Peas are green, wrinkled, large, productive and of excellent quality. Pkt., 4c.; ½ pint, 12c; pint, 20c prepaid; qt., 25c; peck, $1.60, not prepaid.

Horsford's Market Garden.

## Peas, Second Early and Late,

Telephone.

**ABUNDANCE**—A good second early variety, growing about 15 to 18 inches high. It is remarkable for its branching habit, forming large bushes which are loaded with long pods full of large wrinkled Peas of the best quality; one of the most productive of all Peas and the best of its season. Pkt., 4c.; ¼ pint, 10c.; pint, 18c., prepaid; qt., 20c.; peck, $1.50, not prepaid.

**TELEPHONE**—The best main crop variety; height, 4 feet. Peas large, green, wrinkled, enormously productive, and of delicious flavor. Pkt., 4c.; ½ pint, 10c.; pint, 18c., prepaid; qt., 20c., not prepaid.

**PRIDE OF THE MARKET**—Is a strong growing Pea 2 feet high, wonderfully productive. The pods also are of large size and handsome appearance, and the Peas are of splendid quality. Similar to Stratagem and Telephone. Pkt., 5c.; ½pint, 12c.; pint, 20c., prepaid; qt., 23c.; peck, $1.60; bu., $6.00.

**EVERBEARING**—Grows from 1½ to 2 feet high, of branching habit. Pods are 3 to 4 inches long, containing from 6 to 8 large wrinkled Peas. It produces new blossoms after repeated pickings, continuing remarkably long in bearing. Pkt., 4c.; ½ pint, 10c.; pint, 18c., prepaid; qt., 20c., peck, $1.50, not prepaid.

**DWARF TELEPHONE, OR DAISY**—The most productive of all large podded Dwarf Peas. This new Pea is a cross of Stratagem on Telephone and a most excellent sort. The vines grow about 16 to 18 inches high, are dwarf, stocky and vigorous, and bear a tremendous crop of large, well-filled pods. Pkt., 5c.; ½ pint, 12c.; pint, 20c., prepaid; qt., 25c.; peck, $1.50, not prepaid.

**WHITE MARROWFAT**—Pods large, round, light colored and well filled; very productive; 3 to 4 feet high. Pkt., 3c.; ½ pint, 8c.; pint, 16c., prepaid; qt., 15c.; peck, 85c.; bu., $3.00, not prepaid.

Improved Stratagem.

**STRATAGEM**—Late variety for family or market use. Half dwarf, and an enormous cropper. Pods are very large and filled with 7 to 9 large Peas of extra fine quality. Pkt., 4c.; ½ pint, 12c.; pint, 20c., prepaid; qt., 20c.; peck, $1.50, not prepaid.

**CHAMPION OF ENGLAND**—One of the very best in every respect of the older late varieties. It is very productive, and the Peas are of a delicious flavor. Height 4 to 5 feet; Peas green, wrinkled and very large. Pkt., 3c.; ½ pint, 10c.; pint, 18c., prepaid; qt., 20c.; peck, $1.50, not prepaid.

Champion of England.

**PRINCE OF WALES**—A bushel of pods will give about twice the quantity of shelled Peas of any other sort, and in quality they are unsurpassed. Pkt., 4c.; ½ pint, 10c.; pint, 18c., prepaid; qt., 20c.; peck, $1.50, not prepaid.

**TALL MELTING SUGAR**—Well deserves its name, for this Pea is unquestionably the best in size of pod, prolific bearing, and delicious quality. They snap without any string. The pods when cooked are very sweet and tender. Pkt., 5c.; ½ pt., 12c.; pt., 20c.; qt., 40c., postpaid.

**DWARF GRAY SUGAR**—Has edible pods, is early and productive. Pods are broad, flat and crooked, and are cooked when young the same as string beans; they are very sweet, tender and delicious. Pkt., 4c.; ½ pint, 10c.; pint, 18c., prepaid; qt., 20c., not prepaid.

FOR FIELD PEAS, SEE FIELD SEED DEPARTMENT.

## Rhubarb. Pie Plant.

**LINNAEUS**—The best in cultivation. Early, large, very tender, and free from the tough, stringy skin of other varieties. Pkt., 3c.; oz., 10c.; ¼ lb., 35c.

**VICTORIA**—Grows much larger than the above; it may sell better in market, but is not as good for home use. Pkt., 3c.; oz., 10c.; ¼ lb., 35c.

Roots of either of the above varieties 10c. each; 6 for 50c.; 12 for 75c. By express not prepaid.

## Salsify, or Vegetable Oyster.

**LONG WHITE**—This is a standard variety. Salsify is one of the most delicious and nutritious vegetables and should be more generally cultivated for winter use. Pkt., 4c.; oz., 10c.; ¼ lb., 35c.; lb., $1.25.

**MAMMOTH SANDWICH ISLAND**—A new and improved type, producing roots of nearly double the size and weight of the Long White, and of equally good quality. Pkt., 4c.; oz., 10c.; ¼ lb., 35c.

**SCORZONERA OR BLACK SALSIFY**—Treatment same as Salsify, which it closely resembles, except that the skin is black. Should be soaked in cold water a few hours before cooking to remove the bitter taste. Pkt., 3c.; oz., 15c.; ¼ lb., 50c.

YOUR NEIGHBORS NEED SEEDS and if you go and see them you can get their order, as many of them never think of sending away to a reliable Seed House but buy old and worthless commission seeds from the nearest store. Look over our premium list and you will see that you will be well paid for a few hours' work.

Rhubarb Victoria.

# RADISHES.

*Triumph Radish.*

For the market gardener this is one of the most profitable crops to grow, and for the home garden it is also a very important crop; nothing will taste as nice as the radishes grown in your own garden and put fresh from there on the table. They are very easily grown. One ounce of seed is sufficient for 100 feet of drill; 9 to 10 pounds for an acre.
Our packets of Radishes contain from 800 to 1,000 seeds.

**EARLIEST ERFURT RADISH**—It is a well known fact that the market gardener who brings the first vegetables to market makes the most money out of them, and this is specially true of radishes. Repeated tests which we have made with our "Earliest Erfurt" alongside of other so-called early varieties, such as "Twenty Day," "Early Bird," etc., have proven it to be from 3 to 9 days earlier than any of them and more attractive. Shape is very regular; color of skin a rich scarlet; flesh unusually tender, crisp and delicious, never becoming pithy or hollow. Very good for either forcing or planting in the garden, in spring and through the summer. Pkt., 4c.; oz., 8c.; ¼lb., 15c.; lb., 50c.

Olive Shaped Scarlet.

**OLIVE-SHAPED SCARLET**—The best market gardeners' variety for early forcing and outdoor planting. It is very even, smooth, and of a rich, deep scarlet color; flesh is crisp and tender. It is very early, and is ready to pull in about 20 days. Pkt., 4c.; oz., 8c.; ¼ lb., 15c.; lb., 50c.
**WHITE STUTTGART**—Pkt., 4c.; oz., 8c.; ¼ lb., 18c.; lb., 55c.
**ROSY GEM**—One of the earliest; perfectly globular; color, rich deep scarlet at top, blending into pure white at the bottom; exceedingly tender and crisp. Pkt.; 5c.; oz., 10c.; ¼ lb., 20c.; lb., 60c.
**LADY FINGER OR LONG WHITE VIENNA**—This is of remarkably quick growth; pure white, both skin and flesh; crisp, mild and tender. Pkt., 4c.; oz., 8c.; ¼ lb., 18c.; lb., 55c.
**FRENCH BREAKFAST**—One of the best for forcing. For garden culture or home use it is not excelled. Pkt., 3c.; oz., 8c.; ¼ lb., 15c.; lb., 50c.

**"NON-PLUS ULTRA" RADISH**—This is one of the very best and most valuable Radishes for either the market gardener or the home garden. It is one of the best for forcing, being of a fine, round form and bright scarlet color. The flesh is tender and of delicate flavor. Pkt., 4c.; oz., 8c.; ¼ lb., 15c.; lb., 50c.

**LONG SCARLET WHITE TIPPED**—Very early and attractive, long, and of the brightest scarlet. Tipped White. Pkt., 4c.; oz., 8c.; ¼ lb., 15c.; lb., 50c.

**CHARTIER**—They are quite early, large, long, holding their size nearly to the tip, of great beauty and very attractive, of a bright crimson rose color about two-thirds of the length, then shading through pink to a pure waxy white at the tip. Pkt., 4c.; oz., 8c.; ¼ lb., 15c.; lb., 50c.

**WHITE-TIPPED EARLY SCARLET GLOBE**—A very good forcing Radish, being of extremely quick growth, maturing in about 3 weeks. It is of very attractive appearance, being of a bright scarlet with a white tip; very tender and crisp; superior flavor. Pkt., 4c.; oz., 8c.; ¼ lb., 15c.; lb., 50c.
**WHITE GLOBE RADISH**—Of beautiful, round form, pure white skin and flesh, which is very crisp. It grows quickly and withstands summer heat. Pkt., 3c.; oz., 8c.; ¼ lb., 15c.

**WHITE STRASBURG SUMMER**—This variety is of handsome oblong shape, tapering beautifully to a point. Both skin and flesh are pure white, very tender. Pkt., 4c.; oz., 8c.; ¼ lb., 20c.; lb., 70c.

Chartier Radish.

## Winter Radishes.

**CALIFORNIA MAMMOTH**—Grows very large, about 1 foot long and 2 or 3 inches through; skin and flesh pure white, solid, tender and crisp. Pkt., 3c.; oz., 8c.; ¼ lb., 20c.

**CHINA ROSE**—A good winter Radish; flesh firm, crisp and good flavor. Pkt., 3c.; oz., 8c.; ¼ lb., 15c.; lb., 50c.

**LONG BLACK SPANISH**—One of the hardiest and a good keeper; skin black; flesh firm and white, of good flavor. Pkt., 3c.; oz., 7c.; ¼ lb., 15c.; lb., 50c.

**ROUND BLACK SPANISH**—Grows to a good size, is of oval shape; flesh white, solid, very appetizing; a good keeper. Pkt., 4c.; oz., 8c.; ¼ lb., 18c.; lb., 58c.

**WHITE CHINESE**—(New Celestial)—A large, stump-rooted radish with white skin and flesh. Can be sown from July 1st to August 15th and will keep all winter in prime condition. Mild in flavor, brittle, and never woody. Pkt., 5c.; oz., 10c.; ¼ lb., 30c.; lb., 90c.

Mixed Radishes.

**MIXED RADISHES**—The advantage being that one sowing out of the same package will produce early, medium and late Radishes, both long and turnip shaped. Pkt., 4c.; oz., 8c.; ¼ lb., 15c.; lb., 50c.

## SQUASH—WINTER VARIETIES.

**ESSEX HYBRID**—A very productive Squash of the finest quality, and an excellent keeper, specimens having been kept until June as sound and good as when gathered. It is of excellent quality, quick growth, and can be raised successfully as a second crop, following early potatoes, etc. **Pkt., 4c.; oz., 10c.; ¼ lb., 25c.; lb., 80c.**

**HUBBARD**—A great favorite, and more extensively grown for market than any other variety. Of good size; color dark green; shell very hard; flesh yellow, fine grained, dry and sweet. It is the standard of excellence in quality, and all planters will find it to their advantage to plant our Minnesota-grown seed, and by so doing, not only secure the best strain, but insure earliness at maturity. **Pkt., 4c.; oz., 10c.; ¼ lb., 30c.; lb., 90c.** Write for prices on large quantities.

Hubbard Squash.

**THE FAXON**—The flesh is a deep orange yellow with small seed cavity; excellent to cook while yet green. It matures early and is one of the best keepers. A peculiar and interesting variety, as the fruit produced is not of one type, but of various shapes and sizes and of different colors, but without regard to shape, size and color they cook dry and are sweet and rich. **Pkt., 4c.; oz., 10c.; ¼ lb., 25c.; lb., 80c.**

**GOLDEN HUBBARD**—A perfect type of the Green Hubbard, except in color, which is a bright, deep orange yellow, very showy and attractive. Flesh deep golden yellow, much richer in color than Hubbard, fine grained, cooks very dry, and is of excellent flavor. Its keeping qualities are fully equal to, while in productiveness it far excels, the green variety. **Pkt., 5c.; oz., 10c.; ¼ lb., 30c.; lb., $1.00.**

New Red or Golden Hubbard.

**EARLY ORANGE MARROW**—A decided improvement on the old Boston Marrow, being 2 weeks earlier, far more productive and a much better keeper. Skin of a brilliant red, very thick; flesh orange color, fine grained, and of excellent quality. Cooks dry and is one of the best Squashes from September until January. **Pkt., 4c.; oz., 10c.; ¼ lb., 25c.; lb., 80c.**

**MAMMOTH CHILI**—The "big" exhibition squash, the largest of all, often weighing over 200 pounds. There is a record of one Squash having been grown that weighed 292 pounds. The flesh is very thick, and of a rich yellow color; skin smooth and bright orange color. **Pkt., 4c.; oz., 12c.; ¼ lb., 40c.; lb., $1.50.**

**CANADA WINTER CROOKNECK**—A well known variety of Winter Squash of good quality. **Pkt., 3c.; oz., 8c.; ¼ lb., 25c.; lb., 90c.**

**BOSTON MARROW**—Second early, coming in about 10 days after the Bush and Crookneck sorts. Skin yellowish, very thin; the flesh dry and fine-grained, and of unsurpassed flavor. **Pkt., 3c.; oz., 8c.; ¼ lb., 20c.; lb., 75c.**

## SQUASH—SUMMER VARIETIES.

**VEGETABLE MARROW**—A favorite English variety. Flesh white and of a rich flavor. **Pkt., 4c.; oz., 10c.; ¼ lb., 30c.**

**SUMMER CROOKNECK**—One of the best summer varieties. Skin golden and warted. **Pkt., 4c.; oz., 10c.; ¼ lb., 25c.; lb., 80c.**

**WHITE BUSH SCALLOPED**—Earlier than any other variety; of dwarf habit, very productive, and occupies less room on the ground than any other sort. **Pkt., 4c.; oz., 10c.; ¼ lb., 25c.; lb., 80c.**

**YELLOW BUSH SCALLOPED**—Similar to the White Bush, but of a deep orange color. Flesh pale yellow. **Pkt., 3c.; oz., 7c.; ¼ lb., 16c.; lb., 55c.**

The 1902 crop of Squash, Melon, Pumpkin and Cucumber Seed was very short, and the prices seem very high, but we could not replace many sorts for the price we ask.

**BAY STATE**—The shell is light green, hard and flinty, and is one of the longest keepers known. Flesh very thick and solid, bright golden yellow, dry, fine grained; flavor sweet and excellent; seed cavity very small. It matures very early. **Pkt., 4c.; oz., 10c.; ¼ lb., 25c.; lb., 80c.**

**CHICAGO WARTED HUBBARD**—This is a new type of the well-known Hubbard, produced by careful selection of the large, dark green, warted, rough specimens always seen in good stocks of the Hubbard. It has been bred to this type until it is so fixed that nearly all have very hard warty shells. A Hubbard Squash; large, blackish green, hard and with warty knobs all over it, satisfies everyone that it is the best of its class; rich in quality, thick fleshed, and a good keeper, and such Squashes will sell at sight. **Pkt., 5c.; oz., 10c.; ¼ lb., 30c.; lb., $1.00.**

COPYRIGHT, 1893. BY N.B. FAXON CO.

Faxon Squash.

**PIKES PEAK OR SIBLEY**—One of the sweetest, driest and best of all late Squashes. The form is entirely distinct, being pear shaped. The shell is hard and very flinty, yet thin and smooth, and of a pale green color; the flesh thick and solid, brilliant orange color, very dry, fine grained, and of rich delicate flavor; weigh from 8 to 10 pounds. Vines are remarkably vigorous and wonderfully productive. The whole crop seems to ripen at once, as soon as, or before the Hubbard, and is one of the very best keepers and shippers. **Pkt., 4c.; oz., 10c.; ¼ lb., 25c.; lb., 90c.**

PIKES PEAK (OR SIBLEY) SQUASH

## SPINACH

**LONG STANDING**—A very good new variety, which stands fully 2 weeks longer than any other sort before going to seed. **Pkt., 3c.; oz., 5c.; ¼ lb., 12c.; 1 lb., 35c.**

**ROUND THICK LEAVED**—One of the best market sorts in general use. Leaves are large, thick and somewhat crumpled. **Pkt., 3c.; oz., 5c.; ¼ lb., 12c.; 1 lb., 35c.**

**PRICKLY or WINTER**—This is generally sown in the fall for winter use, and will withstand the severest weather with only a slight protection of straw or leaves. **Pkt., 3c.; oz., 5c.; ¼ lb., 10c.; lb., 35c.**

**NEW ZEALAND**—Stands heat and drought better than the other varieties; planted in May, it will yield a supply of leaves all summer. **Pkt., 4c.; oz., 8c.; ¼ lb., 20c.; lb., 75c.**

**BLOOMSDALE or SAVOY LEAVED**—One of the hardiest and heaviest yielding varieties; leaves are large, thick and curled like Savoy Cabbage. **Pkt., 3c.; oz., 5c.; ¼ lb., 12c.; lb., 35c.**

Boston Marrow.

# TOMATOES.

Our Packets of Tomato contain from 1,200 to 1,500 seeds.

**THE NEW STONE**—This has given great satisfaction to all who have grown it. It ripens for main crop; is very large, flesh exceedingly solid, heavy and firm (hence its name). It is of a bright scarlet color, very smooth; ripening evenly to the stem without a crack; in quality the very best, no hard core, not subject to rot, an excellent keeper, making it a good shipper. For canning it is unequaled. Pkt., 4c; oz., 15c; ¼ lb., 45c; lb., $1.50.

THE EARLIEST TOMATO IN THE WORLD

**ADVANCE**—Very early; the Tomatoes are of fair size, bright red, very solid and with no green core. The vines are loaded with fruit. Pkt., 3c; oz., 15c; ¼ lb., $1.40.

**DWARF CHAMPION**—The extraordinary fruiting qualities of the Dwarf Champion Tomato places it easily in the lead of all other Tomatoes in point of productiveness. The fruit is always symmetrical and attractive in appearance; the skin is tough and the fruit solid. Pkt., 4c; oz., 15c; ¼ lb., 50c; lb., $1.60.

**THE NEW PEACH**—A most delicious and unique Tomato. Fruit uniform, resembling a medium sized peach in form and color, even to having the down or fuzz of the peach. The flavor is remarkably fruity and delicious; the best of all o eating from the hand. Skin very thin and readily peels. Pkt., 4c; oz., 15c; ¼ lb., 60c; lb., $1.75.

**LIVINGSTON'S PERFECTION**—Is shaped like the Acme, larger, fully as early, perfectly smooth, blood red in color, very solid and a heavy cropper. Pkt., 3c; oz., 12c; ¼ lb., 40c; lb., $1.40.

Early Minnesota.

**EARLY MINNESOTA TOMATO**—There is a great demand for early Tomatoes, and no wonder, for all lovers of this delicious fruit await its coming into market with much impatience. This handsome new variety which we now offer we claim to be the earliest Tomato grown. In addition to this, a very important point seems to have been secured in shape, color and flavor. Fruit is of fair size, good shape, smooth, dark red color, ripens even, remains solid a long time and never cracks. For earliness it is not approached by any good Tomato. Another desirable feature is its great solidity, a bushel of them, on this account, being worth more than of any other early Tomato. Pkt., 5c; oz., 25c; ¼ lb., 60c; lb., $2.25.

"Yesterday (July 9th) I took the first ripe Early Minnesota Tomatoes to market and received 10 cents per quart or $3.20 per bushel. Your Early Minnesota Tomato is the best and earliest I ever raised," so writes Mr. J. Schunck, July 10th, 1898, from Celina, Ohio.

**PONDEROSA**—Very large and is highly commended in many localities. Like all other mammoth sorts, however, there is a considerable proportion of misshapen fruit, and some with hard green spots around the stem. Our seed is pure. Pkt., 2c; ½ oz., 7c; oz., 15c; ¼ lb., 40c.

**FAVORITE** (Livingston's)—Large, early and smooth and a good shipper. Pkt., 3c; oz., 12c; ¼ lb., 35c; lb., $1.30.

**ROYAL RED**—Splendid main crop variety for the shipper, market and private gardener, and of special value to the canner and catsup maker. Pkt., 3c; oz., 15c; ¼ lb., 45c; lb., $1.45.

**ACME**—One of the most popular kinds on our list, giving entire satisfaction. A favorite everywhere; large, round, smooth, slight purple tint; one of the best. Our seed has been grown with particular care. Pkt., 4c; ½ oz., 8c; oz., 15c; ¼ lb., 40c; lb., $1.50.

**GOLDEN QUEEN**—A beautiful new Tomato, large sized and smooth; color rich golden yellow, with a slight tinge of red at the blossom end; the flavor is mild and excellent, not as solid as red sorts. Pkt., 5c; oz., 15c; ¼ lb., 50c; lb., $1.60.

Dwarf Aristocrat.

**DWARF ARISTOCRAT**—This is practically a red variety of the Dwarf Champion type. In size, solidity, productiveness and flavor, it is up to the best standard. Pkt., 5c; ½ oz., 12c; oz., 20c; ¼ lb., 60c; lb., $2.00.

**LIVINGSTON'S BEAUTY**—Ripens as early as the Acme; of smooth form; keeps and carries well. In color a rich, glossy crimson with a light tinge of purple. Pkt., 3c; oz., 12c; ¼ lb., 40c; lb., $1.40.

Bedell's Long Island.

**BEDELL'S LONG ISLAND**—This Tomato is from the famous garden section of Long Island, and is the finest Large Red Tomato to be found on the New York market. Its fine appearance and solid character makes it a favorite wherever known. It is without a peer and stands alone as the best LARGE TOMATO on earth. Cut shows fruit about one-third average size. Pkt., 8c; ½ oz., 18c; oz., 30c; ¼ lb., $1.00.

**RED CHERRY**—Fine for pickling and preserves. Ripens ahead of any other variety. Pkt., 5c; oz., 20c; ¼ lb., 50c.

**YELLOW PLUM**—A clear yellow; splendid for preserves. Pkt., 5c; oz., 20c; ¼ lb., 50c.

**PEAR-SHAPED YELLOW**—Used for preserves and pickles. Pkts., 5c and 10c; oz., 20c; ¼ lb., 60c.

**IMPROVED YELLOW GROUND CHERRY**—It is a great improvement on the wild Ground Cherry. They grow well on almost any dry soil, are easier raised than the Tomato, are prolific bearers, and the fruit is delicious. For sauce or pies they are excellent, and are delicious as preserves. If put in a cool place, they will keep in the shuck nearly all winter. Pkt., 5c; ½ oz., 20c; oz., 35c.

**PURPLE HUSK TOMATO**—This is quite popular in some places. The plants produce handsome purple fruit in great abundance, which is enveloped in a husk similar to the Yellow Ground Cherry. Pkt., 5c; ½ oz., 20c; oz., 35c.

New Matchless Tomato.

**NEW MATCHLESS TOMATO**—The Matchless Tomato is well worthy of its name; in beauty of coloring and symmetry of form it is without a peer. The vines are of strong, vigorous growth, well set with fruit. The fruit is entirely free from core, of a very rich cardinal red color, and not liable to crack from wet weather. It is of the largest size, and the size of fruit is maintained throughout the season, the healthy growth of foliage continuing until killed by the frost. Pkt., 5c; oz., 20c; ¼ lb., 50c; lb., $1.75.

# TURNIPS.

Our packets contain about 3,500 Seeds.

**PURPLE TOP MUNICH**—The earliest variety after the Red Top Milan; with purplish-white top; very productive. **Pkt., 4c.; oz., 8c.; ¼ lb., 16c.; lb. 55c.**

**LARGE WHITE NORFOLK**—Late, one of the best table sorts, and excellent for stock feeding. **Pkt., 3c.; oz., 7c.; ¼ lb., 2c.; lb., 40c.**

**DEVONSHIRE GRAY STONE**—For field culture and stock feeding one of the best varieties. To distribute it as much as possible we will introduce it at a special, low price. **Pkt., 3c.; oz., 6c.; ¼ lb., 10c.; lb., 45c.**

**EARLY RED or PURPLE TOP STRAP LEAF**—A general favorite with all, and more largely grown than any other Turnip. **Pkt., 4c.; oz., 7c.; ¼ lb., 14c.; lb., 45c.**

**TELTAU or SMALL BERLIN**—Esteemed for flavoring soups. **Pkt., 4c.; oz., 8c.; ¼ lb., 15c.; lb., 50c.**

**White Six Weeks.**

**WHITE SIX WEEKS TURNIP**—A new, very early Turnip, with fine, large, smooth bulbs. The flesh is hard, solid, fine grained, and of the choicest quality. It matures very rapidly. **Pkt., 4c.; oz., 6c.; ¼ lb., 15c.; lb., 50c.**

**YELLOW ABERDEEN**—Yellow flesh of fine texture, nutritious, very hardy, productive. **Pkt., 3c.; oz., 7c.; ¼ lb., 12c.; lb., 40c.**

## TOBACCO.

**BIG HAVANA**—A hybrid Havana or Cuban seed leaf.

**CONNECTICUT SEED LEAF**—Staple variety.

**HESTER**—A broad yellow-leaved variety.

**MIXED VARIETIES.**
Prices on all varieties, pkt., 5c.; oz., 20c.; ¼ lb., 60c.

**Hester.**

**LONG ISLAND IMPROVED PURPLE TOP**—This is undoubtedly the finest variety of Purple Top Rutabaga, and is twice the size of the ordinary stocks. **Pkt., 5c.; oz., 10c.; ¼ lb., 20c.; lb., 65c.**

**Early White Strap Leaf, or Flat Dutch.**

**EARLY WHITE STRAP LEAVED or FLAT DUTCH**—An excellent garden variety; differs from the Red only in color. **Pkt., 3c.; oz., 7c.; ¼ lb., 12c.; lb., 40c.**

**POMMERIAN WHITE GLOBE**—One of the best main crop varieties, with snow white flesh and skin. **Pkt., 3c.; oz., 7c.; ¼ lb., 12c.; lb., 40c.**

**White Egg.**

## RUTABAGAS.

**HURST'S MONARCH**—This grand, new and distinct form of the Rutabaga is, we believe, by far the best of all, producing from 2 to 7 tons per acre more than any other Swede. **Pkt., 4c.; oz., 6c.; ¼ lb., 15c.; lb., 50c.**

**SWEET GERMAN**—This is unequaled for table use. It is very sweet, fine grained and mild flavored; grows to a good size. **Pkt., 4c.; oz., 6c.; ¼lb., 15c.; lb., 50c.**

**BUDLONG**—An American Rutabaga, earlier and rounder than any other of the Sweet German. Improved White French, Rock or Russian Turnips. **Pkt., 5c.; oz., 10c.; ¼ lb., 23c.; lb., 75c.**

**IMPROVED AMERICAN**—Very popular and has for years been considered the leading yellow-fleshed variety; very solid, fine quality. **Pkt., 4c.; oz., 6c.; ¼ lb., 15c.; lb., 50c.**

**SKIRVING'S PURPLE TOP**—A fine table or stock feeding variety; flesh solid and sweet. **Pkt., 4c.; oz., 8c.; ¼ lb., 15c.; lb., 50c.**

**Golden Ball.**

**GOLDEN BALL or ORANGE JELLY**—One of the most delicious and sweetest yellow-fleshed Turnips. The bulbs are of medium size with small tap roots, mature early and keep well. **Pkt., 4c.; oz., 8c.; ¼ lb., 15c.; lb., 50c.**

**SCARLET KASHMYR**—A new and distinct variety. The outside skin is of a beautiful deep scarlet color. **Pkt., 4c.; oz., 8c.; ¼ lb., 20c.; lb., 75c.**

**Purple Top Milan.**

**EXTRA EARLY PURPLE TOP MILAN**—The earliest variety. The tops are very small, distinctly strap-leaved, and grow very erect and compact.

**NEW WHITE EGG TURNIP**—For an all-round variety this is one of the best Turnips. It is a good keeper and excellent either for early or flat sowing. **Pkt., 3c.; oz., 8c.; ¼ lb., 15c.; lb., 50c.**

**GREEN TOP SCOTCH (YELLOW)**—Another excellent kind, hardy, productive, good keeper and of fine quality. **Pkt., 2c.; oz., 5c.; ¼ lb., 10c.; lb., 35c.**

**COW-HORN**—It is white, except a little shade of green at the top. It is delicate and well flavored. **Pkt., 3c.; oz., 7c.; ¼ lb., 15c.; lb., 45c.**

**Long White Cowhorn.**

**Improved Long Island.**

# HERBS.

Sweet Marjoram.

**CULTURE.**—Herbs delight in a rich mellow soil. Sow in early spring in shallow drills 1 foot apart. When 2 inches high, thin or transplant, cut when in blossom, dry quickly.

**Aromatic, Sweet, Pot and Medicinal Herbs.**

| | Pkt. | Oz. | ¼ |
|---|---|---|---|
| Anise | 4 | 7 | 20 |
| *Balm | 4 | 12 | 40 |
| Basil (sweet) | 5 | 10 | 35 |
| Borage | 3 | 10 | 35 |
| Chamomile | 5 | — | — |
| *Caraway | 3 | 7 | 15 |
| Chervil | 3 | 7 | 20 |
| *Catnip | 3 | 15 | 50 |
| *Chives | 3 | — | — |
| Coriander | 3 | 7 | 20 |
| Dill | 4 | 7 | 20 |
| *Fennel | 3 | 7 | 25 |
| *Horehound | 4 | 15 | — |
| Hyssop | 4 | 15 | — |
| *Lavender | 4 | 15 | 50 |
| Marjoram | 4 | 15 | 40 |
| *Pennyroyal | 4 | 25 | — |
| *Rue | 3 | 15 | 40 |
| Rosemary | 4 | 20 | — |
| Saffron | 4 | 15 | 40 |
| Sorrel | 3 | 8 | 25 |
| *Sage | 4 | 10 | 35 |
| Summer Savory | 4 | 8 | 30 |
| *Tansy | 4 | 20 | — |
| *Taragon | 5 | — | — |
| *Thyme | 5 | 18 | 65 |
| *Wormwood | 4 | 24 | 75 |

Varieties marked with a (*) are perennials

Rosemary.

## Our Small Vegetable Garden.

This includes the following seventeen packages of Vegetable Seeds and one packet of beautiful mixed Flower Seed, AND THESE EIGHTEEN PACKAGES WE SEND POSTPAID BY MAIL TO ANY ADDRESS FOR ONLY 50 CENTS.

**1 Pkt. Each:**
Wax Beans.
Early Garden Peas.
Early Sweet Corn.
Early Table Beets.

**1 Pkt. Each:**
Early Cabbage.
Early Table Carrots.
Pickling Cucumber.
Kohlrabi.

**1 Pkt. Each:**
Early Lettuce.
Musk Melon.
Onion.
Curled Parsley.

**1 Pkt. Each:**
Early Radish.
Spinach.
Early Tomatoes.
Early Flat Turnips.

**1 Pkt. Each:**
Marjoram.
Choice Flower Seed Mixture.

These **Vegetable Gardens** are adapted for any garden, and a very great number of our customers plant them every year, as they contain just what they want. These varieties are of our own selection, and we cannot make any change, considering the low price.

## Our Large Vegetable Garden.

This includes the following thirty-five packages of Vegetable Seeds and one packet of beautiful mixed Flower Seed that will please you when you see it bloom, AND THESE THIRTY-SIX PACKAGES WE SEND POSTPAID TO ANY ADDRESS FOR ONLY $1.00.

**1 Pkt. Each:**
Wax Beans.
Green Podded Beans.
Early Beets, round, red
Kale, early curled.
Early Cabbage.
Late Cabbage.
Carrot, early red.
Cauliflower, early.

**1 Pkt. Each:**
Celery.
Celeriac.
Sweet Corn, extra early
Garden Cress.
Pickling Cucumber.
Long Cucumber.
Kohlrabi.
Leek.

**1 Pkt. Each:**
Lettuce, early curled.
Head Lettuce.
Musk Melon.
Water Melon.
Yellow Danvers Onion.
Red Wethersfield Onion.
Parsley, curled.

**1 Pkt. Each:**
Parsnips, long white.
Early Garden Peas.
Pumpkin.
Radish, round, red.
Radish, long.
Rutabaga.
Summer Spinach.

**1 Pkt. Each:**
Squash.
Tomato, early red.
Turnip, early, flat.
Marjoram.
Thyme.
Choice Flower Seed Mixture.

## Large Family Garden.

Weight, packed for shipment, 6 lbs., price, $2.00, transportation charges paid by purchaser.

**Beans.**
Dwarf Green Pod (snap), ½ pt....10c.
Yellow Pod, ½ pt...15c.
Dwarf Limas, ½ pt.15c.
Pole, 1 pkt....... 5c.

**Beet.**
Blood Turnip, 1 oz.. 7c.
Long Blood, 1 oz... 7c.

**Cabbage.**
Early, 1 pkt....... 5c.
Late, 1 oz..........15c.

**Carrot.**
Early Scarlet Horn, 1 pkt. ........... 4c.
Danvers, 1 oz...... 5c.

**Celery.**
1 pkt. ............. 4c.

**Cucumbers.**
For slicing, ½ oz..10c.
For pickles, ½ oz..10c.

**Egg Plant.**
1 pkt. ............. 6c.

**Leek.**
1 pkt. ............. 4c.

**Lettuce.**
Early, 1 oz......... 8c.
Best Summer, 1 oz.. 8c.

**Melons.**
Best Musk Variety
Water, best early,
1 oz. ..............10c.
1 oz. ............... 8c.

**Onions.**
White, 1 oz........15c.
Red, 1 oz...........10c.

**Onion Sets.**
1 pt. ...............18c.

**Parsley.**
1 pkt. .............. 4c.

**Parsnip.**
1 oz. ............... 5c.

**Peas.**
Early, ½ pt.......15c.
Medium, ½ pt......15c.
Late, ½ pt.........15c.

**Pepper.**
Large, 1 pkt....... 5c.

**Pumpkin.**
Best, 1 pkt........ 4c.

**Radish.**
Round Red, 1 oz.... 8c.
Long Red, 1 oz.... 8c.
Long White, 1 oz.. 8c.

**Salsify.**
1 pkt. ............. 4c.

**Spinach.**
Best, 1 oz.......... 8c.

**Squash.**
Summer, ½ oz..... 8c.
Winter, ½ oz...... 8c.

**Tomato.**
Best Red, 1 pkt.... 5c.

**Turnip.**
Early, 1 oz......... 7c.
Fall, 1 oz.......... 8c.

**Sweet Corn.**
Early, ½ pt....... 9c.
Late, ½ pt........ 9c.

This fine collection would cost you (even at our very low Catalogue prices), if selected, $3.55. We offer it to you for only $2.00, purchaser paying express charges. These collections are put up before the busy season, and cannot be changed.

## Village Garden.

**Beans.**
½ pt. Green Pod (snap) .........12c.
½ pt. Yellow Pod Wax ...........15c.

**Beet.**
1 pkt. Blood Turnip ............. 4c.
1 pkt. Long Blood.. 4c.

**Cabbage.**
1 pkt. Early....... 5c.
1 pkt. Late........ 5c.

**Carrot.**
1 pkt. Early Scarlet Horn ........ 4c.
1 pkt. Danvers ½ Long ........... 4c.

**Cucumber.**
1 pkt. for slicing.. 4c.
1 pkt. for pickling.. 4c.

**Sweet Corn.**
½ pt. Early....... 9c.
½ pt. Late........ 9c.

**Lettuce.**
1 pkt. Early var.... 4c.
1 pkt. Summer .... 4c.

**Melons.**
1 pkt. Best Musk variety ......... 5c.
1 pkt. Best Water variety .... .... 5c.

**Onion.**
1 oz. Best Red....10c.

**Parsnip.**
1 pkt. Hollow Crown 4c

**Peas.**
½ pt. Best Early..15c.
½ pt. Best Late...15c.

**Radish.**
1 oz. Mixed ....... 5c.
5 pkts. Flower Seeds ...........25c

This collection, amounting to $1.71, will be shipped you charges prepaid at the very low price of $1.25, or charges paid by purchaser, for $1.00.

# FLOWER SEEDS.

**OUR SELECTED LIST OF BEAUTIFUL FLOWERS**—Our patrons will find here an up-to-date list of the most desirable, choicest and popular varieties, and nearly all easy of cultivation. Space does not permit of many illustrations, but the few that we add will be of material aid in your selections. Cultural directions with a correct illustration in colors are printed on each package; only a few varieties excepted out of the several hundred we have. In the size of our packets we aim to be as liberal as possible, almost without exception a little more than others can give. While our prices are lower than any other reliable house can offer good seed for, our expenses are reduced to the minimum and our customers have the benefit. Everybody can have an abundance of Flowers, at our popular prices. ABBREVIATIONS: A., annual; P., perennial; H., hardy. PLEASE ORDER BY NUMBER ONLY; if you write the name do not omit the Number.

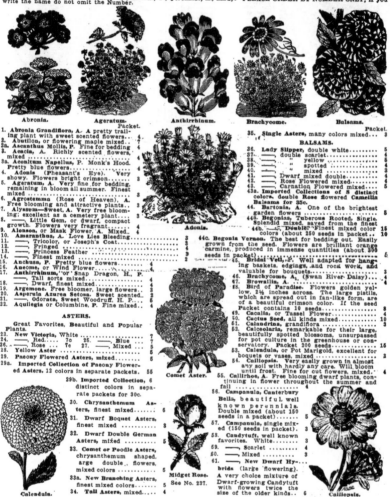

Abronia.       Ageratum.       Anthirrhinum.       Brachycome.       Balsams.

Adonis.

Comet Aster.

Calendula.

Midget Rose.
See No. 237.

Calliopsis.

Packet.
1. **Abronia Grandiflora, A.** A pretty trailing plant with sweet scented flowers.. 4
2. **Abutilon, or flowering maple mixed.** 7
2a. **Acanthus Mollis, P.** Fine for bedding 4
3. **Acacia, A.** Richly scented flowers, mixed ...................................... 4
3a. **Aconitum Napellus, P.** Monk's Hood. Pretty blue flowers....................
4. **Adonis** (Pheasant's Eye). Very showy. Flowers bright crimson...... 3
5. **Ageratum, A.** Very fine for bedding, remaining in bloom all summer. Finest mixed ............................................ 3
6. **Agrostemma** (Rose of Heaven), A. Free blooming and attractive plants.. 3
7. **Alyssum**—Sweet, A. Very free blooming; excellent as a cemetery plant.... 3
8. ——. Little Gem, or dwarf, compact growth. Flowers very fragrant....... 4
9. **Alonson, or Mask Flower, A.** Mixed.. 4
10. **Amaranthus, A.** Love Lies Bleeding............
11. ——. Tricolor, or Joseph's Coat................. 3
12. ——. Fringed ..................................... 4
13. ——. Princess Feather ............................ 3
14. ——. Finest mixed ................................. 2
15. **Anchusa, P.** Pretty blue flowers......
16. **Aneome, or Wind Flower........**
17. **Anthirrhinum, or Snap Dragon, H., P.** Tall sorts mixed................... 4
18. ——. Dwarf, finest mixed.......... 4
19. **Argemone.** Free bloomer, large flowers.. 3
20. **Asperula Azurea Setosa.** Sweet scented.. 3
21. ——. Odorata, Sweet Woodruff, H. P.... 5
22. **Aquilegia or Columbine, P.** Fine mixed.. 4

## ASTERS.

Great Favorites, Beautiful and Popular Plants.
23. **New Victoria,** White .................... 7
24. ——. Red... 7c   25. ——. Blue ... 7
26. ——. Rose ... 7c   27. ——. Mixed ... 5
28. **Yellow Aster** ........................... 5
29. **Paeony Flowered Asters,** mixed........ 5
29a. **Imported Collection of Paeony Flowered Asters,** 12 colors in separate packets. 55
29b. **Imported Collection,** 6 distinct colors in separate packets for 30c.
30. **Chrysanthemum Asters,** finest mixed...... 5
31. **Dwarf Boquet Asters,** finest mixed .......... 5
32. **Dwarf Double German Asters,** mixed .......... 5
33. **Comet or Poodle Asters,** chrysanthemum shaped, large double flowers, mixed colors ............ 5
33a. **New Branching Asters,** finest mixed colors....... 5
34. **Tall Asters,** mixed..... 4

Packet.
35. **Single Asters,** many colors mixed... 3

## BALSAMS.

36. **Lady Slipper,** double white......... 5
37. ——. double scarlet............... 4
38. ——. " yellow............... 4
39. ——. " spotted............... 4
40. ——. " mixed............... 3
41. ——. Dwarf mixed double......... 5
42. ——. Rose Flowered mixed.... 4
43. ——. Carnation Flowered mixed.... 5
43a. **Imported Collections of 8 distinct colors,** double Rose flowered Camellia Balsams for 35c.
44. **Bartonia, A.** One of the brightest garden flowers ........................ 5
44a. **Begonias, Tuberous Rooted, Single.** Splendid mixed, saved from the finest
44b. ——. **Double.** Finest mixed color colors (about 250 seeds in packet.. 10
44c. **Begonia Vernon.** The best for bedding out. Easily grown from the seed. Flowers are brilliant orange carmine, produced in immense quantities (about 300 seeds in packet)............................ 5
45. **Bridal Veil, P.** Well adapted for hanging baskets, edgings, and rock work, and valuable for bouquets.................. 3
46. **Brachycome, A.** (Swan River Daisy)... 4
47. **Browallia, A.** ............................. 4
48. **Bird of Paradise.** Flowers golden yellow, 2½ inches across. The large pistils, which are spread out in fan-like form, are of a beautiful crimson color. If the seed Packet contains 10 seeds.................. 8
49. **Cacalia, or Tassel Flower............** 4
50. **Cactus Seed,** all kinds mixed........ 10
51. **Calandrina, grandiflora** .................. 3
52. **Calceolaria,** remarkable for their large, beautifully spotted blossoms, unsurpassed for pot culture in the greenhouse or conservatory. Packet 200 seeds.......... 15
53. **Calenduls,** or Pot Marigold, excellent for boquets or vases, mixed............. 3
54. **Calliopsis.** Very easily grown in almost any soil with hardly any care. Will bloom until frost. Fine for cut flowers, mixed. 4
55. **Callirhoe, A.** Free blooming dwarf plants, continuing in flower throughout the summer and fall .................................. 4
56. **Campanula,** Canterbury Bella, beautiful, well known perennials. Double mixed (about 150 seeds in a packet)....... 5
57. **Campanula,** single mixed (150 seeds in packet). 3
58. **Candytuft,** well known favorites. White........ 3
59. ——. Scarlet ......... 4
60. ——. Mixed ......... 3
61. ——. New Dwarf Hybrida (large flowering). A very choice mixture of Dwarf-growing Candytuft with flowers twice the size of the older kinds.. 6

Coleus, No. 80.    Chrysanthemum, No. 72.    Castor Bean, No. 75.    Japan Dianthus, No. 97.    Mourning Cloak, No. 95.

Clianthus.

Clarkia.

Geranium, No. 132.

Eschscholzia No. 105

Heliotrope. No. 124

**Packet.**

62. **Canna.** Fine mixed . . . . . . . . . . . 5
63. **Carnations.** (Perennial varieties). For both pot culture in the green house, window garden and open ground culture. Finest German double mixed, of innumerable colors and delicious perfume, 125 seeds in packet . . . . . . . . . . . . . . . . 5
64. **Carnation, New, Margaret.** Blooms in 4 months from sowing the seed. Richest colors . . 5
64a. **Catchfly, A.** . . . . . . . . . . . . . . . 3
65. **Celosia, A.** (Coxcomb), scarlet . . . . . . . . . . . . . . . . . . . . 5
66. **Celosia, mixed** . . . . . . . . . . . . . 4
67. **Centaurea Cyanus,** also called Bachelor's Button. A. Mixed colors . . . . . . . . . . . . . . . . . 4
68. **Centaurea Cyanus,** blue (Emperor William) . . . . . . . . . . . . . . 4
69. **Centaurea Cyanus,** white . . . . . . . 3
70. **Centaurea,** or Dusty Miller, P. These are foliage plants. Very fine silvery leaves . . . . . . . . . . . 5
**Chrysanthemum.** Double in the following colors:
71a. **Golden,** 71b. Scarlet and 71c White. Per packet of each . . . . . 5
72. **Chrysanthemum,** Double, mixed . . . . . . . . . . . . . . . . . . . 5
73. **Chrysanthemum Maximum,** large oxeyed daisy. Fine, large, single white flowers . . . . . . . . . . . . . 6
74. **Chrysanthemum,** Single, mixed . . 3
74a. **Chinese and Japanese Chrysanthemums.** Sown in February or March they will bloom in the Fall. Mixed . 10
75. **Castor Bean,** (Ricinus). Mixed . . 4
76. **Cineraria Hybrida,** P. Mixed . . . 8
77. **Clarkia, A.** Finest colors mixed . . 2
78. **Cleome Pungens, A.** The Giant Spider Plant. One of the best honey producing plants. The flowers are very showy . . . . . . . . . . . . . . . . . . 4
79. **Clianthus Dampieri,** (Glory Pea). One of the most gorgeous flowers cultivated, bright, scarlet . . . . . . . . .
80. **Coleus, P.** The handsomest foliage plant in a variety of colors and shadings. Easily grown from seed . . . . 5
81. **Collinsia, A.** Free blooming, easily grown . . . . . . . . . . . . . . . . . . 2
82. **Convolvulus Minor, or Dwarf Morning Glories.** All colors, mixed . . . 3
83. **Cosmos, A. Mammoth Perfection,** finest mixtures of all colors . . . . . 5
84. **Cosmos.** Giants of California. Best mixed . . . . . . . . . . . . . . . . . . 8
85. **Cuphea,** or Cigar Plant, A. . . . . . 8
86. **Cynoglossum, A.** Few flowers are more easily grown and more free flowering . . . . . . . . . . . 3
87. **Chinese Lantern Plant.** The husks are brilliant scarlet, presenting a beautiful appearance among the green branches. In these husks or "lanterns" is the fruit of deep red color, which is superior to the Winter Cherry for cooking; preserving or eating raw . . 3
88. **Datura,** or Trumpet Flower. Mixed . 4

89. **Dahlia.** Easily grown from seed. Single and double mixed . 5
90. **DIANTHUS Chinensis.** Best double mixed . . . . . . . . . . 5
91. **DIANTHUS, Double,** white . . . 4
92. **DIANTHUS, Heddewigi,** double, crimson . . . . . . . . . . . . . 5
93. **DIANTHUS, New, Large Flowered, Dwarf, double Hybrid.** Finest mixed colors . . . . . . . . . 5
94. **DIANTHUS, Diadematus.** Double Diadem Pink . . . . . . . . 5
95. **DIANTHUS, Mourning Cloak.** The large double flowers are almost black, edged with white . . 5
96. **DIANTHUS, Double : Japan Pink,** mixed colors . . . . . . . . 5
97. **DIANTHUS, Single Japan Pink,** mixed colors . . . . . . . . 5
98. **DIANTHUS, Plumarius** (Pheasant's-Eye Pink). The old-fashioned Grass Pink, very double . . . . . . . . . . . . . . . 5
99. **Digitalis,** or Fox Glove, P. . . . . 4
100. **Double Daisies or Bellis, P.** Fine German Double mixed . . 5
101. **Double Daisies or Bellis, Snow Ball.** Large double white . 7
102. **Double Daisies or Bellis, Longfellow.** Large, double dark rose . 4
103. **Dracaena,** or Club Palm . . . . . 8
104. **Edelweiss,** Famous Alpine plant . 8
105. **Eschscholtzia,** or California Poppy, A. Finest mixed colors . . . 4
106. **Euphorbia,** or Fire Plant, A. . . . 5
107. **Eutoca, A.** . . . . . . . . . . . . . 4
108. **Feverfew,** or Matricaria, a lovely old-fashioned plant, double, white . 3
**FORGET-ME-NOT or Myosotis.**
109. **Palustris.** The true marsh Forget-Me-Not . . . . . . . . . . 6
110. **Alpestris robusta grandiflora.** Large, sky-blue flowers . . . . . 5
111. **Alba.** Pure white flowers . . . 4
112. **Roses.** Pretty rose flowers . . . 4
115. **Freesia.** Easily grown from seed . 4
115. **Fuchsia.** Finest varieties, double and single, mixed . . . . . . . . 10
116. **Four O'Clock,** Mirabilis or Marvel. Finest mixed . . . . . . . . 3
117. **Gaillardia, H. A.** Picta Lorensiana. Charming double varieties, mixed . 4
118. **or Blanket Flower.** Single mixed . . . . . . . . . . . . . . . 3
119. **Geraniums, P.** Can be easily grown from seed. Splendid mixed . . 5
120. **Gilia, A.** Choice mixed . . . . . . 2
121. **Gypsophila,** or Angel's Breath, H. A. Finest mixed . . . . . . . . 3
122. **Godetia, H. A.** Many sorts and colors mixed . . . . . . . . . . . . 3
123. **Golden Rod, H. P.** . . . . . . . . 5
124. **Heliotrope, P.** Finest mixed. (Pkt. 100 seeds) . . . . . . . . . . . . . 5
125. **Hesperis,** or Sweet Rocket . . . . 5
126. **Hibiscus.** Mixed . . . . . . . . . 3
127. **Honesty, A.** . . . . . . . . . . . . 3
**HOLLYHOCK,** P. Chater's Prize, finest double separate colors: 128a, white; 128b, red; 128c, yellow; and 128d, black. Per Packet (70 seeds) . 8
129. **Finest mixed, double** . . . . . . 6
130. **Single** mixed, all colors . . . . 4
131. **New Mammoth Allegheny.** Blooms the first year from seed . . 10

Packet.

133. **Ice Plant, A.** Mesembranthemum. Handsome and curious plant. Flowers frosted, wax-like, foliage thick. Adapted for basket and rock work ............................................ 4
**Ipomoea.** See "Climbers."
134. **Impatiens Sultani, P.** One of the most beautiful plants for summer bedding or Pot Culture. Flowers, rich carmine. (Pkt. 25 seeds) ...... 8
135. **Kaulfussia, A.** Pretty little free flowering plant, exceedingly effective in beds or borders. Mixed colors.... 5
**LARKSPUR** or Delphinium. Annual varieties.
136. **Larkspur,** Double Dwarf Rocket, splendid mixed....................... 4
137. **Larkspur,** Giant Hyacinth, flowered, splendid mixed............... 3
138. **Larkspur,** Emperor, finest mixed.. 3
139. **Perennial Larkspur Formosum,** fine blue................................ 5
140. **Lantana Hybridis, P.** Splendid bedding plants, choice mixed....... 5
141. **Lavatera, A.** ....................... 3
142. **Linum Grandiflorum.** Scarlet... 2
143. **Lobelia Cardinalis.** Scarlet..... 6
144. **Lobelia, Erinus, Emperor William,** Dwarf, dark blue..................... 5
145. **Lobelia, White Gem**.............. 4

Giant Machet, No. 154.

Packet.

146. **Lobelia, Paxtoniana,** white and blue ..................................
147. **Lupinus.** Tall, fine mixed....... 3
148. **Lupinus.** Dwarf varieties. Mixed 3
**LYCHNIS.** Handsome and highly ornamental, of easy culture.
149. **Lychnis, Chalcedonica,** Scarlet..... 3
150. **Lychnis, Haageana.** Splendid, bright scarlet...................... 8
151. **Marigold,** Double French, finest mixed .............................. 3
152. **Marigold,** Double African, finest mixed .............................. 3
153. **Marigold,** Legion of Honor, dwarf, single ............................. 5
**Matricaria.** See Feverfew, No. 108.
**Marvel of Peru.** See Four o'clock, No. 116.
**MIGNONETTE.** A well known old favorite.
154. **Mignonette, Giant Machet.** The best for all purposes.............. 5
155. **Mignonette, Golden Queen.** Fragrant, golden flowers............. 3
156. **Mignonette, Imperialis.** Deep red flower spikes.................... 4
157. **Mignonette, Sweet Scented,** large flowering. The most fragrant variety; oz. 10c.......................... 2
158. **Mimosa Pudica, A.** Sensitive plant 3

Marigold, No. 151.   Lobelia, No. 143.

Mimosa Pudica, No. 158.

Nigelia, No. 179.   Larkspur, No. 138.

Packet.

**Mimulus** or Monkey Flower.
159. **Mimulus Cardinalis.** Splendid scarlet.................. 4
160. **Mimulus. Moschatus.** (Musk plant)........................... 4
161. **Mimulus, Hybridus** Grandiflorus. Mixed.............. 5

**NASTURTIUMS—Dwarf.**
165. **Beauty.** Striped, red and yellow.
166. **Chameleon.** Crimson, yellow and bronze.
167. **Crystal Palace Gem.** Sulphur spotted.
168. **Empress of India.** Dark foliage, crimson flowers.
169. **King Theodore.** Dark maroon.
170. **Pearl.** Creamy white.
171. **Ruby King.** Ruby.
172. **New Bronze.**
Price any of the above, packet, 5c.; oz., 25c.
173 **Dwarf Nasturtiums,** finest mixture many colors, packet, 4c.; oz., 10c.; ¼-lb., 40c.

Empress of India, No. 168.

Lantana Hybridis, No. 140.
**TALL OR CLIMBING NASTURTIUMS.**
174. **Finest Mixture of Lobbs Nasturtium.** Packet, 5c.; oz., 20c.; ¼-lb., 70c.
174a. **Madam Gunther's Hybrids.** Large flowers of the most brilliant shades; packet, 5c.; oz., 20c.; ¼-lb., 70c.
175. **Tall Nasturtiums.** Splendid mixture of many colors; packet, 3c.; oz., 10c.; ¼-lb., 30c.

Packet.
176. **Nemophila.** Fine mixed........... 5
177. **Nicotiana Affinis, A.** Sweet scented 4
178. **Colossus,** 6 feet, immense leaves... 6
179. **Nigelia,** (Love in a Mist), A. Double blue and white mixed.............
180. **Oenothera, A.** (Evening Primrose) 4
181. **Oenothera, Rosea.** (Mexican Primrose) ............................... 5

Packet.

182. **Oxalis.** For hanging baskets, mixed. Packet ......................... 4

**PANSIES.**
The following varieties are all Large Flowering Pansies; Packets about 100 seeds.
183. **Dark Blue or Black-Blue**........
184. **Dr. Faust or King of the Blacks**.. 5
185. **Emperor William.** Brilliant blue 5
186. **Fire King.** Red...................
187. **Golden Queen.** Beautiful yellow.
188. **Improved Striped**................
189. **Peacock.** Coloring truly beautiful
190. **Prince Bismark.** Bronze........
191. **Rainbow.** Very beautiful........
192. **Snow Queen.** Beautiful white.... 5
193. **Violet Blue**........................
194. **Silver Edged.** White margin....
195. **Gold Edge.** Yellow margin...... 5
196. **Chicago Parks Bedding Pansies.** Finest mixture of these varieties....
197. **Good Mixed.** Fine Strain. Oz. 1.25 3
198. **Giant Prize Pansies.** Enormous.. 10

Giant Prize, No. 198.

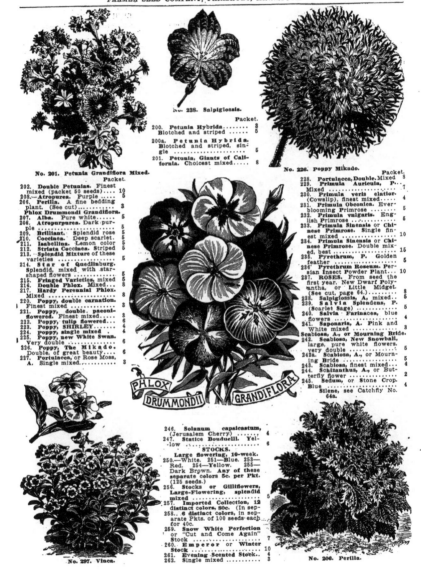

No. 238. Salpiglossis.

Packet.
200. **Petunia Hybrida** ......... 3
Blotched and striped ...... 5

200a. **Petunia Hybrida**.
Blotched and striped, single ...................... 5

201. **Petunia, Giants of California.** Choicest mixed..... 8

No. 201. Petunia Grandiflora Mixed.

Packet.
202. **Double Petunias.** Finest
mixed (packet 50 seeds).... 10
203.—**Atropurea.** Purple ..... 5
206. **Perilla.** A fine bedding
plant. (See cut) .......... 3
**Phlox Drummondi Grandiflora.**
207. **Alba.** Pure white..... 5
208. **Atropurpurea.** Dark purple ..................... 5
209. **Brilliant.** Splendid rose 5
210. **Coccinea.** Deep scarlet. 5
211. **Isabellina.** Lemon color 5
212. **Striata Coccinea.** Striped 5
213. **Splendid Mixture** of these
varieties ................ 5
214. **Star of Quedlinburg.**
Splendid, mixed with star-
shaped flowers ........... 5
215. **Fringed Varieties,** mixed 5
216. **Double Phlox.** Mixed... 8
217. **Hardy Perennial Phlox.**
Mixed .................... 8
220. **Poppy, double carnation.**
Finest mixed ............ 3
221. **Poppy, double, paeoni-**
**flowered.** Finest mixed.... 3
222. **Poppy, tulip flowered....** 4
223. **Poppy, SHIRLEY.......** 4
224. **Poppy, single mixed** . 3
225. **Poppy, new White Swan.**
Very double ............ 6
226. **Poppy, The Mikado.**
Double, of great beauty.... 6
227. **Portulacca, or Rose Moss,**
A. Single mixed.......... 3

No. 226. Poppy Mikado.

Packet.
228. **Portulacca, Double.** Mixed 3
229. **Primula Auricula, P.**
Mixed .................... 7
230. **Primula veris elatior.**
(Cowslip), finest mixed.... 4
231. **Primula Obconica.** Ever-
blooming Primrose ....... 5
232. **Primula vulgaris.** English Primrose ............ 5
233. **Primula Sinensis or Chi-**
**nese Primrose.** Single finest mixed ............... 10
234. **Primula Sinensis or Chi-**
**nese Primrose.** Double mixed, best ................. 15
235. **Pyrethrum, P. Golden**
feather ................. 5
236. **Pyrethrum Roseum.** Persian Insect Powder Plant... 10
237. **ROSES.** From seed the
first year. New Dwarf Polyantha, or Little Midget.
(See cut, page 64.)........ 8
238. **Salpiglossis, A,** mixed.. 5
239. **Salvia Splendens, P.**
(Scarlet Sage) ........... 5
240. **Salvia Farinacea,** blue
flowers ................. 5
241. **Saponaria, A.** Pink and
White mixed ............. 4
**Scabiosa, A,** or Mourning Bride.
242. **Scabiosa, New Snowball,**
large, pure white flowers,
very double ............. 5
242a. **Scabiosa, A,** or Mourning Bride ............... 4
243. **Scabiosa, finest mixed...** 4
244. **Schizanthus, A,** or Butterfly flower ............ 2
245. **Sedum, or Stone Crop.**
Blue ................... 4
**Silene,** see Catchfly No.
64a.

PHLOX DRUMMONDII GRANDIFLORA

246. **Solanum capsicastum,**
(Jerusalem Cherry) ....... 4
247. **Statice Bouduelli.** Yellow ................... 6
**STOCKS.**
Large flowering, 10-week.
250.—White. 251—Blue. 253—
Red. 254—Yellow. 255—
Dark Brown. Any of these
separate colors 5c. per Pkt.
(125 seeds.)
256. **Stocks or Gilliflowers,**
**Large-Flowering,** splendid
mixed ................. 5
257. **Imported Collection,** 12
distinct colors, 80c. (In sep-
258.. 6 distinct colors, in separate Pkts. of 100 seeds each
for 40c.
259. **Snow White Perfection**
or "Cut and Come Again"
Stock ................. 7
260. **Emperor** or **Winter**
Stock ................. 10
261. **Evening Scented Stock.** 4
262. **Single mixed** .......... 3

No. 297. Vinca.

No. 206. Perilla.

**Sweet Peas, Eckfords.**

## SUNFLOWERS.

### HELIANTHUS.
Packet

286. **Helianthus Cucumerifolius**, new miniature Sunflowers. Flowers are single, bright yellow with a dark center.

287. ——, **Stella**, new ever-blooming Sunflower............ 4
288. **Silver-Leaved.** *Argophyllus.* Beautiful yellow and black single flowers and silvery foliage.... 8
289. **Nanus fl. pl.** Very double, rich golden yellow flowers. Dwarf variety. 2½ feet high............. 4
290. **Californicus.** Very double, extra large flowers ... Tagetes, see Marigold, No. 151-158.          5
291. **Verbena, candidissima**, pure white............... 5
292. ——, **Scarlet**, large flowered................... 5
293. ——, **Dark blue**, very fine...................... 5
294. ——, **Golden-Leaved**, mixed colors............. 5
295. ——, **Splendid Mixture**........................ 5
296. ——, **Grandiflora.** New Mammoth flowered, beautiful colors mixed............................ 7
297. **Vinca, Periwinkle Rose.** Mixed................ 5
298. **Violet, P.** Sweet scented, mixed.............. 8
299. **Virginia Stocks, A.** Pretty free flowering plants with red flowers. Easily grown................ 8
300. **WALLFLOWERS, P.** Extra double, splendid mixed colors................................ 7
301. ——, Imported collection of 6 varieties, each 100 seeds, in separate colors, *extra double,* 60c.
302. ——, **Finest Mixed**, single...................... 8

**Zinna Zebra.**

303. **Zinnia, double white**.......................... 4
304. ——, **double scarlet**........................... 4
305. ——, **double yellow**........................... 4
306. ——, **splendid mixed**......................... 4
307. ——, **Carnation striped**....................... 5
308. ——, **Crested and curled**..................... 5
309. ——, **Largest Flowering, double**.............. 5
310. ——, **Double Liliput.** Exceedingly pretty plants, bloom all summer and until late in the fall.... 6
310a. ——, **"Zebra."** Flowers of perfect shape, of orange, crimson, pink, yellow, white, etc., all striped, spotted and blotched with different shades. Mixed colors........... 7

317. **Dolichos, or Hyacinth Bean**............... 8
318. **Humulus Japonicus, A.** or *Japanese Hop*; a rapid growing climber............. 4
319. **Ipomoea Grandiflora, Moon Flower** or **Evening Glory** ......... 10
320. **Ipomoea, Heavenly Blue.** Produces clusters of large blue flowers............ 8

**Japanese Hop.**

D) NOT FAIL to try our Flower Seeds. They are the finest to be had. All fresh, home grown and imported.

## SWEET PEAS.

Our stock of these popular flowers is second to none, and will please our customers. Our packets contain from 50 to 75 seeds.
Pkt.

265. **Cupid**, new dwarf, *white*......................... 7
266. ——, new dwarf, *pink*........................... 7
267. **Blanche Burpee**, the largest pure white Sweet Pea; oz., 12c. 5
268. —— **Ferry**, pink and white flowers, very fragrant. The earliest. ¼ lb., 25c.; oz., 10c.................
269. **Apple Blossom**, rose, shading to pink; very beautiful; oz.,10c. 4
270. **Captain of the Blues**, blue, very large and full; oz., 10c... 4
271. **Butterfly**, white, shaded and edged with blue; ¼ lb., 20c; oz., 10c................................... 4
272. **Crown Prince of Prussia**, salmon flesh color; oz., 10c... 5
273. **Emily Henderson**, white, large flowers. Very early. Oz., 10c. 5
274. **Firefly**, the best scarlet, very brilliant and fragrant; oz., 10c. 4
275. **Invincible Scarlet**, a beautiful rich scarlet, very fragrant; oz., 8c.......................................... 5
276. **Mrs. Eckford**, the best yellow; oz., 10c............... 5
277. **America**, large flowering, white with scarlet blotch in center; oz., 8c....................................... 4
278. **Stanley**, rich dark maroon. The best dark variety. Oz., 10c. 4
279. **Finest Mixed Sweet Peas:** lb., 70c; ¼ lb., 20c.; oz., 8c... 3
280. **Eckford's Giant Sweet Peas**, in Finest Mixture; ¼ lb., 30c.; oz., 10c.................................... 4
280a. **New Double Sweet Peas**, they are very beautiful and interesting; the flowers are extra large; they usually produce 25 to 50 per cent of double flowers; the best colors mixed; oz., 15c................ 5
281. **Everlasting Pea.** *Lathyrus latifolius.* Equally as beautiful as Sweet Peas, and perfectly hardy, bearing magnificent clusters of flowers; mixed colors............ 8

**SWEET WILLIAM.** This is one of, if not the finest, hardy perennials. Exceedingly beautiful and showy plants, producing an abundance of rich-colored flowers throughout the season. Large and beautiful flowers.

282. ——, **Auricula flowered.** Large and beautiful flowers.................
283. **Sweet William, finest double mixed**.... 4
284. ——, **best single mixed** .................. 8
285. **Sweet Sultan.** *Centaurea Moshata.* Handsome, profuse flowering and sweet scented, of very easy culture......................... 8

**Sweet William.**

400. **Wild Flower Garden.** We prepared this mixture from choice, fresh seeds of the *leading varieties* of *beautiful, easily-grown flowers,* which will give a constant and varied bloom the whole season. Oz., 20c.; Packet (about 500 seeds)... 5

400a. **Fragrant Annuals.** A mixture made from seeds of fragrant flowers, giving rich perfume throughout the day and evening; some are suitable for cutting ... 5

400b. **Flowers for Bouquets.** This mixture contains seeds producing flowers suitable for cutting for vases and bouquets, nearly all having long stems ...... 5

**Verbena.**

## SELECTED CLIMBERS

311. **Adlumia Cirrhosa, A.** Allegheny Vine, or Mountain Fringe............. 4
312. **Ampelopsis Veitchi, P.** Japanese or Boston Ivy.. 4
313. **Balloon Vine, A.** Love in Puff. One of the prettiest rapid growing climbers.... 5
313a. **Bignonia, or Trumpet Vine**................... 6
314. **Canary Bird Vine, A.** *Tropaeolum canariensis* ... 4
315. **Cobaea Scandens.** The best quick-growing climber, one that will make a show the first year, both in vines and flowers............... 5
316. **Cypress Vine.** *Ipomoea Quamoclit.* Many colors mixed; a very handsome climber ................ 4

**I Love Flowers, Don't You?**

**No. 316. Cypress Vine.**

326. ———, New Japanese. The colors, tintings and markings are of incomparable beauty .............. 5
327. **SCARLET RUNNER**.......... 4
328. **Smilax, A.** The most desirable house climber.................
329. **Passion Flower.** Mixed......... 4
330. **Wild Cucumber.** Echinocystis Lobata 4

**IMMORTELLES.**

338. **Eeroclineum.** Mixed rose and white 4
339. **Ammobium.** White flowers........

340. **Gomphrena.** Globe Amaranth. Mixed ........... 3
341. **Helichrysum, Monst.** Double mixed ........... 4
342. ———, Imported collection of 6 varieties and colors ........ 30
343. **Rhodanthe.** Finest mixed colors ....... 5
344. **Sanvitalia, Procumbens.** Double ........ 3
345. **Xeranthemum.** Mixed, double flowers. 4
346. **Mixed Everlastings** ....... 4

**No. 341. Helichrysum.**

GLADIOLUS—These are the most attractive summer flowering bulbs grown. Wonderful improvements have been made in the past few years. We offer choice mixtures which we are sure will please. Doz. 30c. postpaid; $1.50 per 100 by express.

Gladiolus.

**CLIMBERS—Continued.**

321. **Ipomoea, Grandiflora, Setosa, Brasilian Morning Glory.** Handsome, rapid grower ....................... 10
322. **Kenilworth Ivy, Linaria Cymbalaria, P.** A charming climber............... 4
323. **Maurandia, P.** A beautiful climber. 4
324. **Morning Glories,** finest mixed; oz., 10c 4
325. ———, Imported Collection of 6 distinct colors ..................... 20

4 **No. 319. Moon Flower. No. 329. Passion Flower.**

**Pampas Grass.**

347. **Coix Lachrymae.** Job's Tears ........ 4
348. **Erianthus Ravenna.** Resembles Pampas Grass .... 3
349. **Eulalia Japonica** 4
350. **Gynerium Argentum.** Pampas Grass 5
351. **Laguarus Ovatus.** (Hare's - Tail Grass) ........ 4
352. **Stipa Pennata.** (Feather Grass)... 4
353. **Finest Mixed.** Ornamental Grasses 4

**12 PKTS. BEAUTIFUL FLOWER SEEDS FOR 30 CTS**

ABRONIA · ASTER · BALSAM · CALLIOPSIS DRL · CELOSIA · CHRYSANTHEMUM

GYPSOPHILA · LANTANA · MARIGOLD · PANSY · POPPIES · PYRETHRUM

F. S. CO'S CELEBRATED ⚜ SEEDS

FARMER SEED CO'S LITTLE GEM COLLECTIONS OF FLOWER SEEDS—12 packets Flowers for only 30 cents. To meet the demand of those who wish a neat display of Flowers at a small expenditure, we have selected 12 of the most beautiful annuals that will bloom in a short time. To beautify home surroundings it is not necessary to go to a great expense.

## EVERGREENS.

A class of indispensable trees for windbreaks, and they are particularly valuable for ornamental planting.

All Evergreens by express or freight; charges to be paid by the purchaser. All stocky, well branched and well rooted.

**DOUGLAS SPRUCE**—It is the most rapid grower of all the conifers; it is a grand tree. 12 to 18-inch, per 10, $3.50; per 25, $7.00.

**COLORADO BLUE SPRUCE** — Very hardy; beautiful steel blue. It is incomparable in beauty. 12 to 18-inch, each, 60c.; per 10, $5.00.

**SCOTCH PINE**—A strong, hardy grower, fine for windbreaks. 12 to 18-inch, per 10, $1.25; per 100, $8.50. Transplanted trees, 18-24 inch, 25c., each; per 10, $2.00.

**WHITE PINE**—A well known native sort. 12 to 18-inch, per 10, $1.25; per 100, $8.75. Transplanted trees, 18-24 inch, each, 35c.; per 10, $3.00.

**NORWAY SPRUCE**—A lofty, elegant tree; one of the best Evergreens for hedge and windbreaks. 12 to 18-inch, per 10, $1.25; per 100, $8.00; 18 to 24-inch, per 10, $2.00; per 100, $16.00.

**BALSAM FIR**—A very regular, symmetrical tree. 12 to 18-inch, per 10, $1.25; per 25, $2.50; 18 to 24-inch, per 10, $2.00; per 25, $4.50.

**AMERICAN ARBOR VITAE** — Grows rapidly and forms a most beautiful hedge, very dense. 12 to 18-inch, per 10, $1.00; per 100, $8.00.

Douglas Spruce.

**Hydrangea Paniculata.**

## Hardy Shrubs and Roses.

A few plants cost but little, and you will never regret the purchase, as it adds beauty and value to your home.

**SPIRÆA (Van Houtti)**—The hardiest of all the Spiræas. The bushes form fine, compact clumps. The pure white flowers are borne in such masses that they form great plumes, drooping gracefully, giving the clumps the appearance of "a snow bank of white bloom." Each, 25c.

**LILAC (PURPLE)**—A well-known, strong-growing shrub, bearing large, fragrant clusters of flowers early in spring. Each 20c.

**LILAC (WHITE)**—Like above, but has white flowers, making it more desired by some. Each 25c.

**SNOWBALL**—A well known and popular shrub, which grows to large size, covered with dense spherical clusters of white flowers, which gives it its name. Each, 25c.; large, 40c.

**WEIGELA ROSEA**—A very fine variety, bearing beautiful and showy rose-colored flowers in May; hardy, and easy of cultivation. Each, 25c. and 50c.

**SNOWBERRY, WHITEFRUIT**—*Symphoricarpus racemosus*—A medium native shrub; flowers small and numerous; berries abundant; snow white. Each, 25c.

**HYDRANGEA, PANICULATA, GRANDIFLORA**—One of the finest hardy shrubs ever introduced, and in size and magnificence of bloom not excelled by any shrub in cultivation. The bush in time attains a large size, growing in beauty year by year. It is in the full glory of bloom from August until the middle or last of October, when every branch is crowned with an immense panicle of fleecy, pure white flowers, changing later to a pinkish hue, sometimes a foot long and nearly as broad as the base, presenting an aspect of majestic grandeur that absolutely defies description. Entirely hardy. 2 years, 12 to 18 inches, by mail, each, 30c.; dozen, $2.25; strong, 1½ to 2 feet, each, 45c.; dozen, $3.25. Plants not prepaid at dozen rates.

**Moss Rose.**

## Moss Roses.

Extra plants, field grown, dormant, 40c.; 3 for $1.00, postpaid. By express, 30c.; 4 for $1.00; dozen, $3.00.

**PERPETUAL MOSS (Blanche Moreau)**—The best white Moss Rose. Flowers are produced in clusters and are large, full and sweet. Color is pure white; both flowers and buds have an abundance of dark green moss.

**CRESTED MOSS**—Rose color, beautifully crested.

**HENRY MARTIN**—Rich, glossy pink, tinged crimson; large, globular flowers; full and sweet; finely mossed.

**SALET**—Color bright rose, with blush edges. An extra fine, cupped sort.

## Hardy Creeping Roses.

**SOUTH ORANGE PERFECTION**—Double flowers, soft blush changing to white, about one and one-half inches in diameter. Perfect rosettes in shape.

**TRIUMPH**—This may well be called the DOUBLE "MEMORIAL ROSE," as it preserves the color of the parent with its characteristics of growth and foliage, but the flowers are double and very fragrant. They are produced in clusters of from 12 to 18 flowers on each cluster on small side shoots.

Price: 1st size, 40c. each; $4.00 per doz.; 2nd size, 30c. each; $3.00 per doz.

**Crimson Rambler Rose.**

## Hardy Field Roses.

**GENERAL JACQUEMINOT**—One of the grandest Roses in existence. Sure to delight every lover of the beautiful, as nothing can surpass them in beauty. Color a rich dazzling scarlet, shaded with deep, velvety crimson, making a superb glowing color. Flowers large; free bloomer. Each, Dormant 30c.

**LA FRANCE**—Peach-blossom pink, the model-garden Rose; blooms all summer. Undoubtedly the most perfect type of a cut-flower Rose. No variety surpasses it in delicate coloring—silvery Roses, shaded pink with satiny sheen. Each, Dormant 30c.

**COQUETTE DES BLANCHES**—One of the best white Roses of its class; fine form, pure white with beautiful shell-shaped petals. Very suitable for cemetery planting.

**BARON DE BONSTETTEN**—Blackish crimson, with vivid red shadings.

**PERSIAN YELLOW**—Hardy yellow Rose; best of its color.

**CRIMSON RAMBLER**—*Polyantha*—This wonderful new Japanese Rose has rapidly obtained popularity and has been eagerly in demand. It is a climbing Rose of vigorous habit, rapid growth and produces in marvelous abundance large clusters of bright crimson semi-double flowers. A splendid climber for covering walls, verandas, pillars, etc., and its profusion of bloom is astonishing.

**YELLOW RAMBLER**—Grand new variety like above except that it is golden yellow and is one of the most satisfactory sorts. Each, Dormant 30c.

**CLIMBING WHITE PET**—Very rapid climber, making a wonderful growth, often 10 to 15 feet the first year. Blooms profusely. Flowers pure white, medium size, very double, ever-blooming, fragrant and hardy. Bound to become a great favorite.

**BALTIMORE BELLE**—Pale blush, shading to rose color; very double; flowers in beautiful clusters.

**GREVILLE or SEVEN SISTERS**—Blooms in large clusters, with flowers varying from white to crimson. Perfectly hardy.

**PRAIRIE QUEEN**—Clear, bright carmine-pink, sometimes with a white stripe; large, compact, and globular; very double and full; the best hardy climber in this climate.

Any of the above large-sized Dormant Roses, 40c. each; prepaid; $4.00 per doz., not prepaid.

# SMALL FRUIT PLANTS.

### Grape Vines, Strawberry Plants, Raspberry, Blackberry, Currant and Gooseberry Bushes.

As we receive a great many inquiries from our customers asking us to supply them with fruit plants, we have finally concluded to add them to our list again. Years ago when we were yet doing business in Chicago, we were connected with a nursery, but, moving to Faribault, Minn., we had to drop the nursery line entirely.

Our previous experience in handling nursery stock and raising small fruit ourselves on our farm, places us in a position to supply our customers with the best and most reliable varieties in the Small Fruit line.

## GRAPE VINES.

The soil for Grapes should be naturally dry, or artificially drained. Grapes will not thrive on low and wet soils, but succeed best on high and dry ground, having a free circulation of air, which helps guard against the diseases of the vines—mildew, rot, etc., and should have enough slope to carry off the surplus water. Good results may be obtained even on low lands when the soil is dry. Grapes do well on most any kind of soil that is dry enough and has sufficient fertility to produce a good farm crop.

Grapes should be planted in rows 5, 7 or 8 feet apart, and about the same distance apart in the rows.

They do very well trained up by the side of any building or along the garden fences, occupying but little room, and furnishing an abundance of the healthiest of fruits. There is scarcely a yard so small, either in country or city, where there is not room for 1 to a dozen or more of Grape vines.

One and two year old vines prepaid at price per single vine. Dozen and 100 by express or freight at purchaser's expense.

Moyer.

**MOORE'S EARLY** — Bunch and berries large, round, with heavy blue bloom; vine exceedingly hardy, entirely exempt from mildew or disease. Very early, desirable for first market. 1 yr., each, 12c.; doz., 75c.; 100, $4.50. 2 yrs., each, 15c.; doz., $1.00; 100, $6.50.

**NIAGARA**—Vine vigorous and productive, with tough, leathery foliage. Clusters large and compact; berries large, with thin skin, greenish-white, tender pulp, and exceedingly sweet and rich. Ripens with Concord. 1 yr., each, 10c.; doz., 75c.; 100, $4.50. 2 yrs., each, 15c.; doz., $1.00; 100, $6.50.

**WILDER (ROGER'S 4)**—One of the finest in quality of all the hardy black Grapes. Bunch and berry large, black tender, rich. Vigorous, healthy, hardy, and productive. Midseason. 1 yr., each, 10c.; doz., 75c.; 100, $4.50. 2 yrs., each, 15c.; doz., $1.00; 100, $6.50.

**CONCORD**—Popular and well known. The Grape for the people; succeeding everywhere and producing abundantly fruit of good quality. 1 yr., each, 10c.; doz., 75c.; 100, $4.50. 2 yrs., each, 15c.; doz., $1.00; 100, $6.00.

Campbell's Early.

**MOYER**—In habit of growth, hardiness, quality and size of clusters it resembles the Delaware very much; but it ripens with the very earliest and has larger berries; it has stood, unprotected, 35 degrees below zero, without injury. It is very sweet as soon as colored; very desirable for planting. 1 year, 20c.; doz., $1.50; ... er ...

**DELAWARE**—Red; bunch small, compact, sometimes shouldered; berries small, skin thin but firm, flesh juicy, very sweet and refreshing, of best quality for both table and wine; ripens with Concord or a little before; vine hardy, productive, moderate grower. 1 yr., each, 10c.; doz. 75c.; 100, $4.50. 2 yrs., each, 15c.; doz., $1.00; 100, $6.50.

**CAMPBELL'S EARLY** — The king of American Grapes, in all respects better adapted to general cultivation in all sections suited to our native varieties, than any other yet grown and tested. It is a very strong grower; hardy; clusters very large and compact; berries often an inch or more in diameter; flavor rich and sweet; season very early; good keeper and shipper. One-year vines, 25c.; doz., $2.00.

## GOOSEBERRIES.

**REDJACKET**—A true native and one of the finest of American Gooseberries, rivaling the large English varieties. It may be said to be truly mildew-proof. It is very hardy, and a wonderful cropper. The fruit is large, smooth, of a rich ruby-red, and fine in quality. 1 yr., each, 15c.; doz., $1.50; 100, $9.00. 2 yrs., each, 25c.; doz., $3.50; 100, $12.00; 100 rates not prepaid.

**DOWNING**—Universally known and always reliable. It is the old standard native sort that has for years been so largely planted for the market. Berries, medium to large, pale green, and of excellent quality. 1 yr., doz., 60c.; 100, $3.50. 2 yrs., doz., 80c.; 100, $4.50. 100 rates not prepaid.

Red Cross.

## CURRANTS.

**RED CROSS**—A strong grower; cluster long; berry larger than Fay; color bright red; quality better than Cherry or Fay and very much more productive than either.

**RED DUTCH**—An old, well known, standard variety. A strong, tall upright grower; berries medium, dark red; productive. 1 yr., doz., 50c.; prepaid; 100 by express, $3.00.

**VERSAILLES**—La Versailles—A vigorous, somewhat spreading grower. Very similar to Cherry Currant in habit of growth and character of fruit.

**VICTORIA** (Raby Castle).—Bush a very strong, upright grower; foliage rather pale bronze-green. Clusters above medium length; berries medium or above, bright red, with mild acid pulp. One of the most valuable late varieties. Very productive. 1 yr., doz., 50c., prepaid; 100 by express, $3.00.

**WHITE DUTCH**—Bush an upright grower, vigorous and very productive. Clusters two to three inches long; berries average medium size, are translucent and a little darker than White Grape; quality xcellent. Ripens early.

**WHITE GRAPE**—Bush vigorous, somewhat spreading; productive; clusters long; berries large to very large, but averaging large, of very attractive color, mild flavor and good quality.

**BLACK CHAMPION**—Bush vigorous and productive; fruit averages above medium; pulp nearly sweet, mild-flavored. A desirable variety for general culture.

**LEE'S PROLIFIC**—Bush rather short, dwarfish, moderately vigorous, productive; fruit varies from small to very large, is rather acid and strong-flavored.

Prices: Except when noted—1 yr., doz., 75c., postpaid; 100, by express, charges paid by purchaser, $2.75; 50 at 100 rate. 2-year-old plants, doz., 75c.; 100, $4.00, not prepaid.

# RED RASPBERRIES.

Postpaid at dozen rates. 100 rates not prepaid.

**CUTHBERT**—Deep, rich crimson, medium to large, productive, very firm, one of the best market varieties; season medium to late. **Doz., 40c.; 100, $1.25.**

**LOUDON**—A new variety, very vigorous and very productive. Fruit large, firm, bright crimson; very hardy and very promising. A splendid shipper. Canes grow erect. Ripens medium late. **Doz., 40c.; 100, $1.50.**

**MILLER**—Bright red, large, round, of fine quality. One of the firmest and best shippers for early market. Vigorous, hardy and immensely productive. **Doz., 40c.; 100, $1.50.**

**THE COLUMBIAN**—Of the many promising Red Berries none of this valuable and profitable class come before the small fruit buyers with brighter promise than this. We have no doubt of the wisdom of investing $10 to $50 in this berry. The fruit is cone-shaped, of dark red almost purplish color. Fruiting season extends from July 10th to August 15th. It is an excellent shipper, and its productive habit is well seen in the fact that 3,511 bushes in 1894 produced an average of 5 quarts each. **Each, 15c.; 6 for 75c.; 12 for $1.00; 100, $6.00.**

Loudon.

## BLACK CAPS.

**KANSAS**—Ripens just after Souhegan; berries as large or larger than the Gregg; jet black, firm, handsome and of the best quality; exceedingly productive. **Each, 10c.; doz., 60c.; 100, $2.00.**

**DOOLITTLE**—Early, very hardy, productive; an old variety but still highly esteemed. **Doz., 40c.; 100, $1.50.**

**GREGG**—One of the best of the black varieties; large, good quality, late; requires good, strong land. **Doz., 40c.; 100, $1.50.** Prepaid at dozen rates; 100 rates not prepaid.

## BLACKBERRIES.

**LUCRETIA DEWBERRY or TRAILING BLACKBERRY**—This is the finest of its class; one of several that have proved successful. The fruit is handsome, and has succeeded wherever it has been tried. A strong grower and exceedingly productive. I will say at a venture that the Lucretia ripens at least 10 days before any other Blackberry. This is surely a good record for Lucretia. **Each, 10c.; 12 for 75c.; 100 for $2.00, not prepaid.**

**KITTATINNY**—Large, conical, glossy, black; requires protection in severe climates. **Each, 5c.; doz., 35c.; 100, $1.50.**

**MINNEWASKI**—Very large and melting, a good grower and fair bearer. **Each, 5c.; doz., 50c.; 100, $2.00.**

Lucretia Dewberry.

Snyder.

**SNYDER**—Extremely hardy, and therefore very valuable for the north; enormously productive, medium size, good quality. **Each, 5c.; doz., 40c.; 100, $1.50.**

**TAYLOR**—Cane as hardy as Snyder; berries much larger and somewhat later; fruit of best quality. **Each, 5c.; doz., 50c.; 100, $1.75.**

**ELDORADO**—Of largest size and best quality, and having so little core that it cannot be noticed in the eating. It far surpasses any Blackberry on the list to-day. In addition to this, it is very hardy and productive, never having been injured in the Northwest. **Each, 8c.; doz., 75c.; 50 for $2.00.**

**ANCIENT BRITON**—One of the hardy varieties. Very vigorous, healthy and hardy; fruit stems loaded with good sized berries of fine quality that carry well to the market and fetch highest price. For general planting for home or market in all sections subject to severe winters, the Ancient Briton is recommended as a first-class variety. **Each, 5c.; doz., 50c.; 100, $1.75.** Single and dozen plants prepaid; 100 not prepaid.

## STRAWBERRIES.

For the convenience of those who cannot be reached by the express companies, we will forward by mail, prepaid, plants of all the varieties enumerated in this list. At the dozen rate the plants will be mailed at the prices annexed, without extra charge. At the hundred rate, if sent by mail, 25 cents additional per hundred plants must be remitted for postage.

**NIC OHMER**—(S.) Originated by Mr. John F. Beaver, who is considered to be the most successful amateur fruit grower in Ohio. Named after Mr. N. Ohmer, ex-president of the Ohio State Horticultural Society. The introducer says: "After watching the Nic Ohmer three years, and hearing how it has behaved wherever I sent it for trial, never having received one unfavorable report on it, I am confident that it is one of the most desirable, if not the very best ever sent out. It is probably not surpassed in healthy, vigorous growth and great productiveness by any variety. It has a perfect blossom. The fruit is of the very largest size, a giant among strawberries. It is never misshapen. Its only departure from the regular roundish conical form is when, under high culture, it is somewhat triangular. It is a dark glossy red, firm and of excellent flavor." **Price: Doz., 50c.; 100, $1.50.**

Parker Earle.　　　　　　Nic Ohmer.

**AROMA**—(S.) Plant is strong and healty; fruit is very large, roundish conical, rarely misshapen; glossy red, of excellent quality and an abundant producer. One of the most profitable late varieties. **Doz., 35c., prepaid; 100, $1.00.**

**BEDER WOOD**—Large, roundish conical, bright scarlet, moderately firm, fair quality; plant vigorous and very productive. A very valuable early sort for home use or near market. **Doz., 35c.; 100, $1.00.**

**BISEL**—(P.) This has a great reputation as a profitable market Berry. Plant shows no weakness of any kind, but is well able to carry its great load of fruit to full maturity. Berries are large, regular conical form, bright red, quite firm, with seeds but slightly imbedded; flesh is light red and of good flavor. **Doz., 35c., prepaid; 100, $1.00.**

**BRANDYWINE**—(S.) This is an introduction by Mr. M. Crawford. It is a late variety of good shape, good size, good quality, firm and productive. We have a true stock of fine plants. **Doz., 35c., prepaid; 100, $1.00.**

**CLYDE**—(S.) This is an immensely productive variety, and berries are nearly as large as the Bubach, of which it is an offspring. The plant is very vigorous and healthy, there being no trace of disease about it. The foliage is light green in color, upright and a sturdy grower. Season of ripening, second early. It is dark scarlet in color and very productive. It thrives on most any soil, and is valuable for family and market use. **Doz., 35c., prepaid; 100, $1.00.**

**PARKER EARLE**—The best variety for family use in the whole list, as it is a perfect-flowered sort and bears immensely. The plant is robust, free from disease, stooling heavily. Berry regular, uniformly large, conical, with a neck, easy scarlet crimson, no hollow core, quality excellent. Its season is medium to very late. Strong plants. **Doz., 40c.; $1.00.**

# STRAWBERRIES---Continued.

**WARFIELD NO. 2—**The plant is a very vigorous grower, exceedingly productive, bears picking daily. The berries are of good quality, dark color, medium size, firm, regular in size; sub-acid. A very profitable berry for nearby or distant market. Season early. **Price, 35c. per dozen, prepaid by mail; $1.00 per 100, not prepaid.**

**SEAFORD (p)—**A new variety from Delaware, exhibiting such fine qualities that it is bound to become popular. It is a better berry than Bubach, which it equals in size, is far more productive and sufficiently firm for market shipment. In color it is a deep glossy crimson and first rate in quality. The plant is exceedingly vigorous, with foliage that endures hot suns with wonderful fortitude. It ripens about second early, and will be found admirable to succeed the early varieties and usher in those ripening in midseason. **Price, 35c. per dozen, prepaid; $1.00 per hundred, not prepaid.** We fruited this one. It is one of our best berries and brought a high price.

**HALL'S FAVORITE (Per.)—**The originator says of this variety: "Plants very strong-growing, with foliage heavy enough and thick enough to protect blossoms from frost and for mulch in winter. I have seen the vines stand 12 to 18 inches high on ordinary land, and upon opening the vines, found as fine fruit as any one would wish to see. The season of ripening is from early to medium, and the whole crop ripens in a very short time. The berries are large, perfectly formed, of uniform shape, coloring evenly to deep, rich crimson; equal to the best in quality. They present a beautiful sight when crated; also keep, ship and sell well. The plant is a heavy cropper, even in old beds of ordinary soil. The Strawberry Culturist says of this berry: 'As seen on Mr. Hall's farm, Hall's Favorite is certainly very large and fine colored. It is better in quality than Bubach by far, and as a grower the Bubach is no comparison.'" **Price, 40c. per dozen, prepaid; $1.25 per 100, not prepaid.**

Hall's Favorite.

### ROCHESTER SPRAYERS.

This Sprayer is made of galvanized steel or of brass, if desired. Capacity from three to four gallons, and has a removable brass air pump. To pour in liquid, the pump has to be removed. The sprayer can be carried in a perpendicular and, in a horizontal position by use of the carrier strap. Before leaving the shop every sprayer is carefully tested at a greater pressure

**THE ACME SEED DRILL—**A garden Seed Drill that will open a furrow and distribute Beet, Cabbage, Carrot, Celery, Lettuce, Onion, Radish, Turnip and all such seeds with perfect regularity. A single packet as well as larger quantities can be sown. Just the thing for those whose gardens are too small to use a Planet Jr., or other drills that cost from $5.00 to $10.00. **Price, delivered to any postoffice, only $1.25. Not prepaid by express, $1.00.**

**EUREKA HAND SEEDER—For Small Sowings and Hot Beds—**It will open the drill, sow and cover Beet, Cabbage, Carrot, Celery, Lettuce, Radish, Turnip and all such seeds with perfect regularity. It sows much more evenly and ten times as rapidly as by hand. The quantity to be sown can quickly be regulated and also the depth. It is the only drill made for sowing in hot beds. Will sow a small packet of seeds as well as larger bulks. Simple, easily understood, and cannot get out of order. Is heavier and stronger than the above, and cannot be sent by mail. **Price, $1.00; delivered per express 50c. extra.**

**SPECIAL OFFER—**Those of our customers who want to take a little trouble can obtain one of these Drills free, as we have decided to send one of them as a premium with an order for Vegetable and Flower Seeds in Packets Only, to the amount of $3.50. Our Collection of Vegetable and Flower Seeds are, however, excluded from this offer. If the Eureka Drill is selected, 50c. should be sent extra to cover express charges.

Considering the low prices which we have made on our large and well filled packages and the quality of our seeds, it would be a very easy thing to obtain orders enough amongst your neighbors for seeds in packages to the amount of $3.50, to obtain one of these Drills.

Eureka Drill.

# BOOKS.

## AGRICULTURE, GARDENING, HORTICULTURE, FLORICULTURE, ETC.

Sent Postpaid on Receipt of Price.    Discounts Allowed on 3 or More Books.    Write Us.

**Keep Yourself Up to Date.    Read the Latest Book of the Specialists.**

SAFETY VALVE

Rochester Sprayer.

than intended to be used at, and fitted with a safety valve, which allows the compressed air to escape after the desired pressure has been obtained.

A force pump is practically worthless where the operator is constantly changing positions as is the case when spraying small fruits, potatoes, etc. The pump and pail cannot be moved without stopping the spray; this means time, and "time is money," especially in spraying season. Use our self-operating Sprayer and you need not stop for anything; just walk right along from one row to another. The work will be done in one-third of the time required in the old way, and the time saved more than pays for this Sprayer the first season.

**Prices. Galvanized Steel,** complete with hose, reversible nozzle for fine or coarse spray, straight stream nozzle and receipts for mixing and applying spraying solutions........................................................**$3.50**

The same style made of copper, **$1.50 extra.**

Brass extension pipes for elevating spray nozzle, per length of 3 feet.....................................**40 cts.**

### UNCLE SAM SPRAYER.

This is made in the same style as the above described Rochester Sprayer, but is smaller, holding about a gallon of liquid. It also gets its force from compressed air, sufficient to wash any large fruit tree or thoroughly wash any upper story window before exhausting its contents. It is made of good material, with removable Brass Air Pump to fill, throws a fine mist spray 8 to 12 feet, or a solid, steady stream 30 to 40 feet, and does the same work as well if not better than more costly machines; where there are only a few trees to spray it fills the bill to a nicety. **Price of Uncle Sam Sprayer.....$1.50**

## PEDIGREE BLUE STEM WHEAT.

This is the only Wheat that yielded a full crop here in this section of the Northwest last year when all the other kinds failed on account of excessive wet weather, rust, blight and other unfavorable circumstances. No matter how promising some fields of wheat appeared shortly before maturing, they were disappointing both in yield and quality when it came to harvesting, as there was hardly any that produced more than 10 bushels of badly shrunken Wheat per acre. The Pedigree Blue Stem Wheat, however, was neither affected by rust, blight nor cold and wet weather, and on account of its stocky and vigorous growth it stored up so much vigor and vitality to withstand all such, to common sorts so serious drawbacks. When it came to threshing it was found that it yielded thirty-nine bushels, machine measure, per acre, and the grain weighed 63 lbs. per struck bushel, or more than three times as much than ordinary Wheat. This Wheat is large and plump grained, hard and flinty, almost translucent, and in milling qualities unsurpassed.

While we do not claim that the yield of the Pedigree Blue Stem Wheat is always so much larger than that of other kinds, we and our customers have experienced, since this so valuable wheat was introduced, that year in and year out it will produce at least again as much grain per acre than these. The difference in the quality between such Wheat should also be considered, for in this case where there is quantity there is also the quality, for Wheat, yielding at the rate of 20-40 bushels per acre must be naturally plump and heavy, and will command always the highest market price. On the other hand, however, Wheat producing only 8-13 bu. per acre is of poor quality, and if it could be properly utilized it would be oftentimes just as profitable if left in the straw, for poor and shrunken Wheat or screening is only fit for feed.

Origination of the Pedigree Blue Stem Wheat—For more than 12 years Mr. Haynes, of North Dakota, labored patiently in the development of this Wheat, and it is safe to say that he has succeeded, not only in having this Wheat pure and unmixed with soft and bearded Wheats, but being more productive also. Mr. Haynes says: "I commenced by planting in my garden in 1884 the grains from two good heads, having three kernels abreast, hoeing it as it grew. From the product of these two heads I rejected the latest and poorest heads, using only the best and earliest for replanting. The improvement made by the process has resulted in increasing the number of kernels abreast in the spikelets from three to four, with the 'fifth kernel commencing to make its appearance. The length of the head is increased about one-third, and the berry much improved in uniformity of color and hardiness. Another important advantage is that it matures about five days earlier."

New kinds of Seed Grain, etc., are introduced every year, but it is seldom that a variety proves itself superior everywhere and under all conditions and meets with so much favor as this Pedigree Blue Stem Wheat has done. Not only here at home in the Northwest where Wheat is the main crop, but everywhere and under all conditions has this **PEDIGREE BLUE STEM WHEAT** proven itself superior to other varieties, outyielding them all. Farmers who ordered 10 bushels or less a year ago write us that they made a great mistake and should have ordered 100 bushels instead, as the Pedigree Blue Stem outyielded their own old Wheat by 10 to 15 bushels per acre on the same fields and under the same conditions, and they would have made big money in the end by paying four times as much for our Pedigree Wheat instead of sowing their own seed. **Price:** Peck, 50c.; bu., $1.50; 2½ bu., $3.50; 5 bu., $6.75; 10 bu., $13.00; sacks included.

For larger quantities please write us.

Mr. W. Haglund, Meeker county, Minn., writes: I had a yield of 29 bushels for every bushel of seed of your Pedigree Blue Stem.

## MINNESOTA KING CORN.

We regard this Corn as the most valuable early Corn for the Northwest, and is certainly the kind to plant in the northern part of Minnesota, Wisconsin and in North and South Dakota, instead of the smaller yielding Flint varieties. There are other kinds of Corn which will yield under favorable circumstances perhaps just as much, but year in and year out, through favorable and unfavorable seasons, there is no other kind that will produce such large average yields as the Minnesota King Corn. On account of its thrifty and vigorous growth right from the start, and its long roots penetrating so deep into the soil, it has more ability to endure the extremes of heat and cold, flood and drought, than any other Corn, and being so extremely early, it is soon out of danger of frost, as the past unfavorable season for raising Corn has fully proven. Due to the very unfavorable, cold and wet season, mostly all the different kinds of Corn were checked so much in growth that when the first frost came, Sept. 13 (here in this section), it was caught when in milk yet, while the Minnesota King came through the season just as good as usual, yielding a good crop of good and well-matured Corn.

The stalks grow only to a medium height, and, as stated above, are well rooted and firm, so they will withstand the strongest winds. In appearance the Minnesota King Corn is remarkably distinct, it being a half yellow Dent Corn. The kernels are very large, broad, and of a rich golden color. The ears are of medium size, and always well filled to the tip. Many seed dealers offer Nebraska grown Minnesota King Corn at a lower price, but such is high at any price, as it will not mature here in our northern latitude.

The stock that we offer we have raised ourselves on our own farm, and will therefore give the best satisfaction, both in early maturity and in germination.

**Price**, express or freight: Qt., 15c.; peck, 75c.; bu., $2.15; 2 bu., $4.00; 5 bu., $9.50; sacks included. Prepaid by mail: Large pkt., 5c.; lb., 18c.; qt., 30c.

For prices on larger quantities, please write us.

H...., Bay Co., Mich.—Your Seed Corn is splendid and gave entire satisfaction. Your Minnesota King Corn especially is fine and it yielded as heavy and heavier as the "Ohio Dent" grown here mostly. "Smut Nose" is also very good, is larger and gives more fodder than the corn grown here. W. HALL.

M...., Marquette County, Wis.—Gentlemen: Ever since 1890 I have ordered seeds from you regularly and always was well pleased. Your Minnesota King Corn has far outyielded any other variety, and was a surprise to me. From 5 acres I had 535 bushels, and this was on sandy and not very rich land, either. C. W. STELTER.

PRESS OF WEBB PUBLISHING CO., ST. PAUL.

Lightning Source UK Ltd.
Milton Keynes UK
UKHW022345030119
334726UK00011B/1182/P